1992

AUTUMN OF THE U-BOATS

By the same author:

The Month of the Lost U-Boats
Night Flight
Raider
Attacker
Under Three Flags
Battleship Barham

AUTUMN OF THE U-BOATS

Geoffrey P. Jones

WILLIAM KIMBER · LONDON

First published in 1984 by
WILLIAM KIMBER & CO. LIMITED
100 Jermyn Street, London, SW1Y 6EE

© Geoffrey Jones, 1984

ISBN 0-7183-0534-5

Typeset by Print Co-ordination, Macclesfield
and printed in Great Britain by
Redwood Burn Limited,
Trowbridge, Wiltshire

Contents

		Page
	Acknowledgments	9
	Introduction	11
1.	Failed to Return	15
2.	The Fiftieth Month	34
3.	A Liberator Story	40
4.	Card's Nap Hand	52
5.	U-Boats at Large	63
6.	Unhappy Anniversary	77
7.	The Azores	99
8.	Escort Group B7 at Sea Again	109
9.	Activity around Convoy ONS20	128
10.	Long Distance U-boats	136
11.	Baby Flat-Tops	146
12.	An Epic Duel	159
13.	Rock Wellingtons	169
14.	Ultimatum	175
15.	The Battle of the Strait	189
16.	Captain Walker and the Second Support Group	207
	Appendix: Boats and Personnel	212
	Glossary	217
	Naval Expressions	218
	Comparative Ranks	218
	Index	219

List of Illustrations

Page

U-377 arriving back at Brest   17
The wounded captain introduces his crew
   to the base commander   17
Diving tanks were just missed   18
Cannon fire damage to *U-377*'s conning tower   18
Halifax of 58 Squadron   32
Grossadmiral Karl Dönitz   36
Liberator of 120 Squadron   49
Grumman Avengers on carrier deck   55
USS *Card*   55
U-402   59
Lockheed Hudson   68
HMS *Oribi*   69
ORP *Orkan*   71
HMS *Orwell*   71
ORP *Orkan* enters convoy   73
HMS *Oribi* prepares to refuel   73
Survivor of *U-419* being rescued   76
Kapitänleutnant Hans Speidel   81
U-643   81
Mattress aerial   84
U-643 sinking   91
HMS *Orwell* to rescue   91
HMCS *Kamloops*   94
Blindfolded prisoners   96
Survivors from *U-643*   97
Landing at Greenock   97
U-306   103
Hedgehog mount   103
U-844   112
HMS *Duncan*   112

U-boat control room   121
Control room close up   121
Motor room   122
Diesel room   123
Main ballast pump   124
Bow torpedo compartment   125
U-848 attacked   144/145
U-378 sinking   149
USS *Core*   152
USS *Block Island*   152
F/L R. Aldwinckle and crew   162
USS *Borie*   162
Wellington of Coastal Command   171
Gibraltar airstrip   171
Lieutenant Hedley Kett   177
U-boat crew prepared to enter harbour   187
Crew of *Ultimatum*   188
HMS *Imperialist*   198
HMS *Fleetwood*   199
Spanish trawlers   204
U-boat crew on Spanish trawler   204

Diagrams
Attack on *U-848*   143
Track chart of USS *Borie* and USS *Card*   166
Technical Data of U-boat types   216

Maps
Mid-Atlantic air gap closed   101
U-boat sinkings for October 1943   126/127
Route of five U-boats   192

Acknowledgements

While compiling this book, I had many questions to raise and I wish to thank the following friends who were able to answer them: Roy Benwell, Gus Britton, Mick Cooper, Peter Diamond, David J. Lees and Jak P. Mallmann Showell. Hans Speidel and I made contact after I had written the chapter on his boat; he was most helpful although he does not yet know what I have written!

I have to thank the editor of *Navy News* for publishing a letter of mine requesting help. It elicited replies from the following people who either offered to help, or were able to help, many of whom are mentioned in the text: A.R. Davies, E.W. Dawson, D.W.V. Evison, T.C. Goddard, D.K. Gowland, W.H. Kett, K. Martin, T.W. McPhail, P. Norfield, I.A. Scrymgeour-Wedderburn, L.V. Silvester and J.A. Wade.

Many of the above mentioned people also contributed photographs, none more than Douglas Gowland. These pictures, together with those from Ernst Gerke, my own collection and from the agencies of Crown, Druppel, The Imperial War Museum, US Navy and the Public Archives of Canada make up the total. All their copyrights are acknowledged.

My brother, Edward M. Jones of Perth, Western Australia, contributed the maps and artwork.

Much of my primary research was carried out in, or through, the offices of the Imperial War Museum in London, the Public Archives of Canada in Ottawa, the Public Records Office at Kew and the United States Department of the Navy in Washington. I wish to thank the kind people in these offices for their valuable assistance.

G.J.

Introduction

The U-boat campaign started on the first day of the Second World War when Oberleutnant Fritz Lemp sank the liner *Athenia*. Soon the exploits of U-boat captains Prien, Schepke and Kretschmer dominated the headlines; Gunther Prien first for his daring foray into Scapa Flow to sink the battleship *Royal Oak*, and then together with Schepke and Kretschmer for the havoc they were causing amongst merchant shipping in the Atlantic and thus to the vital supply lines from North America to the United Kingdom.

Despite the introduction of the convoy system with Royal Navy escorts, shipping losses mounted alarmingly. Admiral Karl Dönitz, veteran U-boat captain, now in command of the U-boat arm, evolved the wolf-pack tactic. Once a U-boat sighted a convoy it must resist the temptation to attack, call up the others of the pack and wait for a favourable opportunity, usually in darkness, to attack.

In May 1941 Fritz Lemp lost his life and from his sinking U-boat codes for the Enigma enciphering machine, by which Dönitz's signals were transmitted, were rescued by the Royal Navy. Information gained from the codes meant that delays in breaking U-boat cipher settings by the decrypting staff at Bletchley Park became shorter and Dönitz's signals to his U-boats were being read in the tracking room at the Admiralty more quickly. But in the U-boat war, counterbalancing this, was the fact that the German observation service, Beobachtungs-Dienst, or B-Dienst as it was usually known, was reading British signals, despite changes in Royal Navy cryptosystems.

In December 1941 the USA entered the war, and in a very short time the U-boat found a happy hunting ground on that coast. Convoys could not immediately be organised, and anti-U-boat patrols were naturally not fully efficient. Once having found this soft spot, the Germans exploited it to the full.

A milestone in the anti-U-boat campaign was reached in May 1942 which saw the introduction of two new weapons, the searchlight Wellington and the Torpex-filled depth charge. The effect of the former under the aegis of Coastal Command was instantaneous and spectacular. The U-boat captain had hitherto considered himself safe by night, but now this was no longer the case. By day he had been able to back his lookouts against those in the aircraft. Now the first indication of the approach of danger was the blinding beam of the searchlight, too late for anything to be done.

Yet despite these innovations, the year 1942 was disastrous for merchant shipping losses. Early in the year the U-boat codes had been changed and until the new code was cracked losses continued to mount.

As the war progressed Coastal Command built up its strength. In the period from May 1941 to November 1942 its U-boat sightings increased fourfold. Thus, from a small force defensively employed and achieving negligible results, Coastal Command became a most important unit in the anti-U-boat campaign. Shortage of aircraft in the Command had severely restricted the scope of Allied offensive operations and the lack of very long range aircraft still left a fatal gap of some 600 miles in the middle of the Atlantic where the wolf-packs continued to take a heavy toll of shipping. The rate of building of merchant ships was increasing apace, but had not yet made good the unfavourable balance between losses and new production. Thus in January 1943 the Combined Chiefs of Staff at the Casablanca Conference laid down that in the coming year the defeat of the U-boat should be the first charge on their combined resources.

Yet in March 1943 B-Dienst intercepted a diversion signal to take two convoys away from a waiting wolf-pack. Dönitz made new dispositions accordingly, and in just three days sank 21 Allied ships for the loss of only one U-boat. Mass attacks by U-boat packs were in full swing and Allied losses that month were very heavy.

Fortunately for the Allies, it was now possible by adding extra tanks to the Liberator to provide Coastal Command with a number of very long range aircraft, and the whole system of convoy escort was reorganised. Some VLR Liberator bases were established in Iceland and these were later supplemented by American and Canadian Newfoundland-based aircraft. The gap was narrowing. Later the introduction of the auxiliary carrier helped to close it yet more securely.

In the Bay of Biscay, the Wellingtons, equipped with the Leigh light and improved radar, had marked success, so much so that the U-boats again virtually abandoned the practice of surfacing by night.

Due to these and other factors, in May the Battle of the Atlantic turned full circle as Dönitz lost 41 U-boats, and withdrew the others to base or other waters.

After a short lull when sightings were scarce, U-boats attempted the passage of the Bay in small packs sailing on the surface and providing mutual support to one another. These tactics continued throughout July and again involved the U-boats in heavy losses, culminating in the sinking of a whole group of three, two by aircraft and one by a hunting group of surface craft – the first which had been made available to co-operate with the Coastal Command Bay patrols.

August opened with the sinking of one U-boat a day, but after about a week there was a lull. At the beginning of September Dönitz was ready to resume the battle, twenty-nine U-boats sailed to the Atlantic, many with their new acoustic torpedoes. The Germans were counting heavily on surprise but the Allies knew of the forthcoming offensive and at times Dönitz must have thought his mind was being read; Captain Rodger Winn in the U-boat tracking room at the Admiralty was doing even better; he was reading his signals with the help of Bletchley Park.

With hindsight this new offensive can be seen as the twilight, or autumn, of the U-boats' successes. So what better time to start the saga than the autumn, the third season, which officially begins in the last week of September?

One cannot turn the clock back forty years, but I have tried to do so while writing this book. I took an October cruise across the Bay of Biscay, on through the cross-seas of the South Atlantic in a ship of the same displacement as the Royal Navy destroyer in which I served in post-war. As a passenger I flew across the Bay several times and landed and took off from the airstrip at Gibraltar. I obtained a video of the Canadian film *K-225*, made aboard a Flower Class corvette in 1943. When preparing the aircraft chapters I visited the RAF Museum complex to look at the Halifax, Hudson, Sunderland and Wellington aircraft, which I had seen flying during the war. I travelled to Kiel and sailed up past the Danish islands, through the same seaway as used by the U-boats four decades ago.

So now, pull back the screens of time, put on your tin hat, bring your ration book and join me at the end of September 1943.

CHAPTER ONE

Failed to Return

Officially autumn begins at the end of the third week of September. The first U-boat attacked at that time, in 1943, was *U-377*, in the North Atlantic.

The VIIC Type U-boat, under the command of Oberleutnant Gerhard Kluth with Leutnant Ernst 'Jumbo' Gerke as the 1WO, was in its tenth war patrol. The boat was escorted out of the Brittany port of Brest in the early evening of Monday, 6 September. Soon afterwards a crew member fell overboard but was rescued and returned by the escort ship. Early the next morning a leak was discovered and *U-377* returned to port, only to be slightly damaged by the propeller of *U-256*. All was soon made right and two days later *U-377* finally set off to be one of twenty U-boats of the *Leuthen* group on the eastern side of the North Atlantic, seeking outward convoys ON202 and ONS18. The U-boats were ordered to keep W/T silence and avoid being observed.

When they were in position, late on the 20th, an R/T signal was received: 'Use radar impulses to find convoy.'

At the time starshells were visible. At 0341 on the 21st *U-377* unsuccessfully shot at a destroyer; the gnat detonation was heard three minutes and five seconds later. Soon after this another R/T message was received, saying: 'Starshells are in the wrong place probably not the convoy.'

But by 0635 *U-377* had the convoy in sight and sent out an R/T signal giving its position. Soon fog came down and *U-377* was driven off by two Free French corvettes, *Renoncule* and *Roselys*. While it was submerged the starboard diesel motor was repaired. When the U-boat surfaced again it sent reports to headquarters on attempts to get at the convoy.

In the early hours of the next day *U-377* had a fortunate escape as a destroyer came in to ram. Turning hard to escape, the U-boat's rudder jammed, but it was able to dive and then had the galling experience of hearing the convoy pass over. Surfacing an hour later, it sighted a steamer and another gnat was fired. There was a malfunction and it detonated after just 26 seconds. The U-boat was then depth-charged. In the early afternoon *U-377* surfaced. There was good visibility at the time and a four-engined aircraft was seen approaching. The aircraft was a Liberator from No 10 Squadron of the RCAF, based at Gander in Newfoundland. There was a moderate wind, but weather and visibility were good at base and six Liberators were airborne before 1130 on convoy escorts.

Air Vice Marshal A. E. Godfrey arrived in the afternoon, inspected a parade and congratulated the squadron on its sinking of *U-341* three days earlier.

Flying one of the six sorties was Liberator L-Lucy, which had been airborne at 0630 and was piloted by Warrant Officer J. Billings. This was the aircraft that was bearing down on *U-377*. The U-boat opened fire immediately and at the same time sent an R/T report saying: 'Am being attacked by aircraft.'

This report was not received by U-boat headquarters but was heard by the nearby *U-402*. The Liberator was driven off, but not before Gerhard Kluth, the captain of *U-377*, had been shot through both arms. He was losing blood and was taken below as the 1WO crash-dived. A further R/T message was transmitted, requesting medical assistance.

Gunfire from the U-boat had been accurate, one of the Liberator's engines had been put out of action and the navigator was wounded; he had a bullet in his leg and a slight scalp wound. However, L-Lucy touched down at base just before midnight.

Aircraft from the squadron reported ten U-boats in the proximity of the convoy.

Three days later, on the 25th, *U-377* was again attacked by aircraft, this time in the early hours. Four bombs were dropped and the boat turned hard to starboard, vibrating badly. It did not fully respond to controls. The top of the conning tower was bent but the U-boat was capable of diving and indeed may have touched bottom. For the next two hours destroyer noises were heard above. After a long spell below, *U-377* cautiously surfaced just before midnight. All was clear, but with a wounded commander and a damaged boat the return journey was commenced. The boat arrived back in Brest on 10 October.

The other U-boats had been signalling in their successes; a total of twelve escorts sunk and three more probably sunk from an expenditure of twenty-four gnats, resulted in the effectiveness of the new weapon being over-estimated. The true figures were three

(Above) *U-377* arriving back at Brest on 10 October 1943

(Right) OL Gerhard Kluth, with his wounded arm bandaged, introduces the crew of *U-377* to base commander KK Lehmann-Willenbrock.

U-377 crawled home badly damaged from an air attack. *(Left)* The diving tanks were just missed. *(Below)* The three jagged holes on the port side of the conning tower were made by the Liberators cannon fire. Forward of them is the grid over the top of the ventilation shaft.

escorts sunk and another damaged.

U-377 had escaped being the first U-boat sunk in autumn on 25 September, but two days later, on opposite sides of the Atlantic two other highly experienced U-boat crews were not to be so fortunate.

Crews of the Martin Mariner flying boats of the US Navy Patrol Squadron 74 at the Aratu air base in Brazil had been searching for a marauding U-boat for some time. The U-boat, *U-161* under the command of Kapitänleutnant Albrecht Achilles, knew it was being hunted but apparently did not seem over-concerned. A reason for this confidence could well have been the successes it had achieved.

The Type IXC boat built by Seebeckwerft at Bremerhaven was launched in February 1941. It did not make its first war patrol until the following January when it left Kiel and put in to Lorient in the middle of the month. Six weeks later *U-161* crossed the Atlantic for a Caribbean patrol, returning at the beginning of April. Sailing to the same area again at the end of the month, the U-boat did not return until early August. After five weeks ashore the crew took *U-161* to a new patrol area off the West African coast and the Atlantic Narrows on 19 September, where there was better hunting. In a two-month spell five ships of about 5,000 tons each were sunk: the British ships *Phoebe* and *Benalder* on 23 October and 8 November; the American *West Humhaw* also on 8 November; the Dutch *Tjileboet* on 29 November and the British ship *Ripley* on 12 December. It was a happy crew that returned to Lorient on 9 January. Two months were spent ashore before *U-161* put to sea again. In mid-March, with U-boats achieving considerable results in the crucial convoy battles, the boat was ordered to the American eastern seaboard. On 19 May the small 255 ton boat *Angelus* was sunk by gunfire. This was the only success recorded when *U-161* returned on 7 June to join most of the other Atlantic boats that had been recalled after their mauling in May.

A photographer snapped a happy-looking and bronzed Albrecht Achilles and the flotilla medical officer in the conning tower of *U-161* just before it left Lorient on 8 August for its sixth and last patrol. The area of operations was to be off the Brazilian coast. It was said at the time of sailing that the medical officer was responsible for the medical care of Atlantic U-boat crews. Two weeks out to sea, in the area of the Azores, *U-161* met a Japanese submarine. Arriving on station off Brazil, the U-boat had to wait until 20 September for its first success. *St Usk*, a 5,000 ton ship, was torpedoed and sunk, but

not before some of the crew were able to get away in lifeboats and
have a good look at the U-boat. Six days later another 5,000 tonner,
Itapage, was torpedoed and sunk and *Cisne Branco*, a 300 ton boat,
was sunk by gunfire. This was to be the ninth and last success for
U-161 – the Mariners from Aratu were after it.

On the evening of the 26th, flushed with the success of two
sinkings that day, *U-161* was on the surface in an area where there
were no clouds for at least twelve miles in any direction. As a
Mariner, camouflaged standard blue-grey with oyster white bottom,
approached, the U-boat crash-dived and had been down for eighty
seconds when the seaplane arrived at the swirl.

Perhaps this escape gave the U-boat crew confidence, but they
should have been warned, for in May a Mariner from the same base
had sunk *U-128*. Albrecht Achilles certainly knew Kapitänleutnant
Ulrich Heyse, the commander of the successful Lorient-based
U-128, for the previous December they had refuelled together from
a milch-cow in the Atlantic. In May, with Kapitänleutnant
Hermann Steinart now in command, together they hunted convoy
SL109. *U-128* fired a spread of torpedoes on the surface at night and
in the counter-attack several depth-charges exploded near *U-161*
when *U-128* had been the original target! A Mariner sank *U-128* on
17 May but the captain and forty-six of his men were rescued by a
US destroyer.

It was the doctrine of the Aratu wing to deliver a decisive and
immediate attack. When the element of surprise had been
eliminated, the doctrine stressed an attack from forward of the beam
of the U-boat, with an attempt to manoeuvre it in such a direction
as to place the longitudinal axis in the trough of the sea and thus
impair the accuracy of fire.

On the morning of 27 September Lieutenant Harry B. Patterson
and his ten crewmen took off from the Brazilian base to search in
the area where the U-boat had been sighted the previous evening.
After being airborne for nearly ninety minutes a radar contact was
reported. The pilot continues with the story:

Aircraft 74-P-2 was flying a barrier sweep at an altitude of 4,500
feet when, at 1050, the radar operator reported a ship bearing
eight degrees to port, 38 miles range. As we closed range, the wake
of a U-boat was first sighted visually by the second pilot about
eighteen miles dead ahead, its course at right angles to ours
headed to our right. Action stations were manned, as we

immediately increased speed and commenced a shallow turn to left to take advantage of the sun, as well as to get in position for a stern attack. No clouds were in the area. I believe we were sighted at this time. About seven to eight miles distant, the U-boat opened fire while in a left turn, apparently attempting to bring his after guns to bear on us. The shells were exploding short, leaving white puffs in a line across our course.

As we came within range, approximately three to four miles distant, some large brown puffs could be seen. The gunners were very accurate and the explosions made the air very turbulent. The front gunner opened fire at about 3,000 yards, the fire was falling short, getting on the target as the range closed. The co-pilot dropped a string of six Mark 44 Torpex filled depth charges as I passed over, or just forward of, the conning tower from the U-boat's port quarter at an angle of about twenty degrees from the stern, between 75 and 100 feet altitude. I made a sharp turn. The U-boat appeared to be just emerging from the bomb slick, most of which seemed to be on the starboard side of the U-boat's track. The U-boat started turning right. When the aircraft was broadside the U-boat again opened fire, the shells exploding off our port side. After reaching 800 feet altitude, I gave orders to standby and commenced the second attack. During this run, the fire was heavier and more accurate. We were hit just forward of the galley door by a shell that exploded just as it struck. Ensign Brett was emerging from the bombing compartment after having reset the intervalometer. He was severely wounded by shrapnel and aluminium from this shell, as was Radioman Bealer. At this time I did not know he was hit, nor where or how badly the aircraft was damaged.

The co-pilot dropped the remaining two bombs as the Mariner passed directly over the target from stern to bow at about 150 feet altitude. I immediately gained height believing that there was a possibility that my engines or fuel tanks were damaged. The navigator carried Brett back aft to a bunk where first-aid was administered. Bealer was still sending signals. The flight engineer reported that we were hit in many places and that our inverter line was shot away putting our electrical instruments out of commission.

Just before reaching 2,500 feet altitude, at which I levelled off, I glanced back and noticed that Bealer was wounded in his right leg. He was still at his station helping with the amplifying report and had never reported being hit. After checking Ensign Brett's injuries and the damage to the aircraft I realised that he needed medical attention quickly. Although we were out of range at this time, the U-boat kept up a continuous fire. It manoeuvred erratically after the second attack and the speed was noticeably reduced. It squared away on a straight course and submerged at 1122. I flew over the swirl and dropped a depth charge marker, and then departed for base.

The Mariner arrived back safely at Aratu where Ensign Brett was found to be seriously wounded and the radioman less so.

A US Navy Ventura arrived at the scene shortly after the Mariner left but nothing further was seen. During the attack the aircraft fired a thousand rounds from the front turret; six hundred from the rear turret; fifty from the port waist. The front gunner believed he killed or wounded the gunners on the conning tower, and possibly wounded others aft. *U-161* remained on the surface throughout, manoeuvring to present its stern to the aircraft for both attacks. The foredeck gun was used when the Mariner was at distance, before and after the attacks. Heavy and constant fire came from the conning tower guns when the aircraft was within range,

After the last attack *U-161* manoeuvred violently and erratically and at reduced speed, its after deck was awash. Light grey smoke was observed in addition to diesel fumes. A small fire was believed to have begun near the conning tower base on the after deck. It was agreed by those who saw the explosions, that the first six depth charges were slightly over to starboard from the conning tower to the stern. The next two were on the starboard quarter, believed within range of the U-boat's stern.

This assessment was probably right, for nothing more was ever heard or seen of *U-161*. As it had been to the east of its reported position of the previous day, it can be assumed it was leaving its patrol area, possibly making for the base it had left seven weeks earlier.

The first autumn success had gone to a twin-engined American flying boat. The second, later in the day was by a four-engined British bomber, the Handley-Page Halifax.

In the early months of 1943 the Battle of the Atlantic undoubtedly went the way of the U-boats but Coastal Command headquarters at Northwood were not without hope. The Coastal Command version of the four-engined Handley-Page Halifax was to make its appearance on the scene in March and ten-centimetre ASV became increasingly available. Before he relinquished command Air Chief Marshal Sir Philip Joubert de la Ferté, C-in-C Coastal Command, had laid down the recommended role of aircraft in submarine warfare after having made a review of past air operations against U-boats. He set out a plan of operations for the future. He suggested that the U-boat be attacked:

(a) At its point of departure, that is to say in the building yards, in the communications that enable it to sail by supplying it with oil, fuel and stores, and at its operational base.

(b) on passage

(c) at its point of arrival, that is to say, in its patrol areas and round the threatened convoy.

His recommendations continued:

All these three operations are essential to ultimate success. Admittedly the attack on the U-boat building yards has only long term consequences. Also it will only become really effective when it is possible to carry out such attacks both by day and by night, thus adding accurate pin point bombing of the building slips to the area bombing designed to dislocate the life of the workers employed in the yards.

The attack on the communications along which the necessary supplies flow to the operational bases can have an immediate effect. The blockade of the Biscay ports by our forces is, so far as supplies to the U-boats are concerned, complete. Only by the overland route can the necessary oil and stores reach the five operational bases of Brest, Lorient, St Nazaire, La Pallice and Bordeaux. If, therefore, attacks are continuously made on the railways and rolling stock that furnish these ports, the operations of the U-boats will be seriously hampered.

The attack on the bases themselves presents a more difficult problem now that we have allowed the Germans time to put the vital portions of their organisation under many feet of concrete. At the same time, however, it is impossible completely to secure all the personnel and material that go to make an efficient base – power and water must always remain exposed, dockyard facilities such as cranes, wharf-sheds and mine sweepers all must remain in the open.

The turn-tables communicating with the various pens and which enable U-boats to be beached and launched are a most vulnerable point. Finally, any reduction in the number of minesweepers due to heavy air attack correspondingly raises the efficiency of the sea mining in the approaches to the ports. The major importance of this form of attack is that the initiative is in our hands; the targets are static if the effort is made, can be continuously under attack.

The second method of attack, on passage, is well recognised in naval strategy as the most difficult form of operation. And when to the powers of evasion possessed by surface vessels are added those of the U-boat, it can easily be seen that a complex problem presents itself. But again, there are great advantages in this form of attack. Firstly, the U-boats must pass through a relatively confined area in which we hold the initiative. So long as they continue to use the Bay ports they must expose themselves to our offensive operations.

Sir Philip then went on to expand the role of the Coastal aircraft round the convoys, that of keeping the U-boats submerged so that they could not locate and report the convoy position.

The most important role of the Command Halifaxes was to attack U-boats on passage; the aim of the pilot on an anti-submarine patrol, on sighting a U-boat, was to deliver his attack with the minimum possible delay so as to catch his target while still on the surface, or at least within a few seconds of diving. For this reason the pilot was given a completely free hand to attack from any direction he wished. Under normal conditions he was expected to attack his objective from whatever direction presented itself and waste no time in jockeying for position. There were occasions when the pilot could select the direction of attack. The fact that the U-boat could remove itself from the danger of aircraft attack in less than two minutes, the very precise bombing problem with which the aircrew were faced, the ineffectiveness of their weapons in the past and the superior look-out which the submarine was in a position to maintain, were some of the factors which previously worked against the majority of attacks. If the U-boat was not going to dive there was no need to attack in the shortest possible space of time. The aircraft could break off the attack before getting dangerously close, then fly round the U-boat at about 800 yards range and bring all guns to bear. These tactics usually produced a high mortality rate among the gun crews on the upper deck, resulting in a sudden decision on the part of the U-boat captain to *zum Teufel gehen* – 'get the hell out of it', therefore leaving the aircraft with a 'sitter'.

This knowledge of U-boat tactics at sea had been hard won and not without cost and so a comprehensive summary of anti-submarine tactics was published, just in time for the pilots converting to Coastal Halifaxes to take advantage of the experience of their predecessors. The main points of the summary were:

U-boats keep a very good lookout – three to four men on the bridge of the conning tower scanning with binoculars a different sector of the sea and sky. It is no use your seeing a U-boat if it also sees you while you are still several miles away. The worst height to fly is 1,000–2,000 feet where the aircraft will easily be seen as it flies over the horizon unless it can make some use of cloud, whereas an aircraft flying at 5,000 feet or more stands a good chance of not being spotted itself, while the crew should have no difficulty in sighting a U-boat wake; in the past this has been seen from 18,000 feet.

Each captain must organize a proper look-out; at least two members of the crew must be keeping watch while the others rest as much as possible. Learn to use binoculars correctly (most people think they know but don't and this is a primary cause of eyestrain). You must scan scientifically. If you look in one direction only, all objects except those fairly close will remain unseen except in an arc of two degrees only. Remember that at 5,000 feet the horizon is 83 miles distant so it is no good looking there.

If the sun is at right angles, the approaching aircraft should achieve almost complete surprise. Remember that unless the U-boat is stationary, it will not normally hear an aircraft until too late. A U-boat can dive within thirty seconds and will be out of harm's way in another thirty seconds, so unless the U-boat crew make a mistake, you must be within three miles before you are sighted. What you've got to do is to get your aircraft with the least possible delay to the position of attack where you must be flying straight and level at a height as near 50 feet as possible. You must practise approaches so that you can always do this first time without a second circuit.

If the U-boat is surprised on the surface and hasn't the time to dive to a safe depth, there is now an increased probability of the commander deciding to remain on the surface and fight it out. In such circumstances you have the choice of going straight into attack or of circling at 800 to 1,000 yards, varying your height, and trying methodically to wipe out the U-boat gun crews.

The month of May 1943 saw the turning point of the U-boat war when a total of 41 were sunk, many of them from the air in the Bay of Biscay. Wing Commander Wilfred E. Oulton was commanding officer of No 58 Squadron, based at Holmsley South, which had been searching the Bay in their Halifaxes for six weeks before the beginning of May without success. This was soon to change.

On 7 May he was responsible for the destruction of *U-663*; this was the thirteenth attempt by No 58 Squadron to sink a U-boat. Eight days later Wilfred Oulton had his second success, sinking *U-463* on the fringe of the Bay of Biscay. His third success came on the last day of May. He attacked and damaged *U-563* before a Sunderland of No 10 Squadron RAAF and another Halifax of 58 Squadron, flown by Flying Officer Eric Hartley, completed the sinking. Wilfred Oulton left the squadron later in the summer.

After a lean summer in the U-boat war the squadron was hoping that autumn would be more fruitful.

There had been revised instructions issued by Air Marshal Sir John Slessor, who had succeeded Sir Philip Joubert as Commander-in-Chief of Coastal Command: In clear weather aircraft would fly at 5,000 feet, but advantage was to be taken of low cloud to gain concealment where possible. As soon as a U-boat was seen, or picked up on radar, the aircraft was to lose height quickly and go in to the attack, aiming to place its depth charges, pre-set to explode at 25 feet, so as to straddle the conning tower. If the enemy dived at once the attack had to be completed within thirty seconds of diving or the depth charges would be ineffective. If a U-boat decided to stay surfaced and fight it out the orders laid down that the aircraft was to attack irrespective of the accuracy of the gunfire.

Having thus placed strong emphasis on speed and accuracy, and on resolution in accepting the very real dangers involved in low attacks, Air Marshal Slessor stressed the vital importance of alertness, in order to sight the enemy as early as possible.

Constant training was carried out to bring up to standard the team work necessary for various members of the crews.

This then was the situation when on 27 September Group Captain Roger Mead DFC, the new squadron commander, who had not previously flown with the squadron, decided to fly as second pilot/observer to Eric Hartley on his twenty-seventh operational sortie, an anti-submarine patrol.

Their Halifax, B-Baker HR982, took off from base on patrol at 1138. The Halifax flew westwards from its Hampshire airfield, out past the South-Western Approaches, on past the south of Ireland when soon after 1700 *U-221* was sighted on the surface

This particular U-boat had been most successful in its year at sea under 27-year-old Hans Trojer. The scene was set for the confrontation between a brave and resourceful U-boat captain and an experienced U-boat killer. What would be the outcome?

At the beginning of hostilities Trojer, a native of Birthähn/Siebürgen, was 2WO in *U-34*, a position he held for fifteen months. For the first six months of 1941 he was 1WO of *U-67* before being given command of the training boat *U-3*. His new boat, *U-221*, was launched in March 1942. The U-boat had been built at the Germania Werft in Kiel. Hans Trojer officially became captain in May. After the drafting officer had crewed the boat and it had survived the rigours of the exercises and trials, it left Germany at the beginning of September for its first patrol.

Hans Trojer and his crew did not take long to make their mark in the Battle of the Atlantic with their new boat, for on 12 October 1942 they attacked convoy SC104. On the first night *U-221* penetrated the ranks of the convoy and sank three ships. The next night the U-boat sank four more. The sinking of 40,000 tons of shipping was a notable achievement for the other U-boats in the group only sank one other ship between them. The largest ship sunk, *Southern Empress* of over 12,000 tons, was torpedoed in the early morning of 14 October and later finished off with gunfire. The U-boat completed its patrol and reported at its French base on 22 October.

After a month ashore, Trojer and his now experienced crew members took their Type VIIC boat to sea again on 23 November. The U-boat was one of a pack positioned to attack convoy HX217 off Newfoundland. Unfortunately *U-221* collided with *U-254* on 8 December south of Cape Farewell. This was an occurrence that was always likely to happen and indeed U-boat headquarters had foreseen such an event, but it was the first collision that had taken place, in action, in over three years of war in the Atlantic.

Kapitänleutnant Hans Gilardone's Type VIIC *U-254* was badly damaged and could not dive. The surfaced U-boat was an easy target for the very experienced Squadron Leader T. M. Bulloch, of whom more later, flying Liberator B-Baker, AM921, of 120 Squadron. The squadron leader depth-charged and sank the U-boat, leaving just three survivors. His wireless operator read a flashed message from below as the Flower Class corvette HMS *Potentilla* signalled: 'You killed him'.

Oberleutnant Hans Trojer and his dejected crew returned to France just two days before Christmas, pleased to be spending the festive season ashore but fearful of their reception after the collision and loss of *U-254*. A subsequent inquiry ruled that nobody was to blame for the collision. Nevertheless the boat did not go to sea again until 27 February 1943.

Convoys HX228 and HX229 were targets at a time of which Winston Churchill said: 'The Germans never came so near to disrupting communications between the new world and the old'. On the morning of 7 March Trojer sank the ship *Jamaica* sailing independently. Three days later Trojer was one of thirteen U-boats in position to attack the heavily escorted convoy HX228. In the evening he sank the freighter *Tucurinca*, the ammunition ship *Andrea F. Luckenbach* and hit the *Lawton B. Evans* but the torpedo failed to explode. The spectacular explosion that sank the ammunition ship damaged *U-221* and another U-boat that was close by. The sinking also resulted in a depth-charge attack from the close escort.

A week later, in the bright spring evening of the 17th, the lookouts in the conning tower did not spot Flying Officer Elser's No 120 Squadron Liberator bearing down on them out of the sun until it was less than two miles away. The captain quickly crash-dived as five depth charges struck the swirl made by the submerging U-boat. The bows and conning tower surged up; it was badly shaken, but survived with just one man injured.

The next day Trojer skilfully manoeuvred his U-boat ahead of HX229, submerged and waited for the convoy. In mid-afternoon, at periscope depth, he fired his stern torpedo which hit a freighter. He then turned his boat and five minutes later fired a salvo of four torpedoes, two of which hit another ship. The periscope of *U-221* was then observed between the convoy lines by the merchant ships *Empire Knight* and *Stephen C. Foster* who quickly opened fire with their machine guns and 4-inch guns. The first ship that had been torpedoed was the American liberty ship *Walter Q. Gresham* on its maiden voyage. The torpedo ripped a large hole in its port side through which its vital cargo of sugar and powdered milk floated out. After the order to abandon ship was given two lifeboats capsized and altogether twenty-seven men were lost before the ship sank four hours later. The second ship, hit with two torpedoes at the aft end on the port side was the British Star line's refrigeration ship *Canadian Star* of over 8,000 tons. After the attack the ship, with its cargo of meat, butter and cheese, settled low in the water and sank less than an hour later with the loss of thirty lives.

It was a much happier crew that returned to port on 28 March. They had survived depth charge attacks from a Liberator and escorts and sunk three more ships; the name of Hans Trojer was becoming known in the U-boat world, and he was awarded the Knights Cross.

The fourth patrol, commenced on 3 May, was to be the longest at sea for *U-221*, lasting until 21 July. On 12 May *U-221* sank the 9,400 ton Norwegian ship *Sandanger*, a straggler from convoy HX237.

Hans Trojer and his crew left the well-equipped St Nazaire base during the evening of 20 September. The crew were relaxed after home leave for some, and the delights of La Baule, a half hour's drive down the coast, for others. At the 200 metre line, Hans Trojer, now a Kapitänleutnant, bade goodbye to his escort and carried out a deep diving test before commencing his patrol. The U-boat captain knew his first task was to negotiate the Bay of Biscay safely – too many U-boats had been caught by air patrols. Hans Trojer, with eleven Allied ships totalling almost 70,000 tons to his credit, successfully overcame this first hurdle and a week later was to the south-west of Ireland when an aircraft was suddenly sighted, low down at 1713 on 27 September.

After over five hours on patrol the Halifax crew were still alert despite the strain of searching in low cloud. At 1700 a possible periscope feather was seen on the surface of the calm sea. The pilot took the aircraft down to fifty feet to investigate. Nothing was seen, but as the Halifax turned away a fully surfaced U-boat was sighted, dead ahead at six miles distant.

As the aircraft was already at fifty feet Flying Officer Hartley decided to approach as low as possible, owing to the cloud. At approximately a thousand yards' range, the U-boat and Halifax opened fire at the same time. The U-boat's fire was at first strong, but wild, and slackened off as the aircraft's fire took effect. A further burst hit starboard No 2 fuel tank as the Halifax attacked from the port bow to the starboard quarter.

Eight 250 lb Torpex depth charges, set to 25 feet and spaced at 60 feet, were released from fifty feet. The stick straddled *U-221*, either between the second and third, or third and fourth depth charge, just aft of the conning tower in a line thirty degrees to the U-boat's track. The mid-upper gunner saw a depth-charge plume either side of *U-221*. The U-boat's stern became awash and its bows rose up into the air; *U-221* then slid backwards into the water and disappeared into the 2,000 fathoms depth of water. No further observation was made.

By this time the hit on the fuel tank caused the starboard wing of the Halifax to catch fire and the aircraft was forced to ditch. With great coolness Flying Officer Hartley, despite serious damage to the controls, crash-landed the Halifax in the sea some three miles from the scene of the attack two minutes later. The aircraft stood on its nose for about five minutes and six of the crew including Hartley climbed into the dinghy; the other two members of the crew were lost.

As neither the Halifax nor *U-221* had time to signal that they were attacking, or being attacked, it is fair to assume they must have seen each other simultaneously. *U-221* was logged on 2 October as 'missing' when nothing had been heard of it, and the Halifax logged as 'failed to return' in 58 Squadron's Operational Record book.

There were no survivors from the U-boat but the Halifax survivors suffered many privations owing to their inability to collect all the dinghy equipment. Group Captain Mead made rough notes in his diary of the ordeal they suffered until they were picked up by a destroyer:

First Day: Decided to eat and drink nothing for two days. All badly shocked. I was knocked about a bit. First wireless operator/air gunner burnt on the face. All seasick but no one seriously hurt.

Second Day: Crew's condition excellent. All chirped up a lot and kept our heads, convinced we would be picked up

Third Day: Drizzle at first, but we dried our clothes when weather cleared up. Tried some fishing, made some lines out of aerial wires and safety pins. No luck. Eat some chocolate half an ounce and two milk tablets each. Between us kept watch all night, guessing hours, those nights were hell.

Fourth Day: Issued one small piece of chewing gum apiece,

given back at lunch time for bait, again no fish, two milk tablets each. Said morning and evening prayer, another bad night, cold and wet, water in dinghy.

Fifth Day: Nice fine day, clothes dry. Decided on one milk tablet each, four times a day. Had my shoes and socks off when sea rose to real Atlantic swell and overturned us. Kept our emergency rations but lost lot of clothes, difficult now to keep warm, especially feet, but all lucky to get back into dinghy. Thoroughly done in and badly shocked after that. Special issue of barley sugar, one each, bucked us up. Sea rough all night, wet and miserable.

Sixth Day: Poor weather drizzle, caught rain water with our hands and drank it. Weather improved afternoon. Ration four milk tablets a day, in evening opened first can of water. Determined to have comfortable night but very cold and all stiff and miserable. At 0200 saw a light on the horizon, fired a signal, then found it was Mars!

Seventh Day: Dried everything out and bathed in afternoon, one after the other. Frightened by a couple of whales basking and bellowing 400 yards away. All wounds healing well. Had discussion. Now obvious searching aircraft unable to find us. Still trying to catch fish. Made fishing net from half a mast and seat of an old pair of pants, no fish but about 1800 caught unlimited number of jelly-fish all sizes, and what looked like baby octopi; tried to make a drink out of them; FOUL.

Eighth Day: Low cloud, turning to warm sun. Made and shipped a two-shirt sail. Most effective. Crew breathing through sea-wetted handkerchiefs and keeping hair and faces wet to reduce evaporation losses. Hope still high, but nights bad. All getting tired easily.

Ninth Day: Very rough. Great strain on all. Night an absolute nightmare. Very rough, raining hard. Afraid of being tipped into water again at any moment. Everything soaked.

Tenth Day: Crew very tired. Special issue of chocolate – two small cubes each.

Eleventh Day: Weather cleared midday. Divided one tin of water among us – two ounces. A little chocolate.

By then Group Captain Mead became too 'dopey' as he said, to write or read his diary.

At 1430 that day, the eleventh day, the survivors saw the mast

Handley-Page Halifax of 58 Squadron Coastal Command.

of a destroyer, and then found there were two destroyers, one on each side of them. They were too weak to realise that they were later being dragged aboard HMS *Mahratta*; they found themselves wrapped in blankets and bound for home. The destroyers came upon them by chance, and when first sighted they were taken for Germans, their soaked uniforms looked so dark. The welcome news was received at Holmsley South on 10 October when at the same time it was announced that the wireless operator and the ASV operator had been killed by the U-boat's fire. One of the squadron flyers later remarked that Group Captain Mead went on the flight looking a comparatively young man but came back looking like an old man.

For their part in the ordeal Flying Officer Hartley and Flight Sergeant Kenneth Ladds were both decorated. Eric Hartley received the Distinguished Flying Cross; part of the citation read:

Flying Officer Hartley and the five survivors remained in the dinghy for 11 days with very little food and water, during which time the weather was sometimes extremely rough . . . during this period Hartley's calm determination and level headedness were largely responsible for the admirable manner in which the remainder of his crew survived their gruelling ordeal.

A mention was also made of his previous success.

Flight Sergeant Kenneth E. Ladds was awarded the Distinguished Flying Medal; his citation read:

> On 27 September 1943 Flight Sergeant Ladds who has taken part in 47 operational sorties, was mid-upper gunner of Halifax B-Baker of 58 Squadron when an attack was made against a surfaced U-boat in the Atlantic. In the face of heavy flak Flight Sergeant Ladds fired his guns with great coolness, and succeeded in silencing most of the U-boat gun positions, and enabled the pilot to carry out a successful depth charge attack. Immediately afterwards the aircraft was hit and forced to descend in the sea. Flight Sergeant Ladds and five other members of the crew reached the dinghy in safety and remained in it for eleven days before being rescued. During this period he conducted himself with exemplary patience and fortitude under conditions of very great hardship.

By the time they were picked up on 8 October the crew of B-Baker had already been given up as lost. Similarly when *U-221* had failed to respond to calls from U-boat headquarters it had been officially reported as lost on 2 October; in fact this date is still given as the date of the sinking in some reference books.

If the gunner aboard the U-boat had fired that round just a second before the Halifax released its charges, thereby escaping, the autumn battles could well have had a different outcome with Hans Trojer and his crew still on the convoy scene.

CHAPTER TWO

The Fiftieth Month

October 1943 was the fiftieth month of the war; hostilities had been going on so long that everybody was becoming war-weary. In the fiftieth month of the Kaiser's war the crews of the German Battle Squadron ships broke into open mutiny. That would not happen this time as crews in the larger German ships were being run down and some men transferred to the U-boat arm earlier in the year after Admiral Karl Dönitz, formerly head of the U-boat service, had taken command of the whole Kriegsmarine.

The Admiral had great faith in his U-boats and their crews. The snorkel U-boat plans were well advanced although he still had plenty of conventional U-boats to put to sea. At the beginning of September, armed with their acoustic homing torpedoes, also known as 'gnats' and 'T5's', the U-boat commanders were ordered to attack convoy escorts with the new torpedoes with the objective of reducing the convoy defences to a point where the merchant ships became easy prey. The commanders were told to attack by night, using old and new devices such as radar, search-receivers, hydrophones and possibly MF/DF to locate convoys and to elude attacks by surface ships and aircraft.

In all previous attempts by the Germans to gain a commanding advantage by the use of some novel weapon, the antidote had been devised so rapidly that the advantage had been merely transient; so it was in this case. The Admiralty came up with the idea of trailing a series of wires, over the stern of escorts, to which long strips of metal were attached at the end. The noise of the strips clashing together in the wake, fifty yards astern of the ship, made more noise than the ship's propeller and so attracted the torpedo. The device, designated FXR, was colloquially known as 'the foxer'.

The Allies had been using their own airborne homing torpedo against U-boats since May without the Germans' knowledge. The aircraft carrying the 'Mark 24 mine' as it was known, would only drop the weapon once the U-boat had dived, for it only acted against a submerged boat.

The conduct of battle, and the constant proximity to death, was a test few mortals could stand over a prolonged period without showing the strain and unfortunately for the Germans, U-boat aces of the calibre of Prien and Schepke had been killed and Kretschmer had been captured. Other potential aces, Achilles and Trojer, had recently been lost. Too many U-boats were returning with no results to report. One U-boat captain had already been executed for cowardice in the face of the enemy; another had been reduced to the ranks for superstitiously refusing to sail on a Friday. Some ratings contrived to get off their boats, or at least delay going to sea again. One stole food from his boat, hoping that he would not be sent back after serving his six-month sentence, but his and other similar ploys were soon seen through. Another scheme was to become drunk and incapable the night prior to sailing and thus miss the boat. Again, after suitable punishment the culprits were put aboard other U-boats. Of course, these were extreme exceptions. Most men coveted the U-boat badge they wore, given after sixty days patrolling, and served their country well.

Despite setbacks in the Atlantic, on the Eastern Front and the loss of 291,000 men, rounded up as prisoners after the failure of the North African campaign, many Germans remained optimistic of the final outcome. Amongst the U-boat men there was open talk of the new secret weapons. Men who had been at Danzig told of the pilotless aircraft with flames at the back, (the V1's). The reasoning went thus: America was hard-pressed in their struggle with the Japanese. The secret weapons would make Britain sue for peace as the Americans would not be able to help them. The way would then be clear for the bulk of the German Army to fight on the Russian Front. The fact that Anglo-American forces were already a third of the way up Italy, and that the Italians had surrendered, was apparently not taken into account.

Allied signals made many advances during 1943, especially in the development of radar and communications equipment. Coastal Command's increased activities resulted in an extension of its communication system. Very close liaison with the Admiralty led to a great improvement in signalling between ships and aircraft. Some new types of airborne communications equipment were introduced, particularly for R/T.

Early in the year an entirely new type of search radar was brought into use. It had the advantages of abolition of external drag-

GROSSADMIRAL KARL DÖNITZ
A signed photograph sent to the author by the former Commander-in-Chief of the
Kriegsmarine and the last Führer of the Third Reich.

producing aerials, plan position display and operation on a wavelength outside the scope of the German search receiver.

The British version of the equipment, used by Coastal Command, was an adaptation of a Bomber Command set, and known as the Mark III, it was fitted into Leigh light Wellington, Halifax, Liberator and Sunderland aircraft. The American version was known as the Mark V, of which there were two variants, and this was fitted to all Liberators delivered to Coastal Command, the installation being done in the United States. This introduction of completely new equipment called for intensive training of operators and maintenance staff. This was made very difficult by the lack of training equipment and a shortage of aircraft. These difficulties were eventually overcome and the new equipment very soon proved its worth. The provision of the new radar enabled aircraft to maintain their effort throughout the twenty-four hours and thus give the U-boats no respite at night in which to recharge and ventilate.

The equipment was put to good use when, from secret transcripts, it was discovered that Dönitz was using a new tactic by sending his boats to sea during the evening. Between May and mid-July 1943 U-boats had sailed from Biscay ports at various times throughout the 24 hours, but after this time the vast majority had sailed within the four hours after 1630. The probable plan was that the boats would then be able to cross the greater part of the Bay in darkness.

Statistics were collated of 127 sailings from the beginning of July to early October: they showed 2 early sailings and 7 post-1630 from Brest; 11 to 41 at Lorient; nil to 42 from St Nazaire; 1 to 14 from La Pallice and 1 to 8 from Bordeaux, totalling 15 to 112 of the 127 sailings. Of course, not all the sailings were from the Biscay ports; Bergen and Trondheim were also used.

Meanwhile on the home front on 2 October Ernest Bevin, Minister of Labour and National Service, told striking Vickers-Armstrong shipyard workers at Barrow that their only honourable course was to return to work. The following day 6,000 Scottish and 800 Durham miners returned to the pits after a four-day grievance. On the 7th a strike by dockyard workers in Malta ended and they pledged not to strike again for the duration of the war.

On 5 October Sir Andrew Cunningham was appointed First Lord of the Admiralty in succession to Sir Dudley Pound. Sir Dudley's retirement lasted only sixteen days for he died on Trafalgar Day. He was a war casualty, worn out by his arduous duty as First Lord and

Chief of the Naval Staff since before the war.

Another to die during October was Sir Kingsley Wood, Minister for Air at the outbreak of war. He had held the West Woolwich seat since the Great War. Although there was a National Government, the democratic parliamentary election process still took place. Major Beech held the seat for the Conservatives, holding off a challenge by the Labour and Independent candidates in a by-election.

Bob Hope, who was born in the constituency, was making *The Cat and the Canary* in Hollywood with Paulette Goddard and in London the quality of stars and shows in the autumn of 1943 has probably never been equalled. There was Ivor Novello's *The Dancing Years* at the Adelphi, Terence Rattigan's *Flare Path* at the Apollo; Anton Walbrook and Diana Wynyard in *Watch on the Rhine*; Nervo and Knox at the Coliseum, Flanagan and Allen at the Stoll, Jack Hulbert and Cicily Courtneidge in *Something in the Air* at the Palace. *The Merry Widow, Lisbon Story* and a host of other shows offered reduced admission for 'Forces in uniform'. For sporting entertainment the Football League offered a North and South competition and on 3 October West Ham defeated Crystal Palace 6-1 at Selhurst Park.

A quarter of a million voluntary workers had contributed three million knitted and made up garments for the Navy League Comforts fund, they also sent honey to submariners. The subject of Dutch Elm disease was brought up in *The Times*.

On 12 October the midget submarines attacked *Tirpitz* in Norway and the following day the Badoglio government in Italy declared war on Germany. In the Caribbean *U-516* sank six ships and escaped despite a week long search. Further north, off Canada, U-boats were showing more signs of activity than at any time since early spring. Their presence in the Gulf of St Lawrence led to the suspension of some independent sailings in the river and reinstitution of convoys. No attacks were made on merchant vessels in the area but mines were laid in the approaches to St John's, Newfoundland. The first floating mine was sighted and sunk six miles off the port on 12 October and the next day eight were destroyed to the north of the swept channel from St John's. The mines were identified as the moored magnetic type. A week later twenty-two mines had been swept but a convoy ran into an unsuspected field south of Cape Spear and lost two ships. On one of the ships, carrying iron ore to the Sydney blast furnaces, twenty-seven of her crew were lost. The loss was serious for the iron works as a large stock pile of iron ore and limestone had to be built up in the navigation season to keep the blast furnaces in operation during the winter.

The Germans also set up a weather station at Martin Bay, near the northern tip of Labrador. The equipment was carried ashore on two rubber rafts from *U-537*, erected and ran for about three.months, until its batteries ran out, giving information on conditions in the North Atlantic Allied shipping lanes. U-boats had previously installed stations in Greenland and Spitzbergen, but this was the only known landing in North America during the war. A second U-boat, sent to re-establish the station in 1944, was sunk en route.

October proved to be Coastal Command's third best month on record despite the unusual run of bad weather in the Bay of Biscay. Weather records show that spring and autumn are always the worst periods for weather in the Bay, the winter months comparing not unfavourably with the summer.

By October the Germans were in a less favourable position than at the turn of the year. Convoys were protected by escort groups, while support groups were given free rein to attack U-boats. VLR aircraft were more plentiful as were the single-engined aircraft from escort carriers.

From July the Germans were unable to break the new naval cyphers and in October their signals were being decrypted so rapidly that the British were reading the signals at the same time as the U-boat captains.

Meanwhile the U-boat losses were a drain on the skilled personnel available for expert seamen and especially technicians. They could not be turned out as quickly as the U-boats were by mass production methods. Perhaps, more important, was the loss of experienced U-boat commanders. Experience could only be gained, not taught, and at this time thirty percent of U-boat captains, at sea, had less than three months' experience of command. Only one had spent more than two years in operational command.

Before going into the events of autumn 1943 more closely, we will look at the role that one aircraft, the Liberator, played in the Battle of the Atlantic.

CHAPTER THREE

A Liberator Story

During August and September 1943, the U-boat killing business in the North Atlantic was poor for Liberators; the veteran H-Harry, AM929, of No 120 Squadron carried out seven trips without any success. Things were to alter in the middle of the next month.

In the early evening of 17 October, D-Dog from 59 Squadron was returning to base on completion of an anti-U-boat convoy escort when at 1817 a U-boat was sighted at ten miles. The aircraft was flying just below cloud base at 1,800 feet, visibility at the time being about thirty miles. Radar was switched on but no contact had been obtained.

The aircraft used cloud cover to approach, hoping to achieve surprise, and circled the stern of the U-boat to attack from the starboard quarter. The Type IXC, *U-540*, was built at the Deutsche Werft in Hamburg, launched 18 December 1942 and was under the command of Kapitänleutnant Kasch. The U-boat opened up inaccurate flak at about 2,000 yards and as the aircraft came in to attack, the pilot noticed for the first time that Liberator H-Harry was also coming in, on a reciprocal course. The 59 Squadron Liberator attacked from the starboard beam, dropping four Torpex Mark XI depth charges. This stick overshot with the nearest depth charge being 200 feet from the U-boat.

The skipper of H-Harry dropped no depth charges on his first run, turned steeply and came in for another attack. The stick of depth charges straddled at 30 degrees to the U-boat's track. The other Liberator then attacked again, but no charge was dropped owing to a malfunction. The pilot made certain of his third attack and dropped four depth charges, straddling the U-boat midway between the conning tower and the stern. In each attack fierce and accurate fire from the aircraft caused casualties to the U-boat's gunners who had been putting up intense anti-aircraft fire. Immediately after this third attack from the 59 Squadron Liberator, *U-540* was observed to be down by the stern and to have lost speed. The railings of the bandstand were twisted and torn and several of the guns' crew appeared to be dead. Others of the crew were seen jumping overboard. Almost immediately after this, H-Harry delivered its own attack, which was a perfect straddle. The bows of the U-boat reared up and *U-540* sank immediately, leaving some twenty to thirty survivors struggling in the sea.

The concentrated and accurate fire from the Liberator's gunners undoubtedly considerably affected the accuracy of the U-boat's flak and this had made it easier for H-Harry to carry out the *coup de grâce*.

For H-Harry this was recorded as a 'shared' kill, but H-Harry had already established a reputation as a scourge of the U-boats. As it survived all but a month of the war, we will look at AM929, and other Liberators, in more detail.

Over 18,000 Liberators were built in various forms during the war; more than any other type of American aircraft, including the Flying Fortress.

Well before the war American aircraft companies, Boeing and Douglas, were working on the problem of four-motor heavy bomber design and produced various designs but of these only the B-17, Flying Fortress, was considered to have a future with the USAAF.

However, early in 1939, the air force called on the Consolidated Company to produce a type whose performance would better that of the Fortress, and not long after the firm was awarded a contract for the B-24. Consolidated promised an early delivery and the first prototype flew on 29 December 1939. This aircraft was powered by four Pratt and Whitney Twin Wasp engines developing 1,200 hp each, giving a top speed of 273 mph.

The fuselage was of aluminium alloy monocoque structure in three main sections, the main bulkheads being forward and aft of the bomb-bay; thirteen transverse frames in the rear section joined by closely-spaced longitudinal stringers of light alloy to which the flush-riveted stressed-skin covering was attached. The wings were an all-metal structure in three main sections comprised of the centre-section which passed through the fuselage and carried the four motor mountings and the undercarriage and the two outer panels which attached outboard of the outer motors; light alloy multi-spar structure with sheet alloy ribs having flanged lightning holes and closely-spaced longitudinal stringers to which the smooth stressed-skin covering was riveted. Special Davis-type aerofoil of thin section was used to offer low profile drag. Fowler-type trailing-edge area-increasing flaps with metal covering were between the ailerons and the wing roots. Statically-balanced ailerons had alloy frames with fabric covering. The tail unit was an all-metal cantilever structure with twin fins and rudders, metal-covered fixed surfaces and fabric-covered movable surfaces. Pulsating rubber de-icers were on the wings and tail. The undercarriage was of the tricycle type with the main wheels retracting outwards into recesses in the wing centre-section and the nose wheel retracting upwards and backwards into a compartment aft of the nose position.

A far-sighted French purchasing commission had ordered 120 B-24's but the equally enterprising British took over the order on the fall of France in June 1940. Altogether a huge production programme was put in hand and the B-24's were delivered in early 1941. The RAF christened the B-24's 'Liberator' and later the Americans also officially adopted this name.

The first batch of Liberators to reach Britain were tested, but found to be not suitable at this time for use as operational day bombers, so were put in service on the 'Atlantic Air Bridge', the trans-Atlantic return ferry service. Liberators were the only military aircraft available and seven were put into commission, flying aircrews from Britain to Canada, a procedure which become known as the Return Ferry Service. Captain Youell, a BOAC pilot, flew the first westbound Liberator in the service, carrying seven members of delivery crews. The flight from Prestwick to Montreal, via Newfoundland, took sixteen hours and forty-five minutes' flying time.

The results of experimental flying and testing in Britain were made known to the Americans and Consolidated set about producing an improved B-24. The upshot was the B-24B, or Liberator I as it became known in the RAF. This was followed by the B-24C, with two power-operated gun turrets and increased fuselage length. This B-24C is the aircraft we are particularly interested in, as they went into service with Coastal Command; their great range bridging the 'Atlantic Gap' – an area where hitherto U-boats could operate reasonably certain of not being located or attacked by aircraft.

The B-24D, Liberator III, was the most widely-used version of the type and differed from the earlier models in having motors with elliptical cowlings and the dorsal turret moved further forward to a point just aft of the control cabin. The aircraft we are following, AM929, was built by Consolidated-Vultee in San Diego, California, code number 29, USAAF No 40.2368. It was completed on 26 May

1941 and flown to La Guardia field for tests. Thence the Liberator flew to Wright Field Daytona, and from there to Dorval Canada, via La Guardia field. The aircraft then flew the Atlantic, touching down at Prestwick on 21 August. It remained at the airport in the hands of Scottish Aviation Limited. Here it underwent preliminary modification taking it from a B-24 to a Liberator of Coastal Command. The next stop was the south coast, to the experimental airfield at Boscombe Down where the RAF gave it thorough performance trials. The aircraft was in their hands until 26 January 1942 when it returned once again to Prestwick for the major part of its conversion into a Coastal aircraft, the work being carried out by Scottish Aviation. This work, much of which was concerned with the installation of four 20mm forward-firing cannon, took over seven months because the necessary spares were not to be had in this country, and their delivery from the United States took a long time due to wartime conditions. Eventually, however, the bottlenecks were straightened out, the supplies came through and AM929 was ready for front-line service.

Although now operational the Liberator, built as a wartime aircraft, was much less comfortable than the pre-war Short Sunderland flying-boat with which it was to share the hazardous sea patrols. In the Liberator there were no bunks for rest periods, no galley to prepare hot food. It was cramped and moving about in the aircraft was an arduous job. Hampered by voluminous flying suits some crewmen had to squeeze through the steel supports in the bomb-bay, wriggling between the depth charges lined up ready to drop, and finally bend low through a narrow door into the rear compartment.

On 3 August 1942 AM929 arrived at Ballykelly County Londonderry, to join No 120 Squadron, and was designated H-Harry. The squadron was now re-equipping with Liberators and AM929 was allocated to Squadron Leader Terrence Bulloch. The squadron leader was a veteran anti-submarine pilot who had flown the slower twin-engined Ansons and Hudsons on this task earlier in the war.

The beginning of the Liberator's operational career was not auspicious. The first trip on 9 August, a fifteen-hour convoy escort, was uneventful, but on its second trip a petrol leak developed, and this combined with poor visibility caused an early return to base. The next sortie also began badly; the pilot found immediately after take-off that one of his engines was giving trouble and circled the airfield for 35 minutes before setting off on his mission. This was considered an important sortie, to search for any survivors of the troopship *Letitia*, reported torpedoed and sunk 610 miles west of Blacksod Bay with 600 troops on board. The ship was not located, as fortunately the report of the sinking was incorrect and it later docked in Canada. After this H-Harry's luck changed. On the next trip it joined a Catalina and naval vessels off the Azores on a U-boat hunt, and finding a most suspicious patch of air bubbles, dropped a stick of depth charges across it. Unfortunately, for the Allies, the U-boat, *U-89*, which was returning from a patrol on the east coast of the USA, was not destroyed, although at the time, with naval forces still harrying it when the Liberator left, it was believed sunk.

Despite its low number *U-89* was only launched the previous September. A Type VIIC boat it was built at Flenderwerft Lübeck. Commissioned in November it joined the 8th Training Flotilla on the Baltic under the command of Dietrich Lohmann, a native of Hamlen, who was then thirty-two years old and something of a veteran having already commanded two other submarines. He had sailed with the legendary Otto Kretschmer during the last two months of 1940 during which time the famous *U-99* sank eight Allied ships. The following month he was appointed captain of *U-544* spending five months aboard before transferring to *U-579*, in command.

So it was as an experienced submarine commander that Dietrich Lohmann took over the new *U-89*. After the working-up period the U-boat sailed from Kiel on 14 May 1941 on its first war cruise, arriving at Brest to join the 9th Flotilla thirteen days later. After a fortnight at the Brittany base the boat left for the American seaboard, but the only action came towards the end of July when the guns' crew were given some practice against a small boat off the Canadian coast. It was returning from its second cruise when attacked by H-Harry. The crew, containing several new recruits amongst its number, were pleased to arrive back safely in France after spending eleven weeks at sea, and under attack from aircraft and naval forces. On its next patrol *U-89* sank three ships. On its fourth patrol *U-89* encountered engine trouble and was returning to base when it was located and attacked by HMS *Anemone*. The corvette attacked with thirty-five depth charges and fired four hedgehog missiles, and considered it 'a certain kill'. But still *U-89*, damaged from the attack, still with engine trouble and short of fuel, until it topped up from *U-463*, struggled on and put into La Pallice on 28 March after two months at sea. That the U-boat survived these two heavy attacks speaks volumes for its Lübeck constructors. Its next patrol was to be its last for after sinking a Greek ship, *U-89* was sunk with all hands five days later by a combined sea and air attack, to become just another statistic among the forty-one U-boats that were sunk in May 1943.

Returning to Terrence Bulloch and his Liberator: More action was soon to follow for on its next patrol on 19 August 1942 a U-boat was sighted while the aircraft was escorting convoy SL118. The pilot went straight in to attack while the enemy was still on the surface. The U-boat, *U-653*, shuddered and remained surfaced for five seconds after the attack and then submerged steeply. The attack was described as 'excellent' by the Naval Staff of Coastal Command headquarters. Certainly Kapitänleutnant Feiler did not molest the convoy again as the boat was so seriously damaged that it had to return to base. Later on in the same day another U-boat was seen and attacked with cannon fire, which forced it to submerge. Three attacks in two sorties was too good to last and the next trip produced nothing more exciting than some French tunny fishing boats.

On 28 August the hard-worked Liberator had an interesting day but was unlucky not to have a sighting. The convoy it was escorting had been attacked the night before and H-Harry did useful work in helping the stragglers to return to the fold. If encouragement was needed, the sight of a listing merchantman limping along with a torpedo in her side must have provided it. While the aircraft was with the main body of the convoy the SNO sent it a signal to investigate a suspected U-boat some distance away. While on this search, another U-boat attacked the convoy and succeeded in torpedoing another ship. H-Harry did not find its U-boat and soon afterwards had to return to base.

The Liberator was not able to have its revenge for some time, as it was soon translated to a more vital area of operations. After three uneventful sorties it was detached to Reykjavik on 6 September 1942 and began to operate in support of the famous Russian convoys. In company with the other Iceland-based aircraft valuable cover was given to these convoys, whose story would have been different had it been possible to give them, all through their journey, the same cover as they received from Iceland in the initial stages.

During September the Liberator sighted three U-boats near the convoys it was protecting and though it was unable to attack any of them they were all put down below the surface where they could do neither damage nor shadowing. On 23 September H-Harry saw an enemy aircraft for the first time. The enemy, probably a Condor, was shadowing the convoy when the Liberator appeared. Shots were exchanged and the enemy was glad to take refuge in a cloud rather than face fire from the four cannons the Liberator mounted. The Liberator was not hit and at the end of the month returned, temporarily, to Ballykelly.

October 1942 turned out to be an exciting month for the Liberator. H-Harry returned to Reykjavik on the 10th and two days later made two attacks on U-boats shadowing convoy ONS136 south-south-west of Iceland. A crew member sighted a wake eight miles to starboard and Bulloch came in behind the track, hoping it was a U-boat. It was soon identified as a Type VIIC, *U-597* in fact. A stick of depth charges was dropped across the Hamburg-built boat and the explosion of the third depth charge was so close to the hull that chunks of metal flew into the air in all directions. One large piece flew past the astonished eyes of the gunner in the rear turret. He reported that the U-boat was completely covered in explosions and lifted out of the water so that the whole deck was clearly visible, with water pouring off it. After the attack a big cylindrical piece of wreckage studded with bolts came to the surface and floated for over half an hour in the middle of a wide patch of oil.

Three days later H-Harry was in the air again, this time flown by Flying Officer S. E. Elser, another veteran U-boat hunter. The pilot was instructed to patrol around convoy SL104 in the North Atlantic. The convoy was picked up nearly a thousand miles from base and the aircraft was instructed to patrol at visibility distance and for the next two hours saw nothing. Then everything happened together. Two U-boats were sighted around the convoy and H-Harry went into action. In the first attack aimed at the further, better placed one, the nearer one was treated to a burst of cannon fire which it was glad to escape by submerging. The second boat, *U-661*, was severely shaken up by depth charges. The pilot was unable to get low enough to drop a really accurate stick but the U-boat was seen again later and finished off by another depth charge attack from H-Harry. Next day the Liberator completed the hat-trick with its third action in three sorties. The U-boat escaped serious damage but was forced to submerge.

Even this did not finish H-Harry's account for the month. After two uneventful sorties, the second of which it did valuable work in reforming a scattered convoy, the Liberator again saw three U-boats round a convoy. One was attacked, though probably not damaged, and the other two escaped by crash-diving. Sighting three U-boats at a time was beginning to be a speciality for H-Harry, for on 5 November, while being flown once more by Terrence Bulloch, it occurred again. This time the Liberator was sent to assist convoy SC107 which had lost fifteen ships in two successive nights

The first one, *U-132*, certainly never worried convoys again, for it became H-Harry's third victim. The pilot mounted a depth charge attack from bow to stern. When the charges exploded, instead of throwing up the usual vivid white plume, the columns of water were dark and dirty. The U-boat's stern rose to an angle of 50 degrees and the screws revolved aimlessly in the air. Soon after the sinking a wide patch of air bubbles foamed on the water for about eight minutes and marked the last resting place for Kapitänleutnant Vogelsang and his crew. The second U-boat of the trio went under before it could be attacked, but the third received the remaining depth charges carried by the Liberator, though it did not sink. The ships below were certainly grateful for their air cover because the U-boats were called off.

When the Liberator took off for its next trip on 20 November it was intended that it should return part of the way home to America. However, the weather in Newfoundland closed in and the crew's hopes of unlimited silk stockings and American cigarettes were deferred for several weeks. The last trip in November was without incident, but in December its first sortie, to protect convoy HX217, was to be the last for the successful combination of Terrence Bulloch and H-Harry, as the squadron leader was about to leave 120 Squadron for a rest tour.

Bulloch reached the convoy at dawn; the weather was stormy but, nevertheless, a U-boat was located astern of the convoy. Six depth charges were dropped but no results were observed. Two further U-boats were sighted approaching the convoy and one received the remaining two depth charges, again without result. As the Liberator still had plenty of fuel left, it continued its job of protecting the convoy by attacking any U-boat observed, with cannon-fire, until it was time to return to Reykjavik.

The Admiralty issued a signal of congratulation which said: 'The six hours escort given to HX217 on 7 December by H/120 at a distance of 800 miles from its base, certainly saved this convoy from serious casualties the following night.'

The Admiralty signal spoke of six hours' escort and working 800 miles from base. The log shows that AM929 was in the air for 16 hours 25 minutes. Time in the air is not all that matters. A Very Long Range aircraft crew's trip can last the full twenty-four hours. Called well before the aircraft is due to set off, which could be four hours before, as the crew have to prepare themselves before breakfast, the pilots go for briefing and to be informed on the latest Intelligence, U-boat report, weather reports; the navigator plots the route, the flight engineer checks his fuel and fuel charts, the gunners that their armament is working. Apart from soon after take-off and the last part of the journey home, when the pilot can switch to 'George', the automatic pilot, the whole time airborne is spent on intense concentration. After the final touch-down all is not over: into the Intelligence Office for interrogation, every facet of the patrol must be reported, ships seen, attacks, weather, all are important. The crew were then allowed to the mess for supper, to bed and the sleep that comes of sheer exhaustion. But there was no more of this for the time being for Squadron Leader Terrence Bulloch, who was having a rest from operational squadron life and operations.

Of the remaining four sorties in 1942 three were uneventful, although one may have been slightly alarming to the crew: the starboard inner engine developed an oil leak when the aircraft was a long way from base, but H-Harry brought the crew safely home on three engines, but this incident should be borne in mind in view of a later event. The other trip produced two attacks. The first, with a full stick of depth charges, damaged the enemy and a good deal of oil was seen. The remaining depth charges may have damaged a second U-boat but the evidence was insufficient.

We now come to the year 1943, which proved so disastrous to the U-boats. So far the story was showing the slow but steady advance towards mastery of the U-boat menace running in direct parallel with the increase in numbers of aircraft, the improvement in airborne weapons and equipment, and the development of air tactics.

Our Liberator began the New Year with a useful sortie on 1 January which rounded up a scattered convoy and ten days later sighted a U-boat near another convoy but was unable to get in an attack before it dived. The next two trips were uneventful; and on 25 January H-Harry returned to its native continent. When a long way from the base in Iceland, the pilot was diverted to Greenland, and set course for the remote Bluie West One base. He was relieved to receive another signal telling him that he could land at Gander if he preferred; he preferred!

After two years' fine service H-Harry was due for an engine change, fortunately there had only been two failures and both of a minor kind. Now was an opportune moment and it was decided that the engines could be most easily changed at Dorval, so the Liberator flew on to the Canadian base. While it was there a major inspection was carried out as well as the engine change. The Liberator, passed fit again for front line action, then flew off to Gander.

On 5 April H-Harry returned to its accustomed area. It took off from Gander on a sweep to Reykjavik and sighted a periscope, which disappeared before an attack could be made. This incident began a period of ill-luck for the Liberator. On the next trip, on 22 April, no fewer than four U-boats were sighted but each time the aircraft went into attack the depth charges hung up. This time H-Harry landed at Goose Bay in Labrador, a novelty for the crew. The aircraft returned to Iceland three days later and had poor luck and uneventful trips for the next two months. Several of the sorties were curtailed or spoiled by bad weather and low visibility. During this time nine sorties were made.

Liberator of 120 Squadron

On 24 June H-Harry made a fitting come-back. While en route to carry out anti-submarine escort to convoy ONS11 south-west of Iceland a fully surfaced Type IXC U-boat was sighted some seventy-five miles north of the convoy. The U-boat, *U-194*, and the Liberator must have seen each other simultaneously for the U-boat began to take violent evasive action. The aircraft dived straight in to attack and opened fire. The U-boat by now was putting up considerable opposition with its guns and as depth charges were released a projectile entered the starboard side of the nose-wheel compartment, rendering all the hydraulics useless. This caused the bomb doors to 'creep' so that only two depth charges released. These straddled *U-194* just forward of the conning tower. The U-boat was not visible after the explosion subsided, but about twenty seconds later, fifteen feet of the bows appeared at a very steep angle and then slid under again. The pilot did not realise that the hydraulics were out of action and he attempted to attack with one depth charge which did not release. On tracking over the position air bubbles and oil were seen coming to the surface, and from twelve to fifteen survivors had appeared, clinging to a long cylindrical object.

In addition to the hit which put the hydraulics out of action, a second shell entered and exploded in the port wing, outside the outer port engine. A serious petrol leak was also started in the starboard tanks, by machine gun bullets. The remaining depth charge load was jettisoned and the aircraft set course for base. A considerable amount of petrol flooded the interior, but the leak stopped when the petrol reached the level of the hole.

On arrival at base the undercarriage and flaps were lowered by emergency methods and for three-quarters of an hour the crew tried to repair the brake hydraulic pipe lines. This was impossible and the pilot then decided to land in tail down attitude. The whole crew, except the flight engineer, took up station in the rear of the aircraft together with all ammunition and movable gear. The mirror camera was removed from its mounting to prevent damage.

A perfect approach was made at very slow speed and a three-point landing made, touching down within a few feet of the end of the runway. Immediately the aircraft touched, the two inboard engines were cut, the two outer ones being kept in case a swing developed. After running a thousand yards most of the speed had been lost but a swing to port had begun. This was checked by opening up the port engine, and the aircraft was eventually brought to rest. The damage from landing was confined to slight buckling of the underskin of the fuselage. The only member of the crew injured was the flight engineer whose neck, back and legs were struck by pieces of shrapnel.

After this magnificent action H-Harry was transferred to 43 Group for repair. A month later it was back in line again but bad weather and poor luck dogged the next few trips, several of which had to be cut short.

The next success did not come until autumn, on 17 October, when *U-540* was sunk, as described earlier in the chapter. As it happened this was to be the final triumph of this successful U-boat killer, for the following month it returned to Scottish Aviation at Prestwick. The Liberator was due for a large-scale overhaul after its long exertions.

H-Harry, AM929, did not rejoin 120 Squadron. The Liberator was still at Prestwick in July 1944. On 17 March 1945 the Liberator joined No 231 Squadron with 45 Group in Canada.

On 9 April, just one month before the end of the war in Europe, AM929 was being flown by two civilian pilots Captains G. Voorhess and D. Mitchell as part of an eight-man crew, and with twelve passengers. At 2000 the pilot attempted a forced landing after the starboard inner engine caught fire at 8,000 feet and could not be extinguished. On its approach to land at Simons, near St Hyacinthe, east of Montreal, it struck high tension cables, crashed, caught fire and burnt out.

The ignominious end to the four-year life of the triumphant AM929 is entered in the record book thus: '9 April 1945 Category E – crashed in Quebec Canada.'

When H-Harry first joined No 120 Squadron it was the only Liberator squadron in Coastal Command. In turn the Liberators of 120 Squadron were the only ones who could reach the real battleground between surface ships and U-boats. The Liberator, which had earlier been deemed 'unsuitable' for daylight bombing in Europe, certainly vindicated itself over the vast waters of the Atlantic Ocean, and none demonstrated this more than AM929.

CHAPTER FOUR

Card's Nap Hand

A U-boat was always liable to attack when entering or leaving harbour, simply because the enemy knew where to look. When Germany captured France in 1940 it wasn't long before Bordeaux, Brest, La Pallice, La Rochelle, Lorient and St Nazaire were selected as U-boat bases. Concrete pens were constructed to house the U-boats while in harbour and to secure them from aerial attack.

Germany, unlike Britain, possessed no bases abroad where their ships and U-boats could refuel, so another solution had to be found. The construction of U-boat tankers was begun, large boats capable of taking fuel, torpedoes, food supplies, medical equipment and spare parts to replenish their colleagues off the main sea lanes and enable them to prolong their patrols without the danger of being attacked while entering or leaving harbour.

These Type XIV boats, nicknamed milch-cows, had a displacement of 1,688 tons, and were only equipped with defensive armament of deck guns. They were insufficiently manoeuvrable for active operations and as well as the 200 tons of fuel they carried for their own consumption they carried an additional supply of over 400 tons to refuel other U-boats. They housed a deck cargo of four torpedoes to supply active service U-boats. It must have taken a special kind of man to command and crew such a potentially dangerous craft, for it stood no chance if attacked by a surface ship and little more if attacked from the air.

Six Type XIV boats were commissioned and the contract awarded to the Deutsche Werke at Kiel. The six boats, numbered U-459 to U-464, were launched between September and December 1941. By the autumn of 1943 the only survivor was U-460, for the rest had all been individually sunk by aircraft attacks.

The survivor started its first war cruise, as a supply tanker, from Kiel, on 7 June 1942 and put in to its French base of St Nazaire on 31 July. After a month in port the U-tanker replenished its stocks and the second war patrol commenced on 1 September and lasted for six weeks. The third commenced at St Nazaire on 11 November and the crew were back six days before Christmas to enjoy the festivities ashore. The first patrol of 1943 began on 31 January and *U-460* returned to St Nazaire on 5 March but then moved further south to Bordeaux, where up to this time the bigger U-boats were stationed. The fifth war patrol, a two-month one from 24 April until 25 June, which survived the forty-one U-boat losses in May, started and ended at Bordeaux. Its sixth, and final, patrol commenced when it slipped from Bordeaux on 30 August.

In April 1941 Winston Churchill, in a letter to President Roosevelt, wrote:

> There are certain areas in the North and South Atlantic off the trade routes in which the enemy maintain their supply ships and where they go to refuel. Up to the present time we have been unable to search out these areas, as we have not had the ships to do it with.

Following that letter the surface supply ships were rounded up, either captured or sunk, and the secret raiders and long distance U-boats were cut off from their sources of supply. This lesson, of preventing boats from refuelling, had been hard learned, so it was no surprise that all the U-tankers, except *U-460*, had been sunk.

U-boat headquarters did their best to ensure the safety of their last Type XIV U-tanker as it cruised to the mid-Atlantic refuelling area off the Azores. All U-boats were ordered to maintain W/T silence within a 250 mile radius of the area, but this tanker now became a priority target for the Admiralty and its progress was carefully monitored from the time it left Bordeaux.

On the other side of the Atlantic the US escort carrier *Card* had been launched on 21 February 1942, five months after *U-460*. The hull was originally intended to be that of a cargo ship. It was acquired from the Maritime Commission while still in the yards of its builders and converted into an escort carrier. It was named for the waters of Card Sound, south of Miami and built by the Seattle-Tacoma shipbuilding corporation of Tacoma, Washington. The ship was placed in commission on 8 November 1942, when Captain James B. Sykes assumed command.

Card underwent a fitting-out period and then sailed on her shakedown cruise in West Coast waters. She left San Diego, California, on 18 January 1943, and after passage through the

Panama Canal, arrived at Hampton Roads, Virginia, on 1 February. The carrier spent the three following months in the areas of Hampton Roads and New York, then, on 14 May 1943, got underway for Casablanca, in convoy, ferrying aircraft and military personnel to the North African theatre of operations

Card departed from the French Moroccan base on 9 June and sailed for Norfolk, Virginia, via Bermuda, arriving on 5 July. On the 29th she was in Bermuda again and, on the following day, put out to sea to engage in anti-U-boat operations in Atlantic waters, west of Flores Island of the Azores Group. The task group consisted of the destroyers *Barry*, *Borie* and *Goff*, with *Card* as flagship.

The Avenger and Wildcat aircraft of the carrier made an immediate impact on the Battle of the Atlantic for in August four U-boats were sunk: *U-117* on the 7th, *U-664* on the 9th, *U-525* on the 11th and *U-847* on the 27th.

The task group arrived at Norfolk, Virginia, on 10 September and remained there and at Hampton Roads, until the 25th when *Card* got underway with *Barry*, *Borie*, *Goff* and *Du Pont*. Two days later they entered Port Royal Bay in Bermuda and the next day were again underway to continue the search for U-boats. *Card* was now commanded by Captain Isbell.

Admiral Dönitz has been quoted as saying: 'Hitherto detection with such promptitude has been unknown and the possibility that the enemy is using a new and efficient type of locating device cannot be ruled out.' Indeed, he was right, the British were reading his signals. Despite W/T silence, and the last message had been received from *U-460* on 26 September the Admiralty knew that the tanker had replenished eight U-boats during September and that other Atlantic boats were waiting their turn in October.

Aircraft from *Card* would provide the answer to the refuelling problem and the carrier was routed to the refuelling area. At 1014 on the morning of 4 October, a patrol Avenger radioed a sighting of many U-boats and two minutes later *Card* launched an attack group to proceed to the area. Within sixteen minutes one of the VP-9 attack group reported contact had been made with four surfaced U-boats. Another attack group was immediately launched to support the first. What the first Avenger pilot, Lieutenant R. Stearns, had seen was *U-460* just completing refuelling *U-264*, with *U-422* and *U-455* waiting. His Avenger was carrying a homing torpedo, so secret it was known as the Mark 24 mine, and orders, which had been in force six months, forbade the dropping of this weapon if

Grumman Avengers on a carrier's deck

USS *CARD*

there was any possibility that the enemy might see or guess its effect. The pilot had a double problem: he could not attack accurately until a U-boat dived and he could not drop it while other U-boats on the surface might see the scale of its destruction. He had to wait for reinforcements. These arrived after half an hour, two Wildcats and an Avenger. In the meantime *U-455* had submerged. Heavy concentrated flak kept the American aircraft from venturing too close while the remaining U-boats prepared to dive.

When the refuelling group had first seen aircraft Hartwig Looks, the experienced and successful captain of *U-264*, suggested to Schnoor that his boat, *U-460*, should dive immediately and the other U-boats would cover him as obviously the tanker was most valuable. The advice was ignored and *U-460* manned its guns. Eventually *U-460* did dive, followed by the others. Of course, this was exactly what the first Avenger was waiting for, and, selecting the U-tanker as his target, Lieutenant Stearns released his homing torpedo at the front of the swirl made by the diving *U-460*. It was all over, oil and debris soon rose to the surface.

Five hours later the captain of *U-422* brought his boat to the surface just three miles from the scene of the morning attack. Possibly he had heard the detonation and breaking up noises and was wondering if he could save any survivors. Whatever his reasoning his action was most imprudent. A Wildcat and an Avenger, complete with homing torpedo, were waiting and as Oberleutnant Poeschel dived the homing torpedo was released and destroyed the Type VIIC boat. In addition to one tell-tale empty life-raft, oil and debris were all that remained. The unfortunate U-boat had been on its first war patrol, from Bergen, and had already reported casualties and damage from an attack by Liberator Y-Yoke of 10 RCAF Squadron.

To return to *U-264*: one of its telegraphists had served on *U-460* when Schäfer was its captain. He left when Kapitänleutnant Schnoor took over. After submerging, he recalls *U-264* heard the destruction of the U-tanker, the sixth and last one and all sunk by aircraft. They heard explosions and then the rushing noise associated with the sinking of boats. He was critical of the tanker's captain, who had been pursued by single-engined aircraft for days on end. He thought a signal 'We are being continually pursued by aircraft' would have caused U-boat headquarters to postpone the refuelling arrangements, and given *U-460* time to disappear for a while. He obviously didn't know that all U-boats were under orders not to signal within a 250 mile radius of the rendezvous, but to any tracker the absence of signals from a particular point would indicate that something was happening there and what better than to send an escort carrier to investigate?

When *U-264* cautiously surfaced, it too was attacked. After eighteen days at sea the captain took it back to base.

Information gained from decoded signals could only be used if corroborated by another avenue of information, thereby protecting the real source. In the autumn of 1943 Dönitz was not the only one to be worried about locating devices for finding his refuelling areas; the British, in supplying information to the Americans, were afraid their source might be compromised. In mid-October the activities of *Card* around the refuelling area were unsettling for U-boat headquarters, but, by continual day air sorties over the area, the Americans could well claim that these patrols were the source of their information. This must also have satisfied U-boat headquarters for they looked into the possibility of only replenishing by night, but by then it was too late.

Aircraft patrols continued throughout the days following the sinking of the milch-cow with no definite sinking resulting from contacts and it was not until 12 October that another strike from the carrier was made against a U-boat. In the late morning an Avenger reported contact with a surfaced U-boat and made an attack. In the early afternoon another Avenger reported another U-boat about fifty miles distant and attacked without result. Nearly three hours later another Avenger arrived at the scene of the contact and attacked unsuccessfully with a 500 lb bomb, the U-boat running on the surface all the while, heading for protective covering of a rain squall. *Goff* was dispatched to the area, but before she arrived another Avenger had sighted the boat and attacked unsuccessfully with four depth charges, and a few minutes later another Avenger was also unsuccessful with its attack.

Early the following day a U-boat was reported about twenty-five miles distant, and immediately thereafter the contacting aircraft made an unsuccessful attack. Later, just after noon, the squadron commander reported another sighting. This indeed was something worthwhile – it was *U-402*, veteran of the Battle of the Atlantic.

In 1943 the average length of all cruises by Type VIIC boats was fifty days. The average stay in port during the last six months of the year was seventy-two days. The U-boat men averaged three patrols a year.

One U-boat that helped keep the average high was *U-402*, a Type VIIC, commanded by Korvettenkapitän Siegfried Freiherr von Forstner. At this time he was the twelfth most successful U-boat commander.

One of four sons, the nobleman was born into a military family: his father was a Kaiser's War general. Siegfried elected to join the Kriegsmarine and graduated in 1933. After early service in *Admiral Scheer* he was posted to *Nürnberg* as ordnance officer. Another baron aboard the cruiser was Freiherr Hans Dietrich von Tiesenhausen, later to become famous as commander of *U-331*, which sank the British battleship *Barham* in the Mediterranean at the end of 1941. Siegfried von Forstner transferred to the U-boat arm in March 1940 and after training was sent to sea in *U-99* on its third patrol as a supernumerary with Otto Kretschmer, already enjoying a high reputation as an ace.

Kretschmer and von Forstner were class contemporaries and both Korvettenkapitäns, and no doubt because of his high rank the baron was marked out for early command without having served as a First Watch Officer. He was married while on a course at the U-boat commanders' school at the end of 1940. He was appointed to command the training boat *U-59* in the early months of 1941.

U-402 had been launched from the Danziger Werft on 28 December 1940 and von Forstner joined as its captain in May. Summer of 1941 was spent on shaking down the crew and the first patrol, in October, proved uneventful but the ice reconnaissance was useful experience for both captain and crew.

The next patrol was more successful and the troopship *Llangibby Castle* was torpedoed on 16 January 1942 in the Western Atlantic. It looked as if the third patrol was going to be uneventful, until on the very last day on station, 2 May, an 850 ton escort vessel *USS Cythera* was sunk. There were only two survivors from the 71-man crew and these were both rescued by the U-boat and returned to France. On its fourth patrol *U-402* was heavily depth-charged off Cape Hatteras and was fortunate to limp back to La Pallice. Repaired and back at sea, in action against convoy SC107 *U-402* sank five ships on the night of 1/2 November. The ships were *Empire Sunrise*, *Rinos*, *Dalcroy*, *Empire Antelope* and *Empire Leopard*. It was an elated crew that returned successfully to its French base, Altogether fifteen ships of 88,000 tons had been sunk in two nights in the convoy whose course had been disclosed to U-boat headquarters by

The successful *U-402*. An early picture.

a wireless intercept.

A confident *U-402* slipped from La Pallice in mid-January 1943. During the first two weeks of the year not a convoy had been seen in the storm-lashed seas of the North Atlantic. However, at the end of the month the German Wireless Interception Service decyphered a course for the 44-ship-strong convoy SC118, and *U-402* was among a pack directed on to the convoy's route. On 7 February *U-402*

signalled that it had intercepted the convoy and in less than 24 hours
sank seven ships. They were, the rescue vessel *Toward*, tankers *R. E.
Hopkins* and *Daghild*, the freighter *Afrika*, a 6,000 ton American
troopship *Henry Mallory*, the Greek *Kalliopi* and the British *Newton
Ash*. This meant that *U-402* had now sunk over 100,000 tons of
enemy shipping. With its torpedoes exhausted the U-boat was
ordered to shadow the convoy, transmitting beacon signals for the
rest of the pack. This nearly caused *U-402*'s undoing for two escort
vessels approached unobserved at night and it was illuminated with
starshell. The captain crash-dived and then had to withstand seven
depth charge attacks which badly damaged the U-boat. It returned
a week overdue to La Pallice with air compressor and engine
troubles including a hot thrust bearing.

At the French base the crew were given a heroes' welcome.
Decorations were awarded to many of the crew, and the captain
Korvettenkapitän Siegfried Freiherr von Forstner was awarded the
coveted Knight's Cross for his very great achievement in sinking
such a large tonnage.

The boat was in the French base for two months while the damage
was being repaired. This gave an opportunity for some of the battle-
hardened crew to be posted to new U-boats, where their experience
would be invaluable, and for new men to take their place and learn
from the veterans still aboard.

U-402 sailed on its seventh patrol in April, its target the eastbound
convoy SC129. The convoy was protected by Escort Group B2 under
Captain Donald Macintyre who could boast that no ship escorted
by him had been sunk in the nine months the group had been under
his command. All this was to change, for 300 miles northwest of the
Azores, in broad daylight, *U-402* sank the 4,500 ton British ship
Antigona and the 3,000 ton Norwegian ship *Grado*.

The counter-attack soon commenced with depth-charge attacks
by four of the escort. No results were seen but the Flower Class
corvette HMS *Gentian* was prudently left at the spot while the other
escorts moved on to protect the convoy. During the evening a depth
charge landed close alongside, which badly damaged the U-boat
and it plunged out of control well below its safe depth of 150 metres
and continued downward to over 200 metres before its dive was
arrested with its hull creaking from the outside water pressure. Once
again the crew sent a silent prayer thanking the shipbuilders at the
Danziger Werft for their thorough job. After *Gentian* moved off at
midnight the badly damaged *U-402* was able to creep back to La

Pallice where a ten-foot tear in the ballast tank was discovered. The boat was laid up for three months for repairs and a refit.

Siegfried von Forstner had made his home in Hamburg and unfortunately for him he was still on leave there at the end of July when the week-long night and day bombers started a fire inferno. Using Window, metallic strips, for the first time the attackers foxed the defences and consequently their losses were low. The von Forstners survived, but it was with heavy heart that the U-boat captain had to say goodbye to his wife when leaving for his eighth patrol. Fortune had so far favoured the brave.

While in port, *U-402*, like the rest of the boats, had been equipped with the new gnat, the acoustic torpedo. In the second week of September the boat sailed from La Pallice and linked up with the *Leuthen* Group which had successfully intercepted the westbound ON202 convoy. On the 20th a gnat directed against the escort sloop HMS *Polyanthus* missed.

On the evening of the 22nd *U-377* surfaced twelve miles astern of the convoy, in good but hazy visibility, and immediately found itself under attack from a Liberator. It sent an R/T signal saying 'Am being attacked by aircraft' and giving its position. Fortunately *U-402* picked up the message and was able to close and put up a heavy barrage of flak against a second aircraft, X-Xray of No 10 RCAF Squadron, that had sighted both U-boats, attacking *U-377* with depth charges and *U-402* with gunfire.

On 24 September *U-402* was one of nineteen U-boats of the *Rosper* Group patrolling in search of another westbound convoy, as described elsewhere in this book. By 9 October the convoy was successfully through the patrol line. By the 13th *U-402* had been at sea for nearly five weeks and was several hundred miles north of the Azores, and the refuelling U-boat. As it headed southward to replenish the boat's nearly empty bunkers and to re-provision, unknown to the captain ahead of him lay a westbound convoy escorted by Task Force 63.

The escort carrier *Card* was screening far to the north of the convoy. Just after noon an Avenger from the carrier, piloted by Lieutenant-Commander H. M. Avery, the squadron commander of VP-9, sighted *U-402* twenty-five miles south of the carrier, and dived in to attack with guns blazing. When the U-boat failed to dive, Avery, who had a homing torpedo that was only good for a submerged attack, and no bombs, circled a mile astern to avoid the U-boat's fire, and called for help. Another Avenger, piloted by Ensign B. C. Sheela, arrived and attacked, catching *U-402* by surprise, but missed the target by 600 feet with a depth bomb. No doubt fearing further such attacks von Forstner saw his chance and dived. This was the opportunity the VP-9 commander needed; he banked his Avenger steeply and raced in, dropping his homing torpedo 100 feet beyond where *U-402* had disappeared. In just 25 seconds it was over, the torpedo homed on to the noisy propeller and caused a violent detonation. Minutes later a spreading oil slick and two cylindrical metal objects marked the last resting place of *U-402* and its gallant captain and crew. The U-boat had been a front boat for two years and all its service was in the Atlantic at a time when the average life span of an operational U-boat was just over eight months.

With its happy band of seamen and airmen, *Card* with her escorts, anchored at Casablanca on 18 October, secure in the knowledge that seven U-boats had already been sunk by her aircraft and many more damaged. However, for some of the crew of her veteran escort destroyer *Borie*, this would be their last run ashore.

CHAPTER FIVE

U-Boats at Large

On the evening of 24 September a group of nineteen U-boats was ordered to a patrol line between 54.20 and 58.45N at 28.30W as a westbound convoy could be expected from the next day. The U-boats were *U-279, U-643, U-388, U-731, U-539, U-666, U-758, U-402, U-584, U-419, U-378, U-952, U-645, U-260, U-603, U-275, U-336, U-610* and *U-448*. On the evening of the 27th the group was further warned to expect the convoy at any time from then on and ordered to use intermediate wave D/F on the convoy R/T, if any. As nothing had been reported by the evening of the 29th a new patrol line was given for the morning of 1 October. This time the signal was to twenty-one U-boats, those previously mentioned, except *U-279, U-388* and *U-731* and the new ones *U-641, U-341, U-305, U-631* and *U-389*; the latter was sailing to the position from the Baltic. *U-448* reported having been sighted by aircraft in the early afternoon of 30 September and *U-279* in the early hours of 1 October. The latter was ordered to take the place of *U-389* in the line. Further aircraft attacks on the 1st were reported by *U-631* and twice by *U-402*. U-boat headquarters expected a slow south-west bound convoy, ONS19, to arrive any time from 1 October onwards. On the evening of that day orders were given for the patrol line to be moved sixty miles as the convoy was expected, but if in the meantime they encountered an eastbound convoy they were not to operate against it, but just to use any favourable opportunities to attack.

A message in special cypher was transmitted on the evening of the 2nd saying the convoy could be expected the next day and again the patrol line was altered. The disposition of the convoy was also being altered, the German signals were being read so the convoy was routed to avoid the waiting U-boats.

By now the Allied VLR Liberators and Hudsons of Coastal Command, together with Venturas, of the USN, were detailed for close cover round the area where U-boat positions had been reported.

A Ventura attacked *U-610* on the afternoon of 3 October and U-boat control assumed the aircraft to be either an advanced reconnaissance plane or an escort. Subsequent reports from *U-275* indicated it was attacked by aircraft that morning but not damaged. The attack was carried out by Flying Officer Jones, piloting C-Charlie of 269 Squadron, and took place south-west of Iceland. The Hudson sighted *U-275* at conning tower depth. The U-boat then surfaced completely, opened fire and took evasive action. The pilot attacked bow to stern, releasing four 250 lb depth charges which were seen to undershoot, the last one fell ten yards ahead of the bow and slightly to port. Contact was then lost in a rain squall although *U-275* had been seen to dive shortly after the attack.

A report from *U-666* said it was heavily depth-charged by two ships of an escort group and forced to move away to repair. The escort ships were HMS's *Dahlia* and *Nene*.

Early on 4 October the patrol line was ordered to move 090 degrees at eight knots, and it was then that aircraft discovered the U-boats running on the surface to catch the convoy. First *U-731* was attacked, three times, by 269 Squadron Hudsons flying south-west from Iceland. In the first attack Pilot Officer Smith, on an anti-submarine swoop, sighted the U-boat on the surface and attacked with four 250 lb depth charges, released from 30-40 feet. Only one depth charge was seen to explode, close to the stern of the U-boat. The Hudson crew opened fire with their machine guns and estimated making hits. There were later two further attacks by another Hudson. The U-boat captain subsequently requested permission to return to base as he, Techand, and five ratings were wounded. *U-539* also reported certain minor defects, including a faulty transmitter. It claimed to have driven off a Hudson and shot down a four-engined aircraft.

The next attack, on *U-336*, was by a Ventura flown by Commander Westhof. The victim had just sent a report to base saying that it had seen aircraft hourly on a westerly course, and had sighted a destroyer the previous evening on the same course. *U-336* was an Emden boat, built at the Nordsee Werke, launched at the beginning of December 1941. The captain, experienced in earlier Atlantic patrols in his Type VIIC boat, was Kapitänleutnant Hans Hünger.

U-336 left Kiel on its first war patrol, to the North Atlantic, on 28 November and put in to Brest on 8 January 1943. Its next patrol was as part of the *Dränger* group attacking convoy SC122 in March. The captain had a victim lined up in his sights but before he could give the order to fire the ship was torpedoed by another U-boat. Nevertheless, *U-336* must have been a happy boat, for when it arrived back at base the 1WO was given the chance to command his own boat, but declined, preferring to stay with Hans Hünger. On its next patrol, to the south-west of the Azores, *U-336* somehow missed the holocaust of May when forty-one U-boats were sunk. It was on patrol from 8 May until 17 July. The boat left Brest on its fourth war patrol on 14 September. Ten days later it was one of the nineteen boats on patrol awaiting the arrival of a westbound convoy. The 1WO who had declined a command was still aboard as the American twin-engined bomber approached, 230 miles away from its Icelandic base.

At 1430 the Ventura, B-Baker of USN 128 Squadron sighted *U-336*. The weather was good, with visibility 15 miles, the wind 15 knots from astern, and the base of five-tenths cumulus cloud lay at 2,800 feet. *U-336* was fully surfaced and on a north-easterly course eight miles on the starboard quarter. An attack approach was begun immediately, and, although advantage was taken of cloud cover on the way in, the U-boat submerged and was out of sight for more than thirty seconds when the bomb release point was reached, so no depth bombs were released. The point of diving was marked by a float light and a marker. After remaining in the area for a short while, the pilot carried out baiting tactics.

Following departure from the point of submergence, Commander Westhof remained thirty miles away from the scene for forty minutes. On his return to the area he saw nothing during a twenty minute search. Departing again, he remained away for one hour and then returned, searched up-track on the original course of the U-boat. Two hours and twenty minutes after the original sighting, the pilot saw a U-boat on the surface ten miles dead ahead. The track of the aircraft at that time was directly out of the sun. Increasing to full speed, the pilot dived immediately for the attack. As soon as *U-336* came within range, the pilot opened fire using short bursts from his bow guns. At about the same time he noticed tracers passing under the Ventura and white smoke puffs about 25 feet in diameter bursting ahead and to each side.

On reaching short range he directed the steady fire of his guns at the conning tower and the gun crews. Crossing the fully surfaced U-boat at an altitude of 50 feet, the pilot released three Mark 44 flat-nosed depth bombs with fuses set to function at 25 feet depth and spaced 75 feet apart. The reported positions of explosions were: first bomb under stern, second bomb under conning tower, third bomb under bow. During the attack *U-336* turned slowly to port and continued to fire at the aircraft, rupturing and tearing the starboard bomb bay door along its entire length and carrying away the radio antenna. None of the aircrew was injured.

Pulling up after the attack, the Ventura was put in a wide turn to port, and the turret gunner, bringing his guns to bear, opened fire on the now crippled U-boat. On the next approach, much confusion on deck was noted. Blue-white smoke and many members of the crew were pouring from the conning tower. The U-boat was almost dead in the water and settling slowly, and a large oil slick was forming on its starboard side. Some of its crew were abandoning ship.

Holding fire until he had reached a position on the U-boat's port bow, the pilot turned in to attack and at short range emptied his guns at *U-336*. Some small rafts were seen in the water at the time of this strafing attack. Circling again, he saw the conning tower of the U-boat disappear. A large black inverted 'vee' shape rose slowly to a height of about fifty feet, nearly vertical, then slowly sank and disappeared. That was the end of *U-336* and its 1WO. In fact no survivors were rescued. The Ventura, having reached the prudent limit of its endurance, returned to base, where it arrived safely despite its damage.

Later in the afternoon, acting on the signal from *U-336*, U-boats were told not to be seen; if weather conditions were unfavourable or the air reconnaissance too strong they were to submerge by day and make up for the loss of speed by a higher rate of knots at night. There followed a reprimand for the captain of *U-336* – in fact a warning for the remainder of the group. It said that the sighting report, of the aircraft and destroyer, should have been sent *immediately*, even if in the thick of an engagement, unless circumstances were very special. The failure to report was a serious error which the captain would have to answer for on his return. It said an earlier report would have been decisive for the whole operation. An earlier movement signal was then cancelled.

The reprimand was, of course, never received in *U-336*, which was already at the bottom of the ocean.

In mid-evening Flight Lieutenant W. J. P. McEwen had been in the air several hours, piloting Liberator X-Xray of 120 Squadron, when he saw *U-279* making for the convoy. Down below

Kapitänleutnant Otto Finke, carrying out his orders in his Type VIIC Bremer Vulkan-built boat which had been launched some nine months earlier, did not immediately see his attacker. Probably he was too intent on reaching the convoy before the impending nightfall.

The Liberator was flying just below cloud base at 3,000 feet when the U-boat was sighted at about six miles' range. The aircraft immediately attacked, making good use of cloud cover and achieved a certain degree of surprise. Flak was encountered at about 1,000 feet, but good shooting with the nose gun from 800 yards silenced the U-boat's gunners.

The aircraft tracked over the U-boat and dropped three Mark XI Torpex depth charges, spaced 90 feet, with the Mark III low level bombsight. The last of the charges entered the water about 40 feet short of the conning tower, exploding right underneath. When the plumes had subsided and black smoke had cleared away, the pilot had the satisfaction of seeing some 30 to 40 feet of *U-279* sticking vertically out of the sea, and about twenty-five survivors wearing lifejackets, in the water. Three large dinghies were dropped, two of which fell among the survivors.

Heeding the warning earlier given to *U-336*, *U-758* reported it had seen aircraft twice earlier and had seen escort vessels searching. Later in the evening *U-260* was ordered to move off southward and return to base due to the sickness of the engineering officer and a leading hand. Before the end of 4 October U-boat headquarters received another shattering blow when *U-422* and *U-460* were sunk off the Azores by aircraft from *Card*, as already recorded.

During the night *U-666*, earlier attacked by the aircraft escorts, reported that it was unable to dive properly and was later given permission to return once the convoy had been found as the forward hydroplane and No 2 battery were defective. A request, from *U-952*, was turned down and the captain told to continue on operations as every eye was needed.

The fact that every eye was needed again shows that B.Dienst were still unable to read Royal Navy signals after the code changes.

Flight Sergeant G.C. Allsop had an early call at his Reykjavik base. After breakfast he checked the rocket projectiles on Hudson FK764, found everything was in order and took off in his 269 Squadron F-Freddie at 0753 on an anti-U-boat sweep. He had only been flying just over an hour when he sighted *U-389* below at one mile range.

The Type VIIC boat was on its first patrol, out from Trondheim,

Lockheed Hudson

to reinforce the patrol line, under the command of 26-year-old Kapitänleutnant Siegfried Heilmann. Built at the Howaldtz Werke at Kiel, *U-389* had been launched less than ten months earlier.

The aircraft was flying at cloud base of 2,500 feet and immediately dived to attack. Fortunately for the pilot the U-boat was nearly ahead on sighting, so no violent alteration of course was necessary. Very heavy concentrated flak was sent up from the U-boat but the firing of the first pair of RP's, from 800 yards so scared the gunners that there was no further opposition. Of the eight RP's fired, five may have been direct hits and the remaining three should have hit underwater. Ten seconds after the attack the entire forward half of the U-boat was enveloped in light blue smoke and *U-389* appeared to have stopped. Shortly afterwards the stern lifted out of the sea at a very steep angle and the U-boat slid under water. The guns' crews opened fire again as the U-boat was diving and about fifteen bodies were seen in the spreading oil patch. No large air bubbles or other evidence resulted, but this was not inconsistent with a successful RP attack. The Hudson signalled its success to base and continued on patrol for another six hours.

At dawn the C-in-C Western Approaches had ordered the 10th

HMS *ORIBI*

Escort Group to detach from ONS19 and join convoy SC143. This eastbound convoy, comprising thirty-nine ships, had sailed from Halifax on 28 September with C.2 Escort Group comprising HM and HMCN ships *Kamloops, Icarus, Drumheller, Sackville* and *Morden*. HM ships *Duckworth, Antares* and *Gateshead* later joined the escort.

The passage of SC143 had been uneventful when the 10th Escort Group comprising HM ships *Musketeer, Oribi, Orwell* and the Polish *Orkan*, joined in the morning of 6 October. HMS *Oribi* and *Orwell* were sister ships, as were *Musketeer* (Senior Officer) and *Orkan*.

ORP *Orkan* had originally been launched as HMS *Myrmidon*. Both 1,920 ton vessels were laid down after the outbreak of war and achieved a top speed of 36 knots. Both had six 4.7 guns, one 4-inch AA gun, light weapons and torpedo tubes. Both were built by Fairfield at Govan; *Musketeer* being launched at the beginning of December 1941 and *Myrmidon* three months later. Their complement was 190.

Myrmidon was crewed by Polish sailors and renamed ORP *Orkan*. As well as serving as a convoy escort with the British Home Fleet in the Atlantic, *Orkan* was involved in escorting convoys to Russia. *Orkan* was among the escorts to His Majesty King George VI when he was inspecting the fleet and patrolled the route taken by him to Africa. In July General Wladyslaw Sikorski, prime minister and C-in-C of the Polish forces, was killed when his Liberator mysteriously crashed into the sea, shortly after taking off from Gibraltar. His body was recovered and returned to Britain aboard *Orkan* for burial in the Polish Forces Cemetery at Newark. The following month, during an operation against U-boats in the Atlantic, in which two were sunk, forty-six survivors were rescued by the Poles and brought back to Britain. Of these thirty-seven were from *U-459*. A 172 Squadron Wellington crashed on the deck of the Type XIV supply submarine while attacking it. The rear gunner was the sole survivor and he was rescued at the same time.

The escort oilers with SC143 had been ordered to be ready to fuel the new arrivals but the senior officer did not consider the state of the sea suitable for oiling, which was not urgent. The 10th Escort Group swept ahead of the convoy to the north and east and on the port bow of the convoy to a depth of thirty to forty miles.

At much the same time a signal was sent to the U-boat pack ordering them to be in a new position by the evening of the next day as an eastbound convoy was expected, SC143 in fact.

The signal was addressed to *U-643*, *U-641*, *U-539*, *U-336*, *U-448*, *U-610*, *U-419*, *U-279*, *U-378*, *U-645*, *U-260*, *U-603*, *U-275*, *U-631*, *U-91* and *U-439*, the latter two recently out of Biscay ports. U-boat headquarters obviously did not know that *U-279* and *U-336* had already been sunk. *U-260* was to return once the convoy had been picked up. In the morning of 7 October *U-309* and *U-762*, freshly out from the Baltic, were ordered to take a position at the northern end of the line.

Although *U-731* had sighted a destroyer just before noon its first sighting report did not get through until 1411 when it was repeated. The U-boat was told to shadow as far as this was possible. Other U-boats in the vicinity were told to operate at top speed, against the escorts if possible, while the other U-boats were to proceed east at cruising speed until the presence of a convoy had been established. At about 1800 *U-448* sighted a destroyer and later reported it had been run over by two destroyers at an interval of forty minutes, but had no hydrophone bearing on the convoy. *U-610* had also seen the same destroyer, submerged and also had not heard the convoy.

The destroyer seen was almost certainly *Orkan*, which reported a close enemy transmission. This was considered by *Oribi*, who had the HF/DF officer on board, to be a shore transmission until the

ORP *ORKAN*

HMS *ORWELL*

Admiralty told them otherwise. However, they swept down the bearing and sighted nothing. The senior officer of the 10th Escort Group correctly concluded that it was his division, and not the convoy, that had been sighted.

The escort group were just taking up stations for the night when another transmission was received and a fix showed it to be ten to twenty miles from the convoy on the port beam. The escort group proceeded to search while the convoy maintained its course into the gathering darkness. Just over an hour later *Orkan* and *Oribi* heard three more U-boat transmissions which gave no fixes but indicated a second U-boat in their immediate vicinity. A short time later *Icarus*, *Oribi* and *Orkan* intercepted a further transmission which it appeared was a U-boat reporting the support group.

What had been happening is this: *U-378* reported having been attacked earlier by aircraft; *U-762* reported being driven under by three destroyers; *U-758* reported sighting two destroyers, firing a stern T5 torpedo at one of them, heard an explosion and sinking noises.

The destroyer was *Orkan*. She experienced a heavy explosion astern and presumed it was a torpedo attack.

U-boat Control appreciated that according to the report by *U-758* their supposition of a convoy was confirmed and all U-boats were to act on the report. There was only a short space left to the eastward. Boats which were on their way to the fuelling position from previous operations with the group, were also to operate if their position and operational efficiency permitted. They were ordered to kill the destroyers and then sink the ships. This would repay them for their long wait.

U-731 broke off operations just before midnight owing to a shortage of fuel and *U-260* began its return passage two hours later. Meanwhile *U-448* reported that it had been repeatedly located. Only two destroyers had been heard, no convoy has been heard on hydrophones and it therefore presumed that the destroyers were from a decoy group.

The ether was thick with traffic; five more transmissions were heard but no fixes obtained. The Senior Naval Officer informed the convoy commodore and the MAC ship *Rapana* that two U-boats twenty miles astern were playing hide and seek with the support group.

The convoy was drawing clear of the danger area. In the early hours of 8 October *U-539* sighted an unidentified vessel and chased

(Above) ORP *Orkan*– the last photograph of the Polish destroyer as it enters the convoy SC143 to refuel. It was sunk early the next morning.

(Left) HMS *Oribi* closes the escort oiler to refuel.

it for two hours before discovering it was a Swedish ship sailing with its lights on. At much the same time another U-boat transmission was heard, fixed at about fifty miles on the port quarter of the convoy. The SNO ordered the support group to search for it. Shortly afterwards he changed his mind as he considered this disposition might allow the original U-boats to get between the convoy and the support group and so decided to recall the latter. As nothing had been heard from the U-boats for thirty minutes, the 10th Escort Group were ordered to create a diversion before returning. Their starshell and searchlights, thirty-five miles clear of the convoy, could just be seen by the main force.

U-610 reported seeing the starshell and searchlights and later reported diving away from aircraft and being depth charged by a destroyer. The captain also reported attacking two destroyers and claimed having heard an explosion eight minutes after firing.

U-boats had to dive immediately after firing their acoustic torpedo, as searching for the noisiest object in the vicinity it would have struck the U-boats' diesel engines. Being unable to see the result and hearing the terminal explosion caused U-boat captains to make optimistic, exaggerated claims, as in this case.

Looking at the situation on their charts, U-boat Control correctly appreciated that as the various sighting reports could not all be of the same destroyers it must be assumed that they were remote escorts of an eastbound convoy. Boats were therefore to carry out searches in wide sweeps at top speed.

Before dawn *U-631* asked permission to move off as the captain had fractured his hand and was not fit to work on the bridge. This was approved. This transmission was heard by the ships as it was from close astern and all ships were told to expect an attack before daylight.

U-378 sighted a destroyer at 0555 and claimed to have sunk it. Indeed this was in fact correct. While steaming at twenty knots with the 10th Escort Group to rejoin, *Orkan* was torpedoed about seven miles astern of the convoy at 0608. She was starboard wing ship. The explosion was seen and heard in her wake followed half a minute later by a large flash and a second explosion of a torpedo hit in her after magazine. Fire spread quickly and within five minutes *Orkan* sank stern first. *Musketeer* closed to pick up survivors while the remaining escorts kept guard. In all one officer and forty-three ratings were rescued. It was concluded that *Orkan* had been hit by one of a salvo of straight running torpedoes.

Immediately after the sinking *U-275* and *U-641* reported seeing searchlights. Later in the morning *U-437* reported that owing to the weather and its distance away it would not be able to take part in operations. *U-641* reported being sighted by an aircraft, probably the Swordfish from *Rapana*, while *U-610* reported being attacked by an aircraft.

U-610 had been attacked by Pilot Officer John Wright flying Liberator R-Rodger of 86 Squadron. In fact all available 15 Group aircraft had been briefed to escort the convoy through the approximate area 30 degrees West to 25 degrees West on Latitude 56 North.

Although the early morning light was not good the wireless officer of R-Rodger on the flight deck saw a wake six miles on the starboard bow and the aircraft set course to investigate. At four miles the wake was identified as a fully surfaced U-boat which began to dive when the aircraft was still three or four miles away. The swirl was clearly visible when at 0856 an attack was made with four 250 lb depth charges. They were aimed fifty yards ahead of the swirl and straddled the U-boat's course at an angle of 45 degrees twelve seconds after it had submerged. While the aircraft was circling, an R/T report was made to the SNO. Ten minutes later the SNO instructed the aircraft to resume patrol. He then ordered the Liberator to return to the scene of the attack and three-quarters of an hour later a wake was sighted eight miles away.

The target was *U-419*, a Type VIIC boat launched at the Danziger Werke at the end of August 1942. The captain was Dietrich Giersberg, who had served in the Navy for seven years, being promoted Oberleutnant in September 1941.

On seeing *U-419*, Pilot Officer Wright went straight in and at three miles the U-boat began zig-zagging. As the final run was made *U-419* turned twenty degrees to starboard presenting an almost stern-on target. Fifteen men were seen in the conning tower and the U-boat was fully surfaced when two 250 lb depth charges were dropped slightly to port, one 80 feet and the other 60 feet abaft the conning tower. When the depth charges exploded there was another and more violent explosion which produced a vivid white flash and a dense, greyish-black plume. The movements of the U-boat were momentarily screened by the depth-charge plume, but when this subsided thirty feet of the bows were seen sticking up out of the water; after twelve or fifteen seconds they sank vertically. Another iron coffin had slid below. Wreckage appeared immediately and the oil patch slowly expanded until at 1020 it was 350 yards across. Fifteen survivors were seen clinging to wooden debris, but during the next twenty minutes all but one disappeared.

The 10th Escort Group had seen the attack from eight miles distance. Homed by the Liberator they arrived and picked up the sole survivor, the captain of *U-419*. Oberleutnant Giersberg was hauled aboard by the crewman of *Oribi* and found to have broken his leg in two places. Afterwards he said:

> My boat was sunk on the surface by an aircraft with a bomb in the stern. In the explosion I was thrown into the water. It was damnably cold. I was trembling all day long on board the destroyer, as she searched for others. There was a whole crew of us on the conning tower. It happened so quickly; the bombs came crashing down and the whole boat disappeared. Then I came to the surface. It was daytime, there was a terrific sea running and I just saw aircraft searching about afterwards. Then I tried to swim about and also I tried to tear off my other rubber boot, but of course I couldn't do that because it was my broken leg.

Willing hands on HMS *Oribi* haul aboard OL Dietrich Giersberg, commanding officer and only survivor of *U-419*

CHAPTER SIX

Unhappy Anniversary

Before continuing with the events of the autumn we will look at the destroyers and the U-boat that were carrying out their duties until the arrival of the Liberator aircraft.

Oribi and *Orwell* were 'O' Class destroyers. They were designed pre-war, ordered on the outbreak of hostilities, constructed under the Emergency War Programme, with *Oribi* being completed in July 1941 and *Orwell* in October 1942.

Oribi took part in the raid on Vaagso Island, off Norway, at the end of 1941. Both ships were on Russian Convoy duty in the winter of 1942 and both were switched to the Battle of the Atlantic in 1943. In May *Oribi* rammed and sank *U-531* and in doing so damaged her bow and had to have a new one fitted at the Boston Navy Yard in the USA. After this was completed, *Oribi* returned to England, escorting the new DE's (destroyer escorts), Captain Class frigates, which had recently been built in the United States and taken over by British crews. At the beginning of July she was at Plymouth, in the middle of the month at Scapa and at the beginning of August out between the Faeroes and Iceland.

Douglas Gowland joined *Oribi* in December 1942 as a signalman, aged just eighteen years and one month, straight from school via the Kingston Sea Cadets. He says he spent a minimum of a third of this time at sea on the bridge where he handled quite a lot of confidential information.

Tom Goddard, an able-seaman, had been on *Oribi* from the time it was launched; he remembers:

Life on board was the best that could be expected considering all the circumstances. The seamen were in four watches which meant a quarter of us were required for cruising stations, half for defence stations and all for action stations!

Pastimes at sea during quiet periods off watch and in harbour were uckers, Monopoly and cribbage. Heaven knows how many hours we spent rolling dice or shuffling cards.

Oribi, like all destroyers, was canteen messing for ship's company; we did fairly well for ourselves when supplies were on hand. On many occasions, however, such as the Russian convoys, after about fourteen days continuously at sea we ran out of fresh meat, bread and potatoes. We then relied on 'corned dog' and 'Chinese wedding cake' and had some hardtack.

Our favourite dish was potmess – meat ration plus dumplings plus two tins of each kind of vegetable available. Dumplings varied from air balls to cannon balls. One new member of the Torpedomen's Mess, when trying his hand as cook, also added two tins of herrings in tomato. Needless to say nobody 'went round the buoy', had second helpings, in fact the seagulls did better than we did that day!

Believe it or not, Scapa Flow was at times thought of as home. Here, at least, we got some mail and were able to get a bath and possibly a run ashore to the Wet Canteen and cinema at Lyness.

Ian Wedderburn was the navigator aboard *Orwell* at the time, he recollects:

We spent a lot of time at sea in the North Atlantic which is hardly ever benign – in the two years I was in *Orwell* we steamed 98,000 miles including ten Russian convoys during the winter months – and when we returned to harbour it was usually to Scapa where the facilities and incentive for a run ashore, at any rate for the destroyers in Gutta Sound, were virtually non-existent. On the other hand in two years we did four boiler cleans at UK ports, which gave 72 hours leave to each watch on each occasion, and two refits in the Humber which gave us another two or three weeks' leave each time; so there were compensations.

Life at sea was uncomfortable and tedious. For the junior ratings who lived in crowded conditions forward on canteen messing, it seemed barely tolerable when it was rough, but there was a certain stoical resignation and little resentment. The senior ratings' mess, on the fo'c's'le deck level was more comfortable but very cramped. In *Orwell* the senior ratings hit it off well together and were a cheerful lot. They included one or two characters whose personality and influence were largely responsible for the contentment of the ship's company. The officers lived in comparative comfort aft but had to endure the hazard – and hazard it was – of fighting their way forward to go on watch in all weathers with the added obstruction of mine rails throughout most of the length of the upper deck. We were a happy lot too and got on well together. The most tiring thing in retrospect, apart from keeping watch one in three and keeping up with one's various jobs off watch, was the continual battle to keep one's balance and retain one's equanimity in the face of abstract frustrations associated with almost perpetual pitching and rolling. We seemed to spend our time fighting the elements and seldom fired a shot in anger.

Looking back I suppose it was a young man's world. Those without too great responsibilities and without family commitments and worries found it easier to be philosophical; those with nervous energy like myself endured better than those who bottled it up. We swore a lot at ourselves and at each other but we seldom if ever bore a grudge.

Now to the U-boat, *U-643*, which had been amongst the pack searching for the convoy since the end of September.

U-643, a Type VIIC boat, was built at the Blohm and Voss yard in Hamburg and launched on 20 August 1942. Kapitänleutnant Hans Harald Speidel was born in Danzig in 1917. He joined the Kriegsmarine in 1936 but in 1938 transferred to the Naval Air Arm and later the Luftwaffe. He flew in torpedo bombers and mine-laying aircraft. He served in the Western and Eastern theatres of war, attacking targets in France, England, and Russia, including the bombing of Moscow. However, in December 1941 Hans Speidel returned to the Kriegsmarine and joined the U-boat service. He was appointed 1WO aboard *U-81*, a U-boat that had found fame earlier for sinking the Royal Navy's most famous carrier *Ark Royal* in the Mediterranean. He took part in five operational patrols in the Mediterranean, including trips to Tobruk.

Kapitänleutnant Speidel was recommended as a commanding officer and after training courses was appointed to command *U-643*. At the time the U-boat was still on the stocks in Hamburg; the commissioning ceremony took place on 8 October 1942. The boat was jinxed – bedevilled with problems throughout its career. There were four different First Watch Officers in twelve months. There was trouble with the diesels and fittings had to be altered. Three times the U-boat went to Hela, on the northern tip of Danzig bay. The boat was going from Hela to the shipyard at Danzig. The diesel was out of action, then the cooling-water pump was out of action. The boat was in the shipyard for three months and everything was ripped open fore and aft. All the fittings and furniture from the wardroom and batteries were removed. Afterwards all the individual cells, sixty-four in each, were removed. The maintenance people couldn't decide whether to repair the cells or replace the batteries. They decided on the latter and then had to wait for a fortnight for them to arrive.

While all this was happening the captain was conducting propaganda visits through Germany, the Sudetenland, the southern Alps, Italy and the Dolomites. Altogether with the trips and leave he was away from the boat for two or three months. The captain was determined not to put to sea until all the defects were remedied.

When the batteries were finally delivered a troupe of young lads, only fourteen or fifteen year-olds, arrived with them. These recent school leavers were known as 'Bilge crabs'. It was their job to wipe down the battery compartments and pressure hull with rags, and then give them a coat of paint. The job was skimped, the youngsters did not clean the surfaces properly but put paint on top of the old dirt instead of doing the job thoroughly. The new batteries were installed. Two months had already been wasted before officials arrived to test the batteries, to see whether everything was now in order. They said that, since the battery and cells – which contained sulphuric acid – had been split, the pressure hull must be examined to see whether it was clean and hadn't become corroded. They took out a cell and looked in underneath and saw that the new paint, that had just been applied, was already flaking. Sulphuric acid, which had been present, had corroded the pressure hull and eaten away the paint too. There was the devil to pay! They had to take out the entire battery again. Both batteries, fore and aft, which had been finished, had to come out.

When, finally, all the problems were sorted out and the boat was ready for acceptance it returned to Hela for special working-up trials. After the first trial the boat returned to the shipyard for adjustments. Once more, after the second and third trials *U-643* again had to return to the shipyard because of battery trouble.

It was only after the fourth and fifth trials that the boat was allowed to proceed to carry out two days' working-up tests, diving on its own. Four extra men were allocated for the new armament, these had taken an eight week gunnery and range-finding course at Swinemünde.

(Right) Kapitänleutnant Hans Harald Speidel, aviator and submariner. Captain of *U-643*.

(Below) *U-643* at Hela

The crew on board, especially the engine room personnel needed refresher training, so long had elapsed since their training days. When, at last, things were more or less alright and they were cleared from the Technical Training Group for Operational U-boats, *U-643* joined the 25th Training Flotilla at Danzig.

At Danzig, at this time, the 25th Flotilla were in *Deutschland* and the 8th Flotilla in *Hamburg*. *U-643* was now ready to commence torpedo firing trials, but on the very day it was due to start firing the flotilla was transferred to Libau, so the whole training flotilla moved north. There the practising began, a week's firing. In the meantime the 1WO had been changed. After Libau *U-643* went to Gdynia for real tactical exercises, – those at Hela had been rehearsals for tactical exercises.

Now, ready for operations, *U-643* proceeded to Kiel. Here the boat spent six days fitting out. By now it was early June. Then came another fateful moment. The conning tower had to be replaced. *U-643* had the old type with one 88 mm (3.5 inch) gun forward of the conning tower and twin 20 mm (.78 inch) guns on the single bandstand. Boats were no longer going on operations so equipped. A new conning tower arrived with two bridge gun platforms, and, had this been installed, *U-643* was scheduled to be operational on 20 July. However, by this time U-boats had adopted the policy of remaining on the surface and shooting it out with aircraft and consequently the anti-aircraft armament had to be increased again. The actual arrangement of anti-aircraft guns varied from boat to boat. *U-643* put into the Howaldts Werke at Kiel. The old conning tower was ripped off and replaced. The new one was supposed to have a quadruple gun and two twins. However, the two twin mountings were not yet there, so two single ones were to be installed. When the new twin guns made their appearance however, the captain determined to have their mountings, for he wanted the best and most modern for his boat. Somehow he managed to get them for ten packets of cigarettes and five bottles of Schnapps, and they were installed on the first bridge gun platform instead of the two single ones. Now *U-643* was right up to date with quadruple 20 mm mountings on the lower step and double 20 mm mountings on the upper step. At the same time the walls of the conning tower on Type VIIC boats were armoured to give gunners extra protection.

All this extra work took time and *U-643* was not ready to put to sea until August. Then came another setback, a signal arrived: 'No boat may put out to sea on operations, await further instructions.'

All fresh provisions had to be unloaded and then re-loaded when the instruction was cancelled. Finally when the torpedoes, ammunition and fuel were taken aboard at Kiel-Wik *U-643* proceeded through the Great Belt and Kattegat to Kristiansand. Then, after slipping from the pier at Soelyst in the Norwegian base, this next sailing counted as an initial patrol as it embraced the Skaggerak barrier area. The U-boat then put in to Haugesund. Next port of call was Egersund, from which *U-643* proceeded past the spectacular scenery, through Bjornefjord and into the harbour of Bergen. At Bergen the crew were accommodated at the U-boat hostel ashore. In town there was a nasty brawl with the Norwegians and many of the crew were involved. A German officer arrived and there were some arrests. Although the boat was only visiting it was decided there must be punishment. One engine room rating received seven days and another two days. The U-boat was in Bergen to have a new type of aerial fitted. The mattress aerial was rectangular about five feet by three feet, trainable through 360 degrees. It retracted into the port side of the bridge when not in use. The aerial was used with the standard Gema set which worked on the standard German naval wavelength. The operational range of the aerial was only about five miles against a surface vessel and ten miles against an aircraft flying at 1,500 feet.

At Bergen, after the aerial had been fitted and last minute adjustments were made to the boat, *U-643* topped up its tanks with fuel and the batteries with distilled water and embarked fresh provisions. Now, at long last, on 14 September *U-643* was ready for its first Atlantic patrol, to join with a pack attacking Allied convoys.

Then the jinx struck again, when, just an hour before sailing time the navigator, a man who had been with the boat throughout and was highly thought of by the crew, fell ill. He was examined by the ship's doctor who pronounced, 'The man can't go to sea any longer; he is unfit to sail; his stomach is completely out of order'. *U-643* sailed without him.

Out at sea, after dismissing his escort and carrying out a deep diving test, the captain had to alter course to pass across the bank, about thirty miles wide, between the Faeroes and Iceland, known to the Germans as the *Rosengarten*. Traversing this area was risky because of the U-boats' vulnerability to air attack. Allied aircraft were often patrolling the area.

Kapitänleutnant Speidel successfully negotiated this first hurdle and on the evening of 24 September was one of nineteen U-boats

A Mattress aerial fitted in position.

forming a patrol line endeavouring to intercept convoy SC143.

We can now continue the storyline where we left off at the end of the last chapter. R-Rodger of 86 Squadron had just sunk *U-419*. The pilot, continuing his patrol, sighted another surfaced U-boat just after the first one had been despatched. The time was 1110.

The U-boat put up what the pilot described as 'ineffective flak' as the aircraft circled at 1,000 to 1,200 yards range, R-Rodger replied with machine gun fire.

Z-Zebra, of the same squadron, picked up the sighting report and was homing on his colleague by means of the radio compass when the U-boat was seen surfaced at seven miles; the other Liberator could be seen circling so the second pilot decided on a direct attack. At three miles the U-boat began to dive. At 1140 an attack was made at 170 degres to the track and four depth charges were released 200-300 feet ahead of the swirl. The depth charges straddled the track, but only a small amount of oil appeared and as this did not spread, the SNO ordered the aircraft to resume patrol and return in an hour.

Piloting Z-Zebra was Flying Officer Cyril Burcher from Rankwick, Sydney. In March he was the first squadron pilot to sight and attack a U-boat and he created something of a record by attacking the enemy once or twice on each of the succeeding five sorties. In April he sank *U-632*. He was later to win the squadron's first Distinguished Flying Cross.

The experienced Australian pilot returned to the scene of the attack at 1250 and twenty minutes later he was rewarded with a sighting, again at seven miles. Another Liberator was about to attack but was meeting serious flak. Flying Officer Webber, flying the other aircraft, T-Tommy of 120 Squadron, was seen to attack and the depth charges appeared to straddle ahead of the U-boat's track. Twenty seconds later Z-Zebra began his run in and although he met intense flak he pressed home the attack. He approached at right angles to the enemy's course and tracked over the U-boat, *U-643*, between the bow and the conning tower. Two depth charges were dropped and the U-boat was straddled. Circling after the attack the Australian pilot saw the other Liberator deliver a second attack which straddled the U-boat's hull and lifted it noticeably. Both aircraft made machine gun attacks. Z-Zebra made four runs and registered hits. *U-643* lost way and besides listing heavily to starboard it was badly down by the bows. At least thirty of the crew came up into the conning tower where they inflated dinghies and put

on life jackets. Later a German naval flag – red with a white circle
and a black swastika – was hoisted. As the Australian was an hour
late in leaving, he set course for base.

Meanwhile T-Tommy was homing escort vessels and keeping the
SNO informed of the situation. Ninety seconds after the last attack
the U-boat exploded forward of the conning tower and immediately
sank by the bows. Survivors were thrown into the sea and many were
killed by the upheaval of water which rose 150 feet in the air.

Twenty minutes later the destroyer escorts arrived. *Oribi* tried to
rescue some six survivors. Tom Goddard recalls:

> The sea was too rough to launch sea boats, we had scrambling
> nets permanently in position on the guard rails ready to be
> released in position to hang down to the sea surface over the ship's
> side. We had managed to get in amongst the survivors who kept
> afloat by lifejackets. The ship came alongside the men, one at a
> time they would attempt to grasp the nets. The ship was
> broadside on to the seas and was rolling to such an extent that
> for one moment practically the whole scrambling net was
> underwater, and the next completely clear. Two of the Germans
> were lucky enough to grasp the net whilst it was going down and
> so had a good hold when it was rising again. The others tried to
> grasp the net when it was rising out of the sea, they had not
> enough grip to take the full weight of their bodies in the air. I, with
> saddened heart, recall seeing some being forced to release their
> hold and with this action re-enter the sea as though dropped from
> a height, and go down like a stone. To see those survivors claimed
> by the sea when life was so near at hand is one of my most vivid
> memories.

An *Oribi* crewman who spoke some German talked to one of the
survivors and found him very despondent. His home was in Cologne
and it had been bombed three times. He was also upset at machine-
gun bullets landing near him in the sea.

Meanwhile, Sub-Lieutenant Ian Wedderburn in *Orwell* recalls:

> By the time our ship reached the scene the U-boat had sunk and
> the survivors were in a life-raft. I remember our skipper,
> Lieutenant Commander John M. Hodges DSO RN, weighing the
> risk of stopping to pick them up and deciding it was acceptable
> if it did not take too long, because he reckoned the other U-boats

would be concentrating on the convoy and its escorts which by this time were about fifteen to twenty miles off and steaming away. I also think he could not harden his heart and bring himself to leave the survivors to their fate; I remember we were relieved when he decided to stop.

It was blowing a moderate gale about force 7 with overcast sky and intermittent rain; a moderate to heavy swell was running. *Orwell* was manoeuvred so as to stop and drift down from windward towards the raft. Scrambling nets were lowered over the port side. A line was fired which was carried by the wind a few yards wide of the raft. I remember one of the survivors, whom we subsequently discovered was the U-boat captain, plunged into the sea, grabbed the line and clambered back into the raft.

As we came alongside the raft *Orwell* was wallowing in the swell and heaving up to about fifteen feet. There was a danger that the raft would be overwhelmed by the bilge keel or that the survivors would be crushed between the raft and the ship's side. They were drenched and exhausted; some were wounded and one or two were completely prostrated. There was no lack of enthusiasm to help them on board amongst *Orwell*'s ship's company as sailors clinging to the scrambling net or guardrail went over the side at risk to themselves to clutch and scoop a survivor as the raft rode up on the swell. I saw one unfortunate German sailor grab weakly for the scrambling net, miss his hold and fall back only to disappear between the raft and the ship and succumb in the sea. One man, the U-boat captain, a blond well-built man, who was the last to leave the raft, steadfastly refused any assistance and heaved himself up the scrambling net in what seemed to be a superhuman feat of endurance. As he climbed over the guardrail he dragged himself to attention and gave a Hitler salute; arrogant he may have been, but he certainly had some guts.

Besides the captain of the U-boat there were two officer survivors – a young doctor and a younger engineer officer who was the second engineer. They were taken to the wardroom. Of the eighteen rating survivors, two with broken limbs and other injuries were taken to the sick bay, the others were accommodated, uncomfortably, in the tiller flat above which a sentry was posted. Subsequently, after some protest, the two or three NCOs, one of whom was an ERA or equivalent, were taken forward and accommodated in the CPO's and PO's mess. In *Orwell* the wardroom was aft, and I remember the U-boat captain voicing his concern about the vulnerability of his surviving ship's company should *Orwell* be hit by a gnat torpedo which of course homed on the propeller noise. He kept wanting to know what speed we were making, and when told it was 15 to 20 knots he said it was his U-boat which had torpedoed *Orkan* earlier in the day. He was also very bitter about the Liberator aircraft, whose bullets had hit survivors in the water. Apart from this he was glum and reticent. The young engineer officer hardly uttered a word and seemed to live in awe and fear of his captain. The doctor was more disposed to talk especially when he was with Surgeon Lieutenant P. A. Adam RNVR, our doctor, helping to attend to the wounded German ratings; he wanted to know where we would be landing the survivors, and would it be the Clyde because he had an aunt living in Argyll.

It was the young engineer officer who had brought up the Kriegsmarine flag hoisted in the conning tower of *U-643*:

> I fetched the ensign out myself, I crawled around on all fours down below in the boat, rummaging around with a torch. The lights had gone, everything had gone. We salvaged a few bottles of Schnapps and all of those up top had one.

Another survivor said:

> We saw the aircraft at ten miles or more. First one and then another came along directly behind when we had already shifted target and were firing at the first one. The second would appear and we would have to shift target again. Then things started to happen. The first depth charges fell absolutely wide. It was the last stick which came much nearer and finished us off.

A German gunner said:

> Up on the conning tower the seas were so big that one could scarcely fire. The waves were so high that they kept washing right over the conning tower. But all this made no difference to the aircraft, they just kept attacking.

Twenty-three survivors were rescued, and *Oribi* failed to save four others; therefore twenty-seven of the crew were accounted for,

meaning just under half were lost, probably the bulk of these in the
150 foot explosion reported by the airmen.

That the pilots acted with humanitarian principles is proved by
their calling rescue ships to the scene of the sinking for what could
only be the recovery of the survivors.

After a time span of forty-one years it is inevitable that there will
be some minor discrepancies, but now Hans Speidel casts his mind
back over four decades:

> After several training courses I was appointed as commanding
> officer of *U-643*. I had a good 49 strong crew, including twenty
> veterans and a naval doctor who was sent aboard as it was
> anticipated there could be injuries from aircraft attacks.
> Originally, after leaving Norway, we should have landed a
> Commando party on the east coast of Iceland to carry out a
> sabotage mission, this was cancelled at the last moment and
> another U-boat took them. South of Iceland *U-643* encountered
> a strong sea and a gale force wind which meant we could only
> surface at night and with the heavy seas delays were inevitable.
> Some of the upper deck structures were damaged by the weather
> including the armoured shields for the gunners' protection and
> the attack periscope was only of limited use due to flooding. As
> part of the *Rosper* Group we were ordered to attack an eastbound
> convoy and on the morning of 8 October I saw an escort destroyer
> *[Orkan]* sunk. A few hours later the boat was attacked by two
> Liberators, one at a time. Had we dived it could have meant the
> loss of our boat. During the first attack the senior gunnery range
> finder was mortally wounded. Depth charges came so close to the
> boat that diving cell one flooded and the boat became bow heavy.
> Both the diesel engines were lifted out of their mountings and the
> batteries started to give off chlorine gas. The central control room
> was one heap of rubble. I ordered the boat to be cleared, so that
> most of the crew were sitting in the conning tower or on the
> multiple gun platform. Rubber dinghies were made ready;
> however, these were shot to pieces in subsequent attacks.

He went on to say, as Wedderburn recalled, that from where he
stood it appeared that men in the water were being hit. He
continues:

> It is a fact that I gave the order to hoist the war flag. This is the

flag that the boat would normally have been flying if it was in port. After the batteries had produced more chlorine gas there came an explosion which led to the sinking of my boat. The men on the conning tower were thrown into the sea by the force of the explosion. So on 8 October 1943, exactly one year after commissioning I, and fourteen of my crew became prisoners of war in *Orwell*. Most had spent an hour in the sea.

An unhappy anniversary!

Instructions issued to captains of aircraft engaged in the U-boat war in 1943 were as follows:

A bold attack with front guns blazing, following surprise, is not only likely to sink the U-boat but it is also demoralizing for the U-boat's crews.

Use the machine guns against the U-boat's gun crews at as long a range as possible and for as long as possible, consistent with not running out of ammunition just when running in to drop a stick of depth charges.

The best targets for cannon and machine gun fire are:
   1) Personnel on the bridge and at the gun positions
   2) The lower aft end of the conning tower
   3) The blister tanks along the midship section of the boat.

Turret guns are usually harmonised at 400 yards, but the bullet drop in travelling an extra 400 yards is only eleven feet.

At no time were instructions issued to fire at men in the water. Orders quite plainly stated that U-boat crews on their vessel were legitimate targets. However, if the guns were not aligned correctly, or the button was pushed a little too early, the first bullets would certainly go into the sea and if any of the crew were already in the water they might well be hit accidentally.

At no time did *U-643* show any sign of surrendering; to the contrary, the hoisting of the Kriegsmarine flag indicated a final sign of defiance. Therefore the aircraft attacked until the U-boat sank.

As *Oribi* and *Orwell* proceed back to protect the convoy, we can reflect that the unfortunate *U-643* may have been unlucky right to the end. When Z-Zebra, after the attack with R-Rodger, returned to the

U-643 is sinking . . .

. . .the Liberator calls up HMS *Orwell* to rescue survivors

position and saw *U-643* at 1310 it was assumed that this U-boat was the one attacked earlier. It probably wasn't; it was almost certainly *U-610* which had reported to U-boat headquarters about being attacked at this time. The jinx continued, for Kapitänleutnant Speidel surfaced at the spot where the Liberator was waiting for *U-610* to appear. We know for certain that they had been close together earlier as both, wrongly, believed they had sunk *Orkan*.

Another U-boat, *U-762*, also reported being attacked by aircraft and said it was moving off because of damage to its engines. A little earlier *U-437* reported that owing to the weather and its distance away from the convoy it would not be able to take part in any operations.

In the early hours the U-boat pack had been signalled by U-boat headquarters that a BV222 would be flying a reconnaissance in the area in the afternoon. The giant six-engined long range flying boat duly appeared over the convoy. U-boats in the vicinity were ordered to close the given position. However, the position given by the BV222 was navigationally unreliable and the object of the exercise was not achieved.

That the Germans were reading air signals, although they couldn't break the new naval code, can be proved by the order they gave to U-boats still in touch. They were told to disregard Allied aircraft as from their cryptographic service they had learned that the air escort would not exceed three aircraft. The U-boats were told that as there was little to lose they were to remain on the surface provided their flak armament was in order. They were ordered if at all possible to get ahead of the convoy, and in an attacking position, before nightfall as that night would be their last chance to attack.

In the afternoon *U-91* reported it had dived to avoid an aircraft attack and later *U-603* reported it had been non-operational as the commanding officer was ill.

The biggest foe, in more senses than one, of the U-boat was the Short Sunderland flying boat. This high wing graceful flying machine with a span of nearly 113 feet and a length of 85 feet was first launched in 1937. Short Brothers of Rochester, on the River Medway in Kent, produced a militarised version of their commercial Empire flying boat. The Sunderlands came into squadron service in the spring of 1938. With its range of 1,780 miles the flying boat was capable of a long patrol and there was every comfort for the crew on board during the flight; including a galley and facilities for crew members off watch to sleep.

Even before *U-643* had been attacked a Sunderland of the RCAF 423 Squadron had taken off from Castle Archdale to protect the convoy. Perhaps this was one of the three aircraft that U-boat headquarters had advised would be on patrol. Although the airmen had put in a considerable number of hours in the air, there had not been many sightings and only one kill in the past four months. This probably prompted HQCC to send the following signal:

> The lack of sightings in moorings area indicated that the enemy is using extreme caution tactics in that region at the expense of his batteries and regardless of the length of time taken. Recent prisoners of war confirm that they were forced to surface when through the *Rosengarten* and when sighted by Iceland-based aircraft were unable to submerge again, both crews and batteries being exhausted. The value of these continuous patrols is considerable and crews should know that their apparently unprofitable patrols have contributed greatly to recent successes further west.

Wing Commander J. R. Frizzle of Halifax, Nova Scotia, had just been appointed as Commanding Officer of 422 Squadron which shared the base in Ireland. He had flown on anti-submarine patrols for eighteen months off the Canadian eastern seaboard without making any attacks. To familiarise himself with operations on the other side of the Atlantic he arranged to fly as third pilot in Sunderland DD863 which slipped its moorings at 1027. Flying Officer A. H. Russell of Edmonton, Alberta, was the first pilot and therefore captain of the flying boat as it sped through the waters of Lough Erne before it became airborne.

The Sunderland reached the convoy area in the early afternoon and then came under the control of the SNO who ordered it to patrol low around the convoy because of the bad visibility. Wing Commander Frizzle was at the controls when *U-610* was sighted below, thirty-five miles from the convoy.

There was also an experienced and senior man as commanding officer of the Blohm and Voss built Type VIIC boat, a nobleman in fact. Kapitänleutnant Freiherr Walter von Freyberg-Eisenberg-Allmendinger had fired his gnat at ORP *Orkan* earlier in the day, and though he was not responsible for sinking the Polish destroyer he was an Atlantic veteran. This 6th Flotilla, St Nazaire-based,

HMCS *KAMLOOPS*

Hamburg-built boat had been involved in the critical convoy battles in March, and, as already recorded had survived an aircraft attack earlier in the day.

The Sunderland was being flown just below cloud base, at 500 feet, in very poor visibility when the U-boat was sighted, fully surfaced, right ahead at 100 yards. Flying Officer Russell immediately took over the controls as the flying boat flew on over *U-610*. He then turned to carry out a low level attack.

Flak from the U-boat was experienced on the turn, but this was inaccurate and was silenced by the aircraft's 0.5 nose gun by the time that the range had been reduced to 200 yards. Three depth charges were dropped, the fourth failing to release. The first two charges fell to port and the third to starboard, abreast the conning tower. The conning tower was seen to lift fifteen to twenty feet as the depth charges exploded. When the disturbance had subsided there was no sign of the U-boat.

As the aircraft manoeuvred for a second attack, fifteen members of the crew of the U-boat were seen swimming in a rapidly spreading oil patch. There was a great deal of wreckage.

Wing Commander Frizzle, standing beside the pilot, watched as he took the Sunderland down for the kill. It was the first attack the new commanding officer had experienced and could not have been a better example of quick thinking in bad visibility, showing a high degree of training and good gunnery.

Just three depth charges had sunk *U-610*. Baron von Freyberg and his crew were all lost. Visibility was bad and night was falling fast, and in the cold and heavy sea the survivors had no hope.

It was an elated Sunderland crew that touched down at Lough Erne in the darkness of the early hours of 9 October after over sixteen hours in the air.

As a result of the previous excellent air cover only a handful of U-boats were still in contact at nightfall. One, *U-91*, fired a gnat at an escort and was depth charged for its trouble.

Headquarters of U-boat Command, in a signal timed at 1410 on 9th, ordered that all boats who could be ahead of the convoy by dawn were to carry on and the remainder to break off and move westward. *U-758* broke off immediately owing to shortage of fuel; *U-275* broke off at 0512 and *U-388* at 0530. *U-645*, under the command of reserve officer Oberleutnant Otto Ferro, torpedoed and sank *Yorkmar*, an American ship of 5,612 tons. *Kamloops* rescued the survivors. This was the only success against convoy SC143, which was by now well within the range of home-based aircraft.

Because of the efforts of Coastal Command aircraft and the support groups the U-boats had not been able to launch a concentrated attack; and the passage of the convoy with the loss of ORP *Orkan* and one merchant ship could be regarded as a well merited victory.

After the sinking of *Yorkmar* all U-boats were ordered to break off and move westwards at 0730. Two and a half hours later there was an ominous call for U-boats *U-279*, *U-643*, *U-419*, *U-336*, *U-610* and *U-448* to report. The latter was the only one able to comply, the rest had already been sunk.

Blindfolded U-boat prisoners are photographed as they line up to go ashore.

Prisoners from *U-643* disembark . . .

. . . on a wet day in Greenock where transport and an ambulance await

The outstanding feature of the operation was the failure of the U-boats to find the actual convoy, or to make any attempt on any more than the one ship sunk, and this when the convoy was without air cover. For the Germans their inability to read the new Royal Naval code had proved disastrous. A great deal of fuel had been expended chasing convoys whereas in the past the U-boats had been waiting in exactly the right position to attack. The disappointed U-boat captains were returning to base with no successes to report. The twenty-four survivors from *U-419* and *U-643* were meanwhile being taken to Greenock, they would take no further part in the Battle of the Atlantic.

CHAPTER SEVEN

The Azores

By the autumn of 1943 the stage had been reached where Allied shipping could sail relatively unmolested so long as an aircraft was present to protect it. However, there was still some way to go. Shortage of aircraft severely restricted the scope of offensive operations. The lack of Very Long Range aircraft still left a fatal gap of some six hundred miles in the middle of the Atlantic where the U-boats had taken a heavy toll of Allied shipping. The rate of building of merchant shipping was increasing apace, but had not yet made good the unfavourable balance between losses and new production, mainly due to the damage inflicted by U-boats earlier in the year.

The obvious way of plugging the mid-Atlantic gap was to secure a base from which aircraft could operate and with this in mind the Allies had long realised the geographical significance of the Azores in relation to the Battle of the Atlantic.

With the invasion of Europe now a certainty it was essential that troops and equipment be shipped from the United States to Britain without being too exposed to the U-boat threat and so for two years the British Government had been negotiating with the Portuguese for the use of the Azores. Already contingency plans had been prepared for an invasion with or without an invitation from Portugal, but as the threat of German retaliation gradually receded the British were given permission to land.

The Azores are a collection of nine islands, further from the mainland of Europe than any other group of islands under Iberian sovereignty. Belonging to Portugal, and some eight hundred miles to the west of that country in mid-Atlantic, they were uninhabited when discovered in 1431. Portuguese colonizers quickly settled and the islands are now a province of that country. Their name was taken from *Açor*, hawk, a bird found there in large numbers.

When Portugal was part of Spain the Azores became a port of call, between 1580 and 1640, for Spanish ships trading with the West Indies. This was an irresistible attraction for the Elizabethan adventurers and it was here, off Flores in 1591, that Sir Richard Grenville in *Revenge* fought his heroic action against a fleet of Spanish war vessels. This action inspired Tennyson to write his ballad taken from the ship's name.

In the First World War Portugal provided the Allies with troops and bases in Africa as well as the Azores. The alliance between Britain and Portugal has extended over six hundred years, possibly because both countries look westwards and depend on the sea. In the Napoleonic wars the Portuguese alliance opened the only way into a hostile continent and it was from Portuguese bases that Wellington began his victorious Peninsular campaign which freed Portugal and helped to break Napoleon. In the seventeenth century the marriage between Catherine of Braganza and Charles II reaffirmed the alliance and brought Britain valuable colonial possessions, particularly in India.

The islands lie on a submerged ridge and are in three groups spreading over a distance of four hundred miles; they are of volcanic origin with oranges, wine and grain as the main produce.

The use of the air bases on Fayal and Terceira islands was permitted from 8 October 1943. The landing force, in three small convoys, left from Britain escorted by three destroyers, oilers, anti-submarine trawlers and the escort carrier *Fencer*. The weather was kind in the initial disembarkation which was carried out with great efficiency and despatch. However, this did not last and the Fortresses of No 220 Squadron, due to fly in to Lagens airfield on Terceira, could not land until 18 October owing to bad weather. In the meantime nine Swordfish aircraft from *Fencer* temporarily carried out anti-submarine duties from Lagens.

The soil at Lagens was lava dust over a subsoil of porous stone so that in rainy periods it soon turned to mud, and became very dusty when it dried. In many places the soil was only a few inches deep and passable roads could only be made by running a scraper over the top, and even the unpleasant reddish mud formed in wet weather did not stop traffic or aircraft landing.

The existing buildings at Lagens were of stone with red-tiled roofs. They were begun by the Portuguese Air Force and completed by the British servicemen, with Portuguese help. They were all on the north-eastern ridge and consisted of the operations block and above that the Area Combined Headquarters. Most of the officers and all the airmen lived in tents in the various squadron dispersal

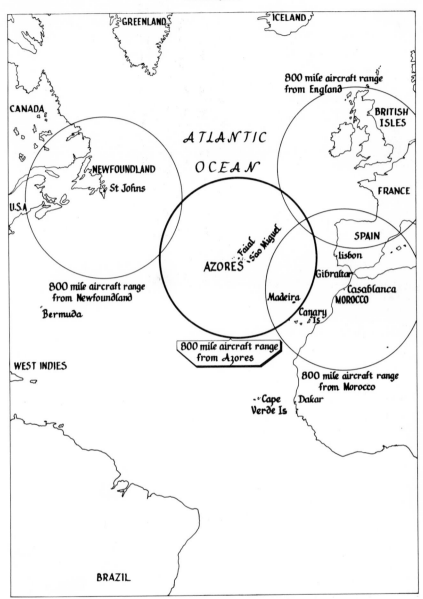

THE MID-ATLANTIC AIR GAP CLOSED
The Azores provided an excellent outpost for anti-U-Boat operations, affording more extensive cover for convoys.

sites. Some were quartered in a dismantled alcohol factory. The stock and plant had been previously removed!

Lagens also had one small hangar with stone walls and a galvanized iron roof. This was used as the main store. Tunnelled into the slopes on the north-eastern side were four or five small sheds which were used as squadron stores.

Lagens is situated on the north-east corner of Terceira in a wide valley which is about four miles wide at the north-western end and about three miles at the south-eastern end. In the centre, at the airfield, the width was about a mile and a half. The valley thus forms a natural funnel which kept the wind always within thirty degrees of the single runway. Taking off towards the north-west the highest ground was sixty feet above the airfield and a mile and a half away. When taking off in the opposite direction the end of the north-eastern ridge was twenty degrees to port and was one hundred feet above airfield level, two and a half miles away from the end of the runway. There was also an obstruction one hundred feet high four miles dead ahead. Thus the approaches from either end were extremely good and pilots could safely come in from about sea-level once they were familiar with the airfield and with the ridges on either side. The circuit was right-handed when approaching from the south and left-handed when approaching from the north. There was initially only a hurricane lamp flarepath and a chance light for night flying.

Lagens airfield was just over a thousand miles west of Gibraltar and only a few hundred miles further from Land's End. These distances speak for themselves and by extending these facilities Portugal put herself on the winning side of the fence. Germany handed a formal note of protest against their yielding military bases under British pressure saying that it constituted a serious breach of neutrality. They threatened to take measures arising from the changed situation.

Within four weeks of the arrival of the convoy all the force and its stores were ashore, base depots and dumps were established. Fifteen days after the initial landing a flight of 233 Squadron Hudsons relieved the Fleet Air Arm aircraft which had covered the landing; by 25 October Nos 206 and 220 had arrived. These were joined during November by detachments of Leigh light Wellingtons from No 172 and 179 Squadrons, and a small flow of transit aircraft from the Newfoundland area were also using the airfield.

U-306 receiving supplies. The Olympic rings insignia on the conning tower signify the captain was a member of the 1936 class – the year the Olympic Games were held in Berlin.

Hedgehog mount aboard an escort vessel.

Every drop of petrol, all rations and equipment had to come eighteen miles over a rather indifferent road and this involved great efforts by the Army and ground staff of the RAF.

Usually on a distant operation communications present a difficulty but in the Azores it was fortuitous that Cable and Wireless Limited had a cable station on Fayal as part of the United Kingdom to South America cable and so coded signals could be exchanged safely.

The Fortresses of 220 Squadron arrived from St Eval on 18 October and almost immediately were flying on anti-submarine patrols.

The first U-boat was sighted by Flight Lieutenant R. P. Drummond, flying E-Easy, while on escort duty with convoy HX262. This was on the morning of the 27th; no attack took place as the U-boat had dived before the Fortress could get into position.

On the same day a homeward-bound convoy of sixty ships, forming convoy SL138/MKS28 from West Africa and the Mediterranean area, was reported by the Luftwaffe off Portugal. A group of eight U-boats, *U-466*, *U-953*, *U-306*, *U-211*, *U-262*, *U-441*, *U-707* and *U-333*, formed a patrol line. They were specifically ordered to remain submerged during the day, surfacing before 1700 only if they were in possession of a clue regarding the convoy.

The Luftwaffe failed to relocate the convoy on the 29th, but *U-262* reported hydrophone bearing to the northward in the evening and the line was ordered to act on this report. Six hours later *U-262* lost contact; the line, however, was ordered to carry out a fan search to the north-west at top speed until dawn and then submerge and move off to the westward.

The convoy was sighted by the Luftwaffe on the morning of the 30th and the patrol line was ordered to operate that evening immediately upon surfacing. During the day a 220 Squadron Fortress from the Azores joined other aircraft, from Gibraltar, escorting the convoy. *U-262* reported being in touch with the convoy, as did *U-707* later.

In the morning of 31 October the action started at 0700. HMS *Whitehall* an old 'V & W' Class destroyer, that had been part of the escort in the Azores invasion, investigated a HF/DF fix some fifteen miles from the convoy. An hour later a U-boat was sighted from the crow's nest at six and a half miles' range; It dived two minutes later. The senior officer was notified and he immediately ordered HMS *Geranium*, a Flower

Class corvette, to join *Whitehall* who was in visual distance.

Whitehall carried out a search and an asdic contact was obtained in nearly perfect conditions. At 0823 the hedgehog was fired and one hit obtained. Considerable timber wreckage and oil came to the surface as a result of this attack. Ten minutes later there was a small underwater explosion, followed immediately by a very heavy one.

The U-boat under attack was *U-306*, a Type VIIC boat launched from Flenderwerft at Lübeck fourteen months earlier. Kapitänleutnant Claus von Trotha was appointed captain. After an initial patrol from Kiel to Bergen, *U-306* left the Norwegian port on 9 March for a two-month North Atlantic patrol before putting in to Brest. A month later it left the Biscay port for a patrol off the West African coast where it torpedoed the 5,882 ton British ship *Kaipara* on 16 July. After returning to France, the boat was in port for two months before leaving Brest on 14 October on its third operation, joining up with the patrol line seeking the United Kingdom-bound convoy.

After the first two attacks on *U-306* the destroyer lost and regained contact several times. Three further inconclusive attacks were made as *Geranium* joined. The corvette carried out three attacks, but at 1000 as neither ship was in contact a box search was carried out, with *Geranium* one mile on *Whitehall*'s beam. The oil slick remained clearly visible and the destroyer recovered samples of this and the splintered woodwork. As no further contact was obtained it was considered the U-boat had been sunk and shortly after 1100 both ships were ordered to rejoin the convoy where other U-boats had been active.

Looking back at the attack by *Whitehall*, the explosion of the hedgehog projectile four seconds after hitting the water indicated that the explosion took place at a depth of 100 feet, which corresponded with the estimated depth of the target. Evidence suggested that *U-306* was mortally hit in this first attack and it finally disintegrated ten minutes later on reaching a great depth when the heavy underwater explosion was recorded in the destroyer. The six further attacks, three by each ship, were probably carried out on the bubble disturbance created by the sunken U-boat.

While the ships were away *U-707* made a submerged attack but was driven off and hunted by a destroyer for six hours; *U-262* attacked submerged firing three single torpedoes and one gnat, it wrongly claimed to have sunk a destroyer; *U-333* also claimed a destroyer sunk with a gnat, it too was depth-charged; *U-466* was depth-charged for six hours and sustained periscope damage.

Later Kapitänleutnant Heinz Franke, in *U-262*, made up for his earlier disappointment when he torpedoed the 2,968 ton steamer *Hallfried*. This was the sole victim of the U-boats during the whole operation of the group.

The remainder of the U-boats were directed on to a southbound convoy but on 5 November they were called off as the convoy was routed too far to the westward.

A new line was ordered to be formed, and in position, by 1700 on 7 November, seeking MKS29. The boats were *U-211*, *U-333*, *U-707*, *U-262*, *U-466*, and *U-228* which was newly out. *U-953* was given freedom of movement until its fuel state necessitated its return.

In the early hours of the 9th, *U-262* reported starshells and later four red lights, presumed to be from a search group. *U-466* fired a gnat at HMS *Havelock* but was heavily depth-charged and suffered such damage that it had to return to base. *U-262* attacked with a gnat but observed no results and *U-228* attacked a straggler, SS *Beckville*, but it was not damaged.

Before all this activity started Flight Lieutenant R. P. Drummond and his crew were having an early call at Lagens. They were briefed to escort the convoy MKS29. The 220 Squadron Fortress took off at 0500 and had reached a point about midway between the Azores and Portugal, some thirty-seven miles south-west of the convoy when suddenly a U-boat was spotted. As this sighting occurred earlier than expected the bombing gear had not been fully set up. It should have been set up immediately the aircraft had left the coast. The U-boat, *U-707* a Type VIIC boat, was built in Hamburg at the Stülcken Sohn works and although launched in November 1941 was only on its third war patrol, having left St Nazaire on 2 October under the command of Oberleutnant Günther Gretschel.

Dawn was just breaking as the pilot went straight in. On his approach he noticed at least one flak gun forward and a number of other guns abaft the conning tower, and they were all firing at his aircraft. The firing was rather wild at first. The pilot turned to port and the navigator immediately began setting up his bombing gear, but he had not finished when the aircraft passed over the U-boat for the second time. The bomb doors were not fully opened and depth charges were not released. During this run up the U-boat's track, the flak was heavy and more accurate. The tail gunner fired long bursts at the conning tower as the aircraft passed over. The Fortress again circled to port and attacked up the U-boat's track, releasing four depth charges spaced at one hundred feet, while below the U-boat was zig-zagging. Due to the bad light the exact entry of the depth charges was not seen, but the U-boat was hidden by the explosion plume. After this attack the U-boat was seen to be stopped and down by the stern, the bow well clear of the water. *U-707* had a 45 degree list to port and all flak had ceased.

The aircraft again circled to port to make a second attack from the port beam and three more depth charges were released which again completely enveloped the U-boat in their explosive plumes. On the run in to this attack the crew of the Fortress thought they saw ten to fifteen men in the water. After the plumes from the second attack had subsided, there was a mild glow under water as if from an underwater explosion, after which the U-boat disappeared stern first. A large oil patch began to form, part of which was thick and treacly and part iridescent. It eventually reached a length of nearly half a mile. Much wooden wreckage was seen, including a large square yellow object like a wooden hatch or raft. Four or five big shapeless objects were seen just beneath the surface.

Half an hour after the attack one man was seen swimming amongst the wreckage and two dinghies were dropped, together with rations. The second dinghy was secured by the survivor, who climbed in. A parachute bag with rations and a Mae West inside was also dropped, but the survivor was unable to pick them up. The aircraft remained circling for an hour and three-quarters, then proceeded to the convoy and reported the sinking and the survivor by visual signal to the SNO, who replied, 'Well done'.

Before returning to base contact had been established with Fortress E-Easy, this time flown by Flight Lieutenant G. P. Robertson DFC. This aircraft arrived at the scene of the sinking and saw the survivor below. A marine marker was dropped and another emergency supply pack, which was gratefully picked up by the German. As no ships had arrived by the time the aircraft was due to leave, a radio and a second supply pack were dropped and recovered by the survivor.

At about this time Flight Lieutenant Drummond and his elated crew were landing to claim a record that could never be beaten; they were the first aircraft from the Azores to sink a U-boat. A more tangible record was to come, for Flight Lieutenant R. P. Drummond was given an immediate award of the Distinguished Flying Cross.

The success provided proof that after four long years of war the mid-Atlantic gap was no longer a gap and that in future any U-boats deployed to that area would receive a similar reception to that accorded to their brothers elsewhere. The days of immunity from air attack were gone for ever. In fact most of the activity for November was concentrated in the South Atlantic, in contrast to that of the previous month when it had been very much in the North. The trans-Atlantic convoys were able to use routes where the weather was less appalling than in the far North Atlantic. This reduced delays and weather damage, which had been such an unfortunate feature of the first fifty months of the war.

As one contemporary chronicler recorded: 'The Azores bases are worth more than a fleet of aircraft carriers to the Allies.'

CHAPTER EIGHT

Escort Group B7 at Sea Again

After three and a half months of inaction as an Escort Group, B7 appreciated the welcome change of operating in support of North Atlantic convoys. Peter Gretton, the senior officer, found invaluable the experience gained in viewing the situation from a different angle and the opportunity of watching other groups in action.

Commander Gretton, in *Duncan*, sailed with *Vidette*, *Sunflower*, *Loosestrife* and *Pink* from Londonderry on 12 October. At 1700 the next day the group joined with Commander R. A. Currie's B6 Group escorting convoy ON206. The senior officer was aboard *Fame*. The corvettes of B7 took up positions on the close screen while *Vanquisher*, from B6, was stationed on the extended screen to reinforce *Duncan* and *Vidette*. *Deveron* also formed part of the outer screen by day.

The next day passed without incident and on the 15th the convoy was diverted to the northward to clear convoy ONS20. The fifty-two ships comprising convoy ONS20 had assembled at the northern end of the Irish Sea and sailed on the morning of 10 October. Close escort was provided by seven Captain Class frigates of the 4th Escort Group: HMS *Bentinck*, *Blackwood*, *Drury*, *Burges*, *Byard*, *Berry* and *Bazeley*, with the addition of HMS *Northern Sky*, *Northern Wave* and the rescue ship *Accrington*.

From HF/DF transmissions at 2203 it was evident that a U-boat was in contact with ON206. This interception was a fortuitous one by a U-boat fresh out from Norway. At the time of the contact the convoy was steaming at eight knots in good visibility. A fix indicated that the U-boat was about ten miles on the port bow; it sent a sighting signal reporting the position of the convoy. Half an hour later *Vanquisher*, about nine miles on the port bow, gained a radar contact which she illuminated with starshell, forcing the U-boat to dive. Four minutes later an attack was carried out on the estimated diving position. *Duncan* closed and both ships listened. Just after midnight *Duncan* obtained a doubtful asdic contact and attacked with hedgehog, but without result. This contact was afterward classified as 'non-sub' and the search was continued for another two and a half hours when both ships set course to rejoin the convoy. While they were still rejoining another fix at 0825 indicated the presence of this or another U-boat about sixteen miles on the port beam of the convoy.

As air escort Flight Lieutenant Eric Bland was flying L-Lucy, a Liberator from No 86 Squadron, he sighted a Type IXC U-boat when flying at 2,500 feet. This was *U-844*, a new boat, only launched from the AG Weser yard at Bremen the previous New Year's Eve and under the command of Oberleutnant G. Möller. The U-boat was on the surface eight miles away, making a speed of sixteen knots and was fifteen miles south of the convoy.

The aircraft made straight for the U-boat which opened fire at some 2,000 yards range. The Liberator took switchback action but, at 100 yards range, the two port engines were hit. During the next few seconds there were repeated hits on the port side and on the fuselage.

The flak was intense and accurate. The aircraft continued its run, attacking from the starboard beam, and attempted to release four depth charges from 50 feet. The U-boat was still on the surface, but the depth charges failed to release. The Liberator turned to port and circled the U-boat at 1,500 yards range while the crew assessed the damage. The port inner engine was feathered, and the port outer had been badly hit though it still ran at half power. The SNO was informed and began homing *Duncan* to the vicinity of *U-844*. After ten minutes of homing, another Liberator was seen. This was S-Sugar of 59 Squadron flown by Pilot Officer W. J. Thomas. The crew had sighted the surfaced U-boat when ten miles away. The other Liberator was then seen circling the U-boat. Flying at 4,000 feet S-Sugar turned towards the U-boat and when he was two miles away Pilot Officer Thomas decided to attack at once as the enemy gunners seemed to be concentrating on the other aircraft. He put the aircraft into a steep dive but realised that he could not possibly get down in time. Steep turns, first to starboard and then to port, put him in an attacking position and he ran in from the enemy's port quarter. Using his low level bomb sight, four depth charges, spaced at 45 feet, were dropped from 70 feet. During the approach the U-boat put up intense flak and hit the aircraft's starboard inner engine when it was still 300 yards away. Two depth charges exploded on each side of the U-boat forward of the conning tower and the vessel was completely hidden in spray.

The Liberator turned steeply to starboard to get into position for another attack, when the pilot was told that the engine was on fire. Meanwhile the U-boat began to submerge and only the conning tower and stern could be seen. Continuing his turn, the pilot saw a deep red flame shooting out of the conning tower. He went in again and dropped four more depth charges, 300 yards ahead of the swirl, half a minute after the U-boat had disappeared. It was seen that the swirl was brownish in colour. The Liberator then climbed away and the damaged engine was feathered. While trying to assess the damage to his aircraft the pilot received a radio message asking him to circle the position. Deciding his aircraft was in no immediate danger he remained on the scene until the destroyer arrived. *Duncan* arrived and dropped a pattern of depth charges on the estimated diving position as it was not then known that the U-boat had been sunk.

Meanwhile, L-Lucy, the first attacking Liberator, attempted another attack just as the U-boat was seen to be diving, that is just after the 59 Squadron Liberator's second attack. Again the depth charges failed to release. As the other Liberator was still on the scene and a destroyer was quite near, Flight Lieutenant Bland jettisoned his depth charges and set course for the convoy, intending to ditch because of the loss of fuel from the starboard outer engine, because of over-heating of the other starboard engine and because there was doubt as to how much longer the other engines would continue to run, even at reduced power. The SNO was informed of this intention. The Liberator had been unable to send a sighting report because of the necessity to home *Duncan* and because of the damage to the aerials. The pilot was instructed to ditch on the port side of the convoy. This was done near *Pink*. The sea was choppy, with no apparent swell. The ditching was made into the wind. The aircraft touched the water tail first at 117 mph and then buried its nose in a wave, apparently ten feet high. The shock of the impact broke up the aircraft and made normal ditching drill impossible. The entire crew were braced on the flight deck and the top turret hatch had been opened before the impact. All the crew were picked up by *Pink* within ten minutes. Two did not survive. *Pink* reported the condition of the survivors to the SNO.

The convoys were so placed when intercepted that it was impossible to evade the advance of the main pack of U-boats which had been formed in a patrol line near 30 degrees west. Thereafter

(Right) U-844. The crew appreciate some fresh air.

(Below) HMS DUNCAN – a pre-war photograph

they were so handled that the Germans would be likely to split their forces between them. In actual fact although both were simultaneously being shadowed U-boat headquarters made the appreciation that there was only one convoy, ONS20, and that the other was a decoy group.

South-west of Iceland, *Duncan* after a fruitless search for the sunken *U-844* decided to rejoin ON206 at 1100 as there were indications that more U-boats were in contact abaft the convoy's beam and it was essential to try and prevent their gaining a bearing.

Later in the day, with three Liberators giving air cover, still several hundred miles off Iceland, E-Easy of 120 Squadron sighted a Type VIIC U-boat about thirty-five miles south of the convoy. The pilot, Flight Lieutenant R. F. Kerrigan, reported the position to the SNO and ran in to attack. The target was *U-470*, a Kiel-built boat on its first patrol, under the command of Oberleutnant Günther Grave, which homed on the convoy from their W/T signals.

As the Liberator attacked, the U-boat manoeuvred stern on and opened fire; the aircraft replied with the nose gun. During the final stages of the run in, the aircraft lurched slightly to starboard. This was at first thought to be due to a flak hit, but it was later found that the lurch was caused by the starboard beam window falling out and hitting the leading edge of the tailplane. Due partly to this and partly to the U-boat's manoeuvring a poor line of attack resulted, and the pilot decided not to release his depth charges. The aircraft circled to starboard and attacked from the port beam, releasing four depth charges spaced at 60 feet. According to visual evidence the depth charges were thought to have straddled, but the evidence of other aircraft suggested that in fact the stick may have just overshot with the nearest depth charge very close to the U-boat's starboard side.

Meanwhile Flight Lieutenant B. E. Peck, flying Z-Zebra of the same squadron, had intercepted his colleague's radio message, and at 1918 sighted the U-boat, but before an attack could be made C-Charlie of 59 Squadron, flown by Pilot Office Loney, which had previously obtained a radar contact, had sighted the U-boat, and at once attacked from the port quarter, obtaining a straddle with six depth charges spaced at 60 feet or a near miss just ahead. Z-Zebra then ran in for the first attack from the beam. This was achieved by flying on a parallel course to *U-470* on the starboard side and then turning to port in a steep curve; but on the approach the U-boat still managed to swing stern on so as to bring the main armament to bear.

Intense flak was encountered, and two bursts were seen just ahead of the nose of the aircraft. The actual attack was carried out from the starboard quarter, and six depth charges spaced at 50 feet were released. The stick overshot slightly, but the U-boat's stern was lifted out of the water by the explosion.

E-Easy then made its second attack from a position forward of the U-boat's starboard beam, and four more depth charges, spaced at 60 feet, were released. During this run up *U-470* appeared to have been surprised, and the gunners concentrated on C-Charlie, which was also making a run. When the aircraft tracked over the U-boat the gun crews were in a state of confusion and did not fire at all, although tracer followed the aircraft after the attack. The depth charges probably overshot, exploding close to the starboard quarter of the U-boat. Meanwhile C-Charlie, owing to the evasive action of the U-boat, decided not to attack, but made a dummy run, and the gunners swept the conning tower and deck with all guns.

The events that led up to the final destruction of *U-470* are somewhat confusing, and it is not entirely apparent whether Z-Zebra or C-Charlie delivered the death blow. C-Charlie made a third run up, but abandoned it at the last moment to allow Z-Zebra to get in an attack as it was better placed. C-Charlie was unable to get out of the way in time and had to pass through the spray from the explosion of the depth charges. Z-Zebra's second attack was carried out from the starboard quarter, and a perfect straddle with two depth charges was obtained with the aid of the Mark III bombsight. C-Charlie also made another attack in the face of intense and accurate light flak, and a stick of charges fell close alongside the hull.

In the end the U-boat's bow rose to a very steep angle, hung there for a few seconds and then sank. The SNO was informed and *Duncan* and *Vidette* were homed to the position and the former picked up two survivors. Owing to the necessity for rejoining the convoy as soon as possible, there was no time to rescue the remainder who were scattered over a wide area – the aircraft had sighted about fifteen survivors.

Duncan, eight miles on the port bow of the convoy, obtained a near HF/DF transmission at 2317. Six minutes later a U-boat was detected by radar and was illuminated with starshell until it dived. *Vidette* had also obtained radar contact at over 9,000 yards while closing. *Duncan* carried out evasive tactics to starboard and dropped a pattern of depth charges on the estimated diving position. *Vidette* then joined in and after obtaining asdic contact, made one attack just after midnight with ten depth charges on the U-boat, which had now gone deep. Contact could not be regained so *Duncan* set course to rejoin, leaving *Vidette* to search for a further two hours.

Another threat to the convoy was averted six hours later by *Duncan* who, nine miles ahead of the starboard column, detected by radar a U-boat coming into attack. It dived almost immediately and was attacked by eye. A search was then carried out with *Vidette* but half an hour later she was sent ahead to counter the possibility of a submerged dawn attack. *Duncan* searched until the convoy had cleared the danger area before rejoining. By this time the weather and visibility had begun to deteriorate; nevertheless, the group topped up with fuel during the day.

When it became known at the Admiralty that U-boat headquarters had assumed there was only one convoy, ONS20, and that the other was a decoy group, B7 was ordered to proceed to support ONS20 some 150 miles away to the north-west.

Shortly afterwards a Liberator from 59 Squadron, on passage to base from ON206, sighted *U-540* some 170 miles to the northward. The pilot, Flight Lieutenant E. Knowles, was then joined by Warrant Officer B. W. Turnbull flying the veteran H-Harry of 120 Squadron and together the Liberators sank the U-boat as described in an earlier chapter.

The escort group proceeded to the slower convoy, disposed to port in the order *Duncan*, *Pink*, *Sunflower*, *Loosestrife* and *Vidette*, when at 2140 *Sunflower* obtained a radar contact on a U-boat which dived almost immediately. The convoy was estimated still to be about thirty-five miles away.

The Type VIIC U-boat was *U-631*, a Blohm and Voss Hamburg-built boat, launched in May 1942 and under the command of Oberleutnant Jürgen Krüger. In March, on its second patrol, it had acted as contact keeper, was credited with sinking a 5,000 ton freighter and had survived two depth charge attacks by Sunderlands, although sustaining damage.

After *U-631* had dived *Sunflower* obtained asdic contact and attacked with depth charges. Amidst the depth-charge explosions the U-boat surfaced at an angle of forty-five degrees and then disappeared. The corvette made a second attack, after which contact was lost, but with *Pink* carried out a search round the spot. The other three ships commenced a search, spaced at six miles, to prevent the U-boat escaping on the surface. *Vidette* followed up an HF/DF bearing but returned without having found anything. Jürgen Krüger and all his crew had been sunk by *Sunflower. Duncan, Vidette* and *Loosestrife* set course at 0215 for the slower convoy then only about ten miles to the north, leaving the remaining two corvettes to carry out a prolonged search.

Group B7 joined ONS20 and the 4th Escort Group in the early hours of 18 October. This convoy, as we have already seen, after being sighted by a U-boat two days earlier, had been diverted to clear the route of ON206. One ship, *Essex Lance*, had been lost on that day torpedoed by Kapitänleutnant Christian Reich in *U-426*, but this had been offset by the destruction of two U-boats, one by air and one by the escorts, as will be revealed in the next chapter.

Duncan and *Vidette* spent the day sweeping on the starboard quarter and astern while *Loosestrife* took the opportunity to top up with fuel, from the tanker. *Vanquisher*, another who had been detached from ON206, joined the extended screen the same evening.

At mid-morning the next day, while the convoy were plodding along at six knots with *Duncan, Vidette* and *Vanquisher* carrying out a sweep about ten miles astern, *Vanquisher* obtained a radar contact. The contact soon disappeared and she carried out an attack in the estimated diving position. The other two destroyers joined and a search was carried out which produced no result. On rejoining the convoy *Duncan* and *Vanquisher* swept up the starboard side while *Vidette* closed to fuel. Later in the day *Vanquisher* was detached for St John's.

Sunflower and *Pink* rejoined in the early hours of 20th, but in mid-morning the latter left for Newfoundland so that two of the crew of the crashed Liberator who had been seriously injured could have expert medical attention ashore. The aircraft crew expressed their appreciation of the fine seamanship of the *Pink*'s captain and the devotion of the ship's medical officer, who undoubtedly saved the life of the seriously injured warrant officer while the ship made for St John's harbour in very unfavourable weather.

During the day *Duncan* and *Sunflower* topped up with fuel and depth charges and, as the convoy was now no longer threatened, the group was detached at 1800 to support convoy ON207.

The next two days were without incident and by 0900 on the 23rd the group was about a hundred miles to the north-north-west of ON207. Shortly afterwards an aircraft signal was picked up by the escort group. A telegraphist reported that an aircraft from 224 Squadron was signalling his base asking them to inform B7 that he was calling them up as he had spotted a U-boat.

The U-boat he sighted, *U-274*, a Type VIIC, was launched from Bremer Vulkan's yard just thirteen months earlier. It was newly out from Norway, under the command of Kapitänleutnant Günther Jordan, apparently on passage to reinforce the dwindling patrol line across the convoy routes.

Coastal Command 224 Squadron had converted from Hudsons to Liberators and it was Z-Zebra from this Squadron that was calling up base. Several new types of airborne communication equipment were introduced into the Command and very close liaison with the Admiralty led to a great improvement in communications between ships and aircraft. However, the introduction of completely new equipment called for intensive training of operators. This was made very difficult by the lack of training equipment. Possibly this was the reason the aircraft was transmitting on the wrong wavelength and a valuable twenty minutes was lost in making the U-boat sighting report to base instead of to the senior officer in *Duncan*, who was not far away at the time. When eventually contact was made between the Liberator and *Duncan* communication and homing were most satisfactory.

Duncan, now alerted to the presence of a U-boat, called the hands to action stations and seven minutes later *U-274* was picked up on the radar screen. When contact was finally established with Z-Zebra homing was easy, more so when plumes of depth-charge explosions were seen over the horizon.

Z-Zebra had first of all made a rocket attack. The RP carrying Liberator was one of several new weapons that came into use during 1943. This was mainly as a result of the impetus given to development by the 'fight back' tactics adopted by the U-boats in the early part of the year, tactics which emphasized the need for weapons which could be released while the aircraft was out of range of the U-boat's flak. The RP was only a secondary weapon and in this instance was followed up by a depth-charge attack. Although the enemy was not seriously damaged the combination of homing procedure and observation of the depth-charge plumes gave *Duncan* and *Vidette* a fix at fifteen miles. An hour later, as the destroyers closed, a sea-marker dropped by the Liberator, was sighted and a search commenced. *Sunflower* and *Loosestrife* later joined.

After two hours *Duncan* obtained a firm asdic contact which was held down to 250 yards in spite of the U-boat's efforts to confuse by using SBT, a device that had thrown many a lesser hunter off the scent. A hedgehog attack was carried out, but without result. Contact was regained astern but the U-boat took violent avoiding action and it was not until 1327 that *Duncan* succeeded in carrying out another hedgehog attack, after losing contact at 500 yards. Sixteen seconds after the projectiles hit the water three explosions were heard by all ships. The estimated depth of 400 feet was immediately passed to *Vidette*. She was by now in contact and, as previously ordered, carried out an accurate depth charge attack three minutes after hearing the explosions. After this attack a firm contact could not be regained. *Duncan* dropped one heavy depth charge with deep setting to ensure complete destruction of the U-boat. A final hedgehog attack was made by *Vidette* but this was thought to have been on the depth charge disturbance.

Duncan then recovered some of the large quantity of wreckage which was identified by U-boat prisoners already on board. Oil and wood wreckage were still rising to the surface when the group left the area at 1500.

Course was adjusted to remain in a position sixty miles to starboard from ON207 which was escorted by C1 Group with the senior officer in *Forester*. No further incident occurred and the group closed the convoy on the morning of the 25th in order to refuel.

Pink joined from St John's, after landing the Liberator survivors ashore, in the afternoon and the now complete B7 Group parted company and proceeded towards ON208.

The convoy, escorted by B3 Group, with the senior officer in *Towy*, was met at 2300 on the 27th and the following day was spent in refuelling. About noon *Duncan* followed up an HF/DF bearing for twenty-five miles but found nothing and returned to the convoy.

Instructions were received from the C-in-C Western Approaches to leave at dusk as the main U-boat threat was considered to have moved to the westward. As the necessary alteration was only twenty degrees from the convoy course, it was decided to sweep along the track during the night and alter course at daylight.

By 0600 on 29th the group was in position about eighteen miles ahead of the convoy, in good visibility. The ships were in line abreast two miles apart in the order *Vidette, Loosestrife, Duncan, Sunflower* and *Pink*. Shortly afterwards *Vidette* obtained a radar contact at six and a half miles. The target appeared to be stopped but when the range had closed to half the distance, it appeared to be proceeding at a speed of ten knots. Starshell was fired but before they burst, the U-boat dived at 4,000 yards. *Vidette*, not in asdic contact, attacked with depth charges on the estimated diving position. A search was then commenced with *Duncan* while the corvettes carried out a wider sweep with legs of six miles. *Duncan* obtained a doubtful asdic contact and attacked with hedgehog. This contact, however, was afterwards considered to be fish.

By 0700 convoy ON208 was only six miles away and altered course to port to avoid the hunting ships. An hour and a half later the convoy was well clear and the group was reformed in line abreast in the order *Sunflower, Pink, Duncan, Vidette* and *Loosestrife*. The ships, one mile apart, then commenced a further search.

While still on the initial course *Sunflower* obtained a firm asdic contact at 0923 at 2,100 yards. She prepared for a hedgehog attack and *Duncan* took over as directing ship, while the rest of the group were ordered to carry out a sweep. The first attack was not a success owing to the failure of the buzzer causing the projectiles to fire late. For the moment *U-282* was reprieved. The reprieve was only temporary for Oberleutnant Rudolf Müller and his crew. Their new Type VIIC U-boat, again from Bremer Vulkan, had only been launched in February, and was on its first war patrol, out of Bergen.

Less than fifteen minutes after the first attack *Sunflower* ran in to attack with hedgehog. Three explosions were heard six seconds after the projectiles had hit the water. There was a short pause, then a loud noise similar to a U-boat blowing tanks, followed immediately by several muffled explosions. *Duncan* followed in astern, as previously arranged, and, four minutes later, attacked with depth charges to ensure the destruction of the U-boat.

Duncan and *Sunflower* remained in the close vicinity until 1015 when wreckage and human remains were sighted, some of which were picked up by *Duncan* as evidence of the kill.

Twelve hours later *Pink* obtained a radar contact which soon disappeared and a pattern of depth charges was dropped in the estimated position. *Pink* and *Duncan* then carried out a search for two hours before rejoining the group. This contact was afterwards thought to have been a whale.

Escort Group B7 joined convoy HX263, escorted by the 4th Escort Group with the senior officer in *Bentinck*, the following midday. The corvettes were stationed on the extended screen ahead, while the destroyers were employed in sweeping on the quarters and astern of the convoy outside visibility distance. During this and the following day the group, with the exception of *Loosestrife*, fuelled from the convoy.

Vidette was detached to proceed to Londonderry at best speed as she required docking. As the convoy did not appear to be threatened the rest of the group left at 1400 after *Loosestrife* had refuelled in very heavy weather.

The group finally arrived at base on the morning of 5 November. They destroyed three U-boats, picked up survivors from a fourth and gave support to five convoys, not one of which was attacked while they were in company. By refuelling from escort oilers whenever opportunity arose, they were able to steam 7,000 miles in the twenty-four days at sea.

Control Room – showing chart table, periscope and periscope shaft. The four canisters contain protosorb which absorbs carbon dioxide.

U-BOAT INTERIORS – Type VIIC

Close up of control room showing port and starboard telegraphs, rudder indicator, voicepipe to the bridge and compass.

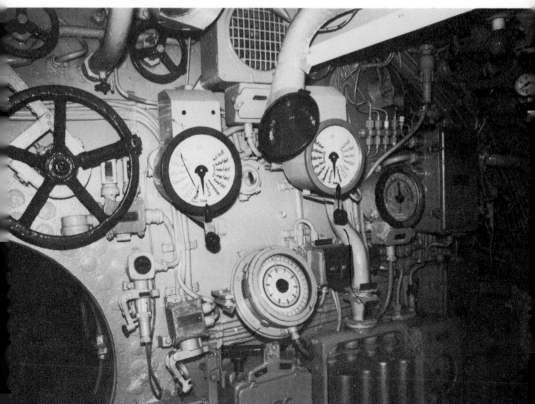

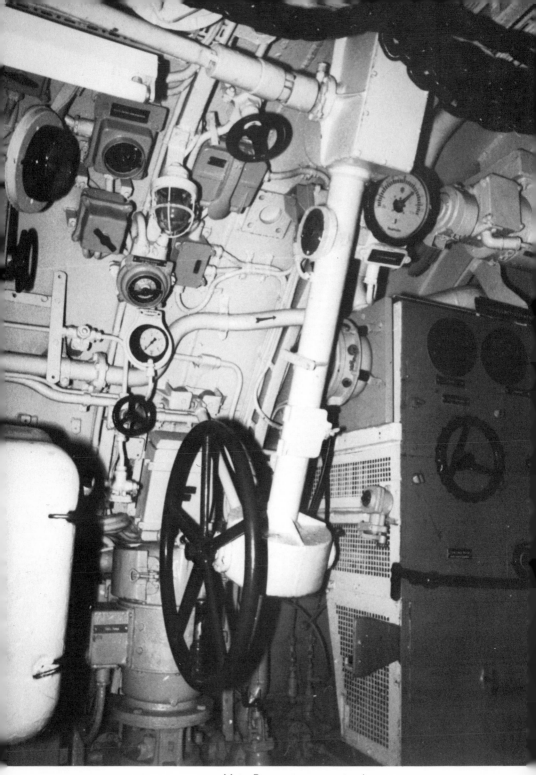

Motor Room, emergency steering.

Diesel Room

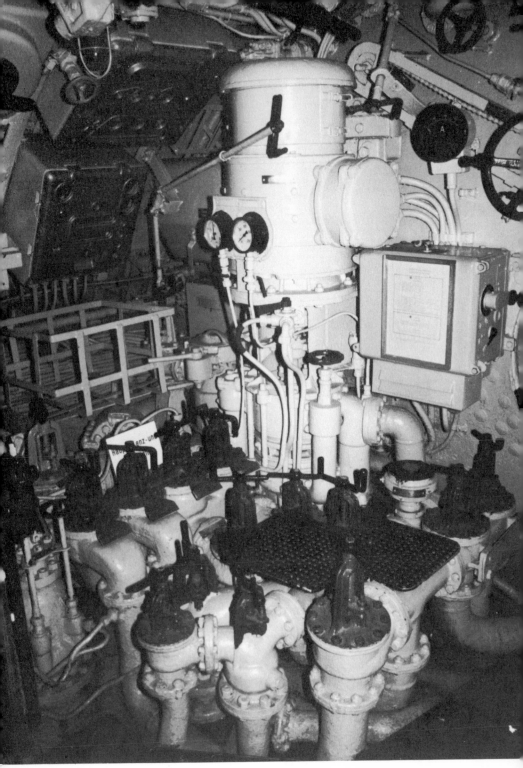

Main Ballast Pump

Bow Torpedo Compartment, starboard side. The bottom torpedo tube is open.

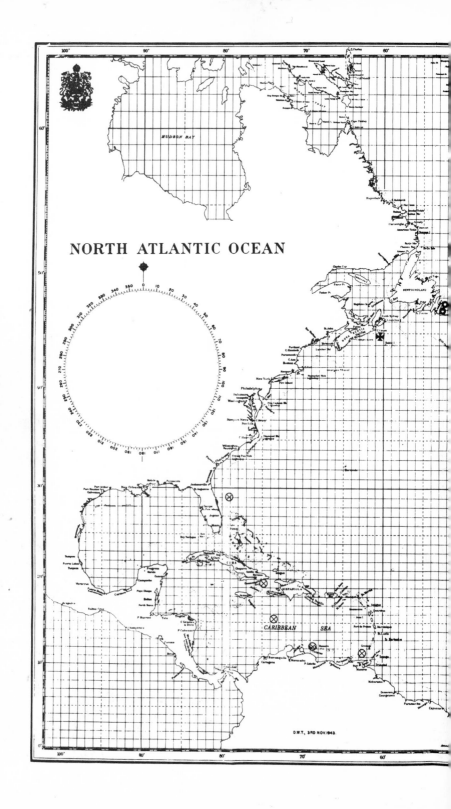

NORTH ATLANTIC OCEAN

D.W.T. 3RD NOV. 1943.

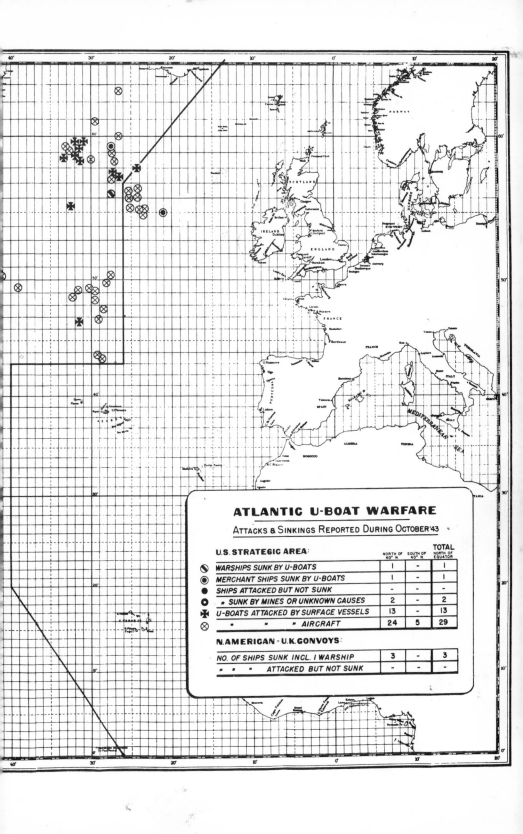

ATLANTIC U-BOAT WARFARE

ATTACKS & SINKINGS REPORTED DURING OCTOBER '43

U.S. STRATEGIC AREA:	NORTH OF 40° N.	SOUTH OF 40° N.	TOTAL NORTH OF EQUATOR
◐ WARSHIPS SUNK BY U-BOATS	1	-	1
◉ MERCHANT SHIPS SUNK BY U-BOATS	1	-	1
● SHIPS ATTACKED BUT NOT SUNK	-	-	-
◍ " SUNK BY MINES OR UNKNOWN CAUSES	2	-	2
✠ U-BOATS ATTACKED BY SURFACE VESSELS	13	-	13
⊗ " " " AIRCRAFT	24	5	29

N. AMERICAN - U.K. CONVOYS:

NO. OF SHIPS SUNK INCL. I WARSHIP	3	-	3
" " " ATTACKED BUT NOT SUNK	-	-	-

CHAPTER NINE

Activity around Convoy ONS20

Convoy ONS20, with fifty-two ships, escorted by the Escort Group, sailed on 10 October, as already recorded. Apart from heavy weather, which elicited some heartfelt comments from the Senior Naval Officer in *Bentinck*, on the lively qualities of his new command in a seaway, the first few days were uneventful.

The expected battle developed during the 16th and 17th and was fought in the area bounded by latitudes 57-60 degrees North and longitudes 36-33 degrees West. At this time convoys ONS20 and ON206 and their escorts were steaming close together.

Formidable air cover was arranged for both convoys during daylight hours, and aircraft were soon sending in reports of U-boats in the vicinity of the convoys.

In the late afternoon of the 16th S-Sugar of No 86 Squadron was on passage to ONS20 when a surfaced U-boat was sighted sixteen miles dead ahead. The Type VIIC boat, *U-964*, was a new one only launched from the Blohm and Voss yard at Hamburg at the turn of the year and was under the command of Oberleutnant Emmo Hummerjohann on its first patrol, out of Bergen.

The aircraft turned 15 degrees to starboard and climbed into cloud. At 2,000 feet the Liberator broke cloud and found itself some five miles from the U-boat. The enemy had evidently seen the aircraft and opened fire at a range of two miles. The Liberator pilot, Flying Officer George Gamble, a native of Warwickshire and a former Hudson captain, decided to go straight in to attack and approached from fine on the port bow, opening fire with the nose gun at 1,000 yards. The U-boat turned to starboard, but the Liberator tracked over the conning tower at fifty feet and dropped three depth charges spaced at 90 feet. Neither the splash of entry nor the explosions were seen, but from the position of the explosion mark and the wake it was seen that the depth charges had exploded correctly, and it was estimated that the stick had straddled. However, the U-boat appeared to be undamaged, although ten minutes after the attack it stopped and remained stationary for five minutes before getting under way again. It circled and put up very intense flak when the Liberator attempted a second attack. The pilot decided to postpone this and circled to port at ranges from 1,000 to 2,500 yards, constantly varying his height. He tried in vain by R/T to contact the convoy escort, then about a hundred miles away, and sent out W/T reports. The U-boat took violent evasive action for twenty minutes and then set off north-west at about 15 knots. The Liberator made other abortive attempts to attack and then asked Group headquarters for instructions in case a naval unit was being directed to the scene. Group ordered the aircraft to try to home the surface escort and, when this failed, to return to the convoy. It was not appreciated at Group that the Liberator had not yet met the convoy

It was then almost dark and with no prospect of surface aid Flying Officer Gamble decided to make another attack in spite of the flak. He made two dummy attacks from ahead and in each case the U-boat's gunners reacted promptly. He then came in a third time from ahead, altering course all the way in. The German turned to starboard and opened up at a thousand yards. The aircraft altered to port and hit the conning tower and gun positions with fire from the nose. Then the Liberator swung to starboard and attacked. Three depth charges were dropped, the third falling alongside the hull just forward of the conning tower.

When the plumes subsided *U-964* seemed to be on an even keel but began making small circles and figures of eight. Flak came up intermittently as long as the aircraft was within range, and the vessel was apparently under control. Three-quarters of an hour later the U-boat's bows seemed low in the water and after a few minutes black smoke came from both sides of the after deck. It slowly lost way and an hour after the second attack, stopped with its bows well under water. Three minutes later the bows sank even lower and *U-964* disappeared from sight heading north. Right up to this moment it kept up spasmodic fire but at no time in the whole action was the aircraft hit, although the gun crew used a prodigious amount of ammunition. As soon as the U-boat disappeared the Liberator flew low over the scene of the attack. In the failing light the crew saw lifejackets in the water and about a dozen men clinging to one dinghy and sixteen or twenty to another. Later five survivors were picked up by *U-231*.

So ended 16 October; three U-boats had been sunk before they could do any damage to the convoys. However, the 6,625 ton British ship *Essex Lance* was torpedoed two miles astern of ONS20 in the late evening. She broke in half and was abandoned, the entire crew being taken off by the rescue ship. Several U-boats were now in contact with the convoy and the escorts hunted many contacts, *Bentinck*, *Drury* and *Berry* each putting down U-boats astern of the convoy.

At this time, in Northern Ireland, the Canadians of No 422 Squadron were entertaining locals at the weekly Saturday evening social at their base at Castle Archdale on Lough Erne. There had been a gale warning since early morning and safety crews were posted aboard the Sunderland flying boats at their moorings.

Among those not present at the social was Flying Officer, Acting Flight Lieutenant, P. T. Sargent of Toronto and his eleven-man crew of S-Sugar who had put in for an early call. They were detailed to escort convoy ONS20. There were to be three pilots aboard and an Englishman, Flight Lieutenant P. A. S. Woodwark from Kent, the group gunnery officer was making a check-up flight.

It was not at all pleasant on the Sunday morning with a high wind blowing and rain falling, nevertheless, at 0411 S-Sugar JM712 slipped from its moorings. The giant Sunderland was cleared to overfly Eire to the nearest shoreline on a prescribed route to the convoy.

Shortly after midday two radar blips were obtained on the screen at a range of five miles. The aircraft was in a rain squall at the time, but on coming out of it the crew saw two surfaced U-boats ahead. The position was about twenty miles south of the convoy.

The sea was rough, with a north-westerly wind of 35 knots, but visibility was about twenty-five miles. The two U-boats were about fifty yards apart and the port vessel kept slightly astern of the other. The Sunderland flew in to attack taking evasive action by undulating. The U-boat opened fire at two thousand yards with every gun that would bear. The aircraft's evasive action and the good shooting of the air gunners, who cleared the enemy's decks, enabled the Sunderland to escape damage in its first run. The attack was made from the U-boat's port beam from fifty feet and three depth charges spaced at 60 feet were released. The stick undershot by thirty feet. The Sunderland then did a tight turn to port at a range of half a mile and came in at 100 feet for a second attack. On this run no evasive action was taken and the aircraft, a huge target for the gunners, was heavily shelled by both U-boats. The R/T was shot away and the front turret recuperator destroyed: the automatic pilot was blown out of the aircraft, the W/T destroyed and the radar damaged; the control quadrant was hit and the throttle and pitch controls shot away: the wing dinghy was blown out, the mid-upper turret and the hull generally riddled. The navigator, Flying Officer Chesley B. Steeves of Elgin, New Brunswick, had been hit by a shell which blew away his left leg and the lower part of his body. Despite his mortal wounds he was able to give the pilot a course for the convoy before he died. The group gunnery officer and the front gunner, Flight Sergeant L. T. Needham, were also killed.

In spite of this heavy and accurate shooting the pilot carried on and from fifty feet released two depth charges across the U-boat's beam. The third failed to release. The U-boat was straddled, lifted noticeably and disappeared without seeming to dive in the normal way. The second U-boat remained on the surface throughout the action and fired continuously while the aircraft was in range.

After the action the Sunderland returned to the convoy, reported the attack by visual signal to *Drury* and informed the ship that it was going to ditch. The Sunderland touched down on the top of the swell at 75 knots about one hundred yards ahead of the escort. After bouncing once the aircraft buried its nose in the oncoming swell and disintegrated. One of *Drury*'s seamen gallantly swam to the aircraft and rescued an unconscious officer who was entangled in the wreckage. Unfortunately the attempt to extricate the pilot was unsuccessful and he went down with his aircraft. The U-boat survived.

Liberator O-Orange of 120 Squadron was returning to ONS20 after attacking another U-boat, when at 1510 a fully surfaced U-boat was sighted about ten miles south of the convoy, The pilot, Flight Lieutenant G. L. Hatherly, at once manoeuvred his aircraft to carry out a head-on or beam attack, but it became obvious that the U-boat intended to keep its stern towards the aircraft and fight back. The pilot therefore decided to make full use of the sun and cloud cover and approached from astern. As soon as the aircraft broke cloud, about two miles from the U-boat, accurate light flak was encountered but the first burst from the Liberator's nose gun silenced the gunners below. Four depth charges were released in a dive from 400 feet, and were seen to enter the water very close to the port side of the U-boat. As the bows of the U-boat emerged from the depth charge plumes it was seen to be badly down by the stern and the bows were lifted out of the water. The aircraft continued circling the U-boat, which was still down by the stern, and considerable flak was again encountered. The SNO was kept informed of the situation and after fifteen minutes the aircraft returned to the convoy having now used up all its depth charges.

After two reverses, the next attack produced a certain kill. HMS *Byard*, a new Captain Class frigate, was returning to her station after chasing off a U-boat reported by aircraft to be seventeen miles away. At this time the convoy was in the mid-Atlantic gap some 300 miles south of Iceland. Before two Devonport based ratings give their graphic accounts of the sinking we will look at the new frigates, for *Byard* was the first of them to claim a U-boat.

During the inter-war years the Admiralty had not foreseen the need for building convoy escort ships and when the U-boats began to take their toll of merchant ships Winston Churchill negotiated a deal with the US President. In the autumn of 1940 fifty US World War One vintage destroyers were transferred to the Royal Navy in return for bases in Newfoundland and Bermuda.

As the home shipyards were working to capacity Britain again turned to the US for more escorts to be provided under the new Lease-Lend Agreement. Seeing what had already happened in the Atlantic the US Navy lost no time in designing ocean escorts and it was these frigates that exactly fitted the bill for attacking U-boats.

The simplicity of shape of the Captain Class frigates greatly facilitated the all-welded assembly work on the structure and allowed mass production of the vessels throughout 1943.

The ships were of 1,940 tons displacement when stowed for sea, were 306 feet long and carried 160 depth charges, more than any other convoy escorts.

Britain arranged to take over, through Lease-Lend, every third ship constructed commencing with *Bentinck*, hull number DE52, then *Byard*, DE55. They were built by Bethlehem-Hingham, near Boston, and HMS *Byard* was launched on 6 March by Lady Darling, the wife of Admiral Darling who at the time held an appointment with the British Delegation in Washington.

The ship, and indeed all of the Captain Class, took its name from a naval captain of Nelson's day. *Byard* was commissioned in June at the builders yard, under the command of Lieutenant-Commander L. H. Phillips from Kent. When the crew filed aboard they were amazed to find a laundry and an ice-cream bar installed. Luxury indeed!

Byard proceeded from the builders yard to Casco Bay. Here the turbo-electric motors produced a speed of 24 knots, more than adequate to catch a surfaced U-boat, and the ship, with its high freeboard, soon acquired a reputation for rolling.

After the working-up period Captain Class frigates were allocated to the special frigate base in Belfast. Here, at Pollock Dock, the American 3-inch ammunition and stores were warehoused. In September the 4th Escort Group was formed with seven Captain Class frigates with *Bentinck* as Senior Officer and *Byard* second-in-command.

We will now don our heavy weather gear, fasten our chin-stays and join Signalman Phillip Norfield in *Byard*, now a week out at sea:

Byard was returning to her station. When about eight miles from the convoy an asdic contact was made. Mr Love, the Warrant Officer Gunner on watch at the time, turned the ship to investigate. The presence of a U-boat was established, a ten-charge pattern dropped and preparations were being made for a second attack when a U-boat broke surface right ahead. The U-boat captain must have been surprised at what he saw, for the new frigate was something of a *rara avis* in the Atlantic. Our commanding officer reported:

'I was in an ideal position to ram but a long way from home, and knew the convoy was threatened, so turned and engaged it with gunfire. A duel with the U-boat now developed on the surface and it was engaged with gunfire. Everything that *Byard* had was brought to bear. The U-boat's conning tower and deck were swept by Oerlikon fire and Bofors fire, and the 3-inch scored a direct hit at the base of the conning tower at a range of three hundred yards with the first round. The Huns, prevented from reaching their guns, soon had enough and started to abandon their ship as it sank by the stern. One officer, five petty officers, and twenty-one ratings were picked up. They were not truculent as the temperature of the water was 40 degrees Fahrenheit. The officer, a young German of twenty-five, whose wife was expecting her first baby that day, had swum over supporting a wounded man and was the only prisoner not distressed. It was nearly dark by now. All the Germans in the water appeared to be dead, and I was some distance from the convoy so I proceeded to rejoin the escort.'

After the account from the signalman and his commanding officer we now turn to the account of Able-Seaman T. W. McPhail:

On the Sunday evening, when we were engaged in shadowing a westbound convoy, and while I was off watch and relaxing on top of my bunk with J. B. Priestley's *The Good Companions*, the alarm bells sounded, and true to our training we were all closed up at Action Stations within a few seconds. We had had so many false alarms in the past that my only reaction was that my leisure time was being wasted as so often before and, of course, I was never able to make it up on another occasion.

However, an asdic contact had been made, we carried out our usual procedure and dropped a pattern of depth charges, my specific Action Station being to pull the depth charge lever when the signal sounded. I think most of us were very sceptical and I don't really think we had any fear, though I had experienced that in the past and was to again in the future, not always on war service!

As we made our first circle after dropping the first pattern the bows of a U-boat suddenly appeared straight ahead, and not too far off, and soon it had surfaced and I could see figures running on the deck. I think my reaction was curiosity as much as anything. However, I heard our skipper yelling 'Fire, Fire!' and soon we had trained on it and opened up with all we had. It didn't seem long until there were bodies bobbing about in the sea and as far as I recall the U-boat just disappeared, I don't remember seeing it go. We picked up several survivors, some of our chaps making gallant efforts to pull them from the sea. Some, alas, were just swept away and some appeared already lifeless. One was badly wounded in the stomach.

The weather during the action was very good for this time of year, although I think there was a heavy swell and I am told the sea temperature was very low. Certainly visibility was excellent, a clear greyish day.

It is difficult to describe my reactions. Certainly I did not feel afraid, though I am no hero. After all the hubbub I continued reading my novel till it was time to go on watch.

Forty years have passed but I still see those chaps in the water like it was yesterday, although strangely enough many more recent memories have faded away.

It did not take long to establish that the sunken U-boat was *U-841*, a Type IXC launched just a year earlier from AG Weser yard at Bremen. It had sailed from Trondheim and was on its second patrol and as the first one had been abortive its commanding officer Kapitänleutnant Werner Bender was another one of the many commanders currently to lose his life in a U-boat without achieving any success in his new boat.

Byard was the first of her class to see action against a U-boat and naturally the crew were very happy; they remained a happy crew for most of them remained in the ship until the cessation of hostilities.

The sinking of *U-841* was the last serious action round the convoys. The sea and air escorts had sunk six U-boats round ONS20 and ON206 in two days for the loss of one merchant ship and two aircraft.

The initiative had been decisively wrested from the enemy and in no case was he able to mount a mass attack nor carry out his pack tactics. Escort commanders reported that a high level of co-operation was achieved and that homing procedure was carried out with efficiency.

CHAPTER TEN

Long Distance U-Boats

When, after their mauling at the end of May, Dönitz recalled his U-boats from the Atlantic, it was only in this area that there was to be a temporary lull. Elsewhere, such as the American eastern seaboard and the Indian Ocean, U-boats were still operating successfully.

Early in June U-boat headquarters detailed nine U-boats and two supply U-boats to the Indian Ocean to relieve those already operating in that theatre. The outgoing U-boats had a rough passage with attacks from the Biscay patrols and American carrier-borne aircraft so that only five reached their destination. Early in September the new group fuelled from a tanker off Madagascar and dispersed to their operational areas.

In October there were two U-boats off the Arabian coast, and one each operating off Bombay, Colombo and Mombasa. Their targets were independently routed ships sailing without escorts. These U-boats, and their forerunners, had caused the British serious dislocation and it was for this reason that No 244 Squadron was at Sharjah. The squadron had been in existence, in the Middle East, since the end of 1940 and since October 1942 had been equipped with Blenheim V's – the Bisley.

The Bristol Bisley was a mid-wing twin radial engined aircraft with a single fin and rudder. In June 1935 the original Bristol Type 142 'Britain First' caused a flurry in official aviation circles when it actually flew faster than the latest fighter then produced. The design was developed by the Air Council into a military bomber. Thus from a high-speed purely commercial aircraft was born the Blenheim which served the RAF extremely well in the early part of the war.

The Blenheim V appeared in late 1942, by which time the medium bomber was being replaced by the Boston and Mosquito. Differing from the earlier Marks in having a solid attack nose, it became known as the Bisley. Production models reverted to a new type glazed nose and operated for a short time in the Middle East, suffering heavy losses when attacking defended positions. The RAF airmen of 244 Squadron, equipped with the Bisley, were therefore flying aircraft nearing the end of their operational life. Their base at Sharjah was under control of the Iraq and Persia Command.

The squadron was another of those that appeared to have been forgotten by those at home, and left to their own devices. They organised football tournaments, had a visit from the RAF Gang Show and flew occasional boring patrols over the Gulf of Oman and Indian Ocean. In mid-October the most important thing that appeared likely to happen was the impending visit of Josephine Baker, the international cabaret star. However, all was to change on Saturday the 16th when Sergeant L. Chapman took off at 1330 in C-Charlie, for yet another patrol.

The temperature was in the nineties as the Bisley took off from the shimmering airfield. No intelligence had been received about the location of a U-boat so it was something of a surprise when Chapman and Sergeants Bonymgre and Murrell, his other crewmen, suddenly saw a U-boat four miles away after they had been in the air for eighty minutes. The U-boat, a Type IXC$_{40}$, was *U-533*, built at Deutsche Werft in Hamburg and launched on 11 September 1942, under the command of Kapitänleutnant Helmut Hennig. It was on its second patrol and left Lorient on 6 July.

U-533 was on the surface making eight knots when first seen. The pilot lost height and manoeuvred his aircraft to such a position that he was able to make a head on attack. The U-boat quickly submerged but ten feet of the stern was still showing as the Bisley made its approach. Four depth charges were dropped, bow to stern, and two were seen to fall in the swirl. The Bisley circled the area and after five minutes the crew were rewarded by the sight of oil rising to the surface. As the oil patch increased air bubbles and two or three white objects were seen. The pilot also thought he saw a survivor. The Bisley was compelled to return, owing to a W/T failure. When it touched down at base at 1620 and reported the attack another Bisley was ordered up and was airborne within half-an-hour. Another aircraft was ordered up from Jask. However, failing light made observation difficult.

The AOC-in-C RAF Iraq and Persia signalled: 'Delighted to hear your news – anxiously await further details.'

The further details emerged the following evening when news was received from Hormuz that the lone seaman survivor had been picked up after 28 hours in the water. The German was taken to Sharjah to 244 Squadron's base. He said that many seamen joined *U-533* without having received any U-boat training at all. Later he was to say more about the outward passage:

> On our way out one destroyer depth charged us the whole night, always at short intervals, the W/T operator kept reporting, 'Destroyer coming nearer', 'right above us'. Whenever she was straight above us the captain proceeded at maximum or three-quarter speed and turned off and then back to silent running. If she is right above us she can't hear us on account of her own propeller noises. The search gear made a sort of singing noise which is always deceptive when it sings like that. We sweated blood that night. How it rumbled, and we were then at a depth of 180 metres too. Finally when we got through to the Gulf of Aden, the officer of the watch said, 'I feel like a new man now'. Even he had never experienced anything like that; he too had sweated blood. He thought that was the end of us; nearly all the lights were smashed, which had never actually happened to us before; we were bombed from the air and depth-charges. None of our fuses was ever affected before, but this time they were all knocked out, although, on the first patrol all six tubes were put out of action as a result of being depth-charged. All the upper deck torpedoes were smashed and all the tubes bent.

The seaman also said *U-533* had come up the Arabian coast and made local purchases.

Unfortunately this German voice was the only note of variety to be heard at the base, for a later note recorded the extreme displeasure felt at the non-appearance of Josephine Baker, the cabaret star.

Some reference books still give the cause of sinking of *U-533* as by Bisley aircraft E and H of 244 Squadron. The U-boat was sunk by Sergeant Chapman's C-Charlie. I believe the confusion arose because the serial number of the Bisley was EH404.

Also constructed for distant waters were the U-cruisers. The Type IXD$_2$ 1,600 tonners were the last conventional U-boats put into production before the advent of the snorkel. These ocean-going boats, designed for extended long distance operations had six torpedo tubes and carried twenty-four torpedoes. They were designed to accommodate a crew of fifty-seven, although more were carried. The boats were powered by a nine-cylinder and a six-cylinder diesel on each shaft and had a bunker capacity of 442 tons so that they could be used to refuel other boats if necessary.

There were only thirty-two boats built of the Type, all by AG Weser at Bremen, more had been projected but were later cancelled. One of the thirty-two, and the only one featured in this book was *U-848*. Launched on 6 October 1942 it was commanded by Korvettenkapitän Wilhelm Rollmann. On 2 November it sank the 4,573 ton British ship *Baron Semple* off the Brazilian coast. This success took Rollmann's personal score over the 100,000 ton mark and into the top thirty of the U-boat captains' table in terms of tonnage sunk. He was a pre-war U-boat captain and was awarded the Knight's Cross as early as July 1940.

On 5 November *U-848* was cruising, surfaced, south-west of Ascension Island. Unfortunately for the U-boat's crew the South Atlantic island had both US Navy and Army aircraft based there.

A Navy Liberator, B-12 of 107 Squadron, took off at dawn on an anti-U-boat sweep; after nearly five hours on patrol the pilot turned to fly the homeward leg. He ordered the transfer of fuel from the outboard wing tanks which required that radio and radar be turned off.

It was just after 1100 and the aircraft was flying at 3,000 feet when the bow lookout reported that he had sighted a ship through a break in the clouds. This was indeed fortunate, for with the radar switched off, had there not been a break in the clouds the pilot might have returned to base with nothing to report.

The sighting was made at five miles. A closer examination identified the wake and stern as that of a U-boat, estimated to be travelling at 15 knots. Radar was turned on as the aircraft headed toward the target. At 1111 the first attack was made. In a diving turn to port, the Liberator flew across the U-boat from its port beam at 75 feet. Six depth bombs were dropped, spaced at sixty feet, landing just forward of the conning tower. The stick straddled the U-boat between bomb number 3 and number 4 but apparently 3 dropped unarmed.

The aircraft pulled up in a steep bank to port, preparing for a second run, Meanwhile *U-848* turned to starboard and the pilot was unable to straighten out in time to get into position, so no bombs were dropped on this run.

After this attack the pilot flew a short distance away from the scene of action, while he contacted another Liberator from the same squadron, B-4, by R/T to advise him of the attack and to home him to the target.

The U-boat, still down by the stern, was losing more oil and moving in an erratic course to the south, making four to five knots. The pilot believed it was unable to submerge.

Turning again to port for a third run, the Liberator approached at about sixty degree target angle with 25 feet altitude, and dropped the three remaining bombs, spaced at sixty feet. The bombs were observed to land and explode short on the U-boat's port bow, the number 3 bomb coming closest but again it apparently dropped unarmed. Still *U-848* did not dive but continued turning, down by the stern and appeared to be losing a large amount of oil.

During the pull-out after the last attack, three puffs of smoke were observed, the only known shots fired by the U-boat at its attacker in all three runs. The element of surprise in the aircraft's attack and the efficiency of the aerial gunners probably prevented the U-boat's crew, who were topside the boat in sufficient numbers, from directing anti-aircraft fire.

Liberator B-4, on receiving the report of the attack, immediately altered course, although it was on a return leg of its 600 mile anti-U-boat sweep, and headed for the reported attack position, twelve miles away. The U-boat at first appeared to be turning to the left in a wide circular turn. Within one and a half miles of it, the approaching relief Liberator was attacked with heavy anti-aircraft fire. Most of the fire was portside and below. Believing the gunners would soon correct and score hits, the pilot lost altitude and turned to port to a position inside the smoke puffs of the fire. Subsequent fire from the U-boat was on the starboard bow and beam, in its former position.

Straightening out for a diving run, with the other Liberator strafing the U-boat from its port side, B-4's mid-upper turret and both bow guns opened up with accurate fire on the conning tower and scored hits which silenced the anti-aircraft fire. As the aircraft approached the target six depth bombs with a 25 feet depth setting, 60 feet spacing, were released at 150 feet altitude, but dropped short. In a sharp pull-out, which lifted the aircraft from 25 to 30 feet altitude, the rear gunner opened with more accurate fire.

The aircraft climbed to 500 feet, then made a sharp left turn to start a second run. The turret guns continued accurate fire, but encountered no anti-aircraft fire from the U-boat. Three more bombs were dropped from 100 feet altitude. Nose down the Liberator crossed over the conning tower at 25 feet and it was established that the closest bombs fell 30 feet short.

Having dropped all its bombs the Liberator climbed and sent a message to base requesting another aircraft to continue the attack while it set course for home. Because it had more fuel the original attacking Liberator remained to home relief aircraft.

Meanwhile *U-848* continued on an erratic course in a southerly direction. By 1330 it had returned to the position of the first attack and appeared able to cruise on a straight course. It then headed west.

Another US Navy Liberator, B-8, had also picked up the signal that was sent out from the scene of action and soon arrived. In the approach, the U-boat's oil slick was noted first, then the U-boat itself at a distance of about ten miles to the west of the slick. The pilot of B-8 contacted B-12 and suggested a combined attack.

Starting a power glide and levelling off at 1,400 feet until five miles from the target, B-8's pilot applied full throttle and began his run at 200 mph. The target angle was 160 degrees when the dive was started, but the U-boat turned to starboard making the final target angle 90 degrees. While still two miles away puffs of white smoke from explosive shells were seen above and to the left of the aircraft. Within a mile to half mile range, something hit and smoke was reported coming from the starboard engine.

With the approach of B-8, whose gunner strafed the deck and gunners, B-12 made a coordinated run on the starboard beam, breaking off at 400 yards and turning to port. B-8 followed up, attacking from broad on the U-boat's starboard beam, crossing just abaft the conning tower at 100 feet altitude, releasing five depth charges. All landed short, the closest about 100 feet. Both waist guns were fired when they could be brought to bear, and the tail gun was fired after the aircraft passed over.

As B-8 pulled out in a climb to the left, it was reported on the intercom that the damaged engine was on fire. The pilot feathered the propeller, cut the engine, and the fire went out in a few seconds. He climbed to 4,000 feet and levelled off, remaining in the area until 1410 before setting course for base. Although four depth bombs remained the pilot decided to return to base for the safety of all, feeling the U-boat was damaged and could not submerge, and knowing Army aircraft were approaching to attack. He knew also that B-4 was being reloaded at the base, only 260 miles away, and would continue the attack.

The original attacking Liberator, B-12, remained in the area to cover *U-848*. By 1515 it appeared to be no longer losing oil, and thereafter cruised at 10 to 12 knots for short periods of time.

Half an hour later a Mitchell of the Army First Composite Squadron arrived to make two bombing runs from 1,400 feet, but the bombs fell short. At 1635 a second US Army Mitchell, of the same unit, arrived to drop 500 lb demolition bombs, but these, too, were reported as not dropping close enough to the target.

When the second Mitchell arrived, the original Liberator left the area for base, having been airborne for more than ten hours. On its way back, it met B-4 returning to the scene, and directed it to the target. At 1700 it met a Catalina, commanded by US Army personnel of the First Composite Squadron, which was also directed to the scene of action.

B-4 sighted a large oil slick at 1650, and five minutes later spotted *U-848*, about eight miles ahead, twelve miles west of the oil slick, moving at between eight and ten knots. The Liberator turned to the right of the target, and began a wide anti-clockwise circle, planning to attack from the bow. The altitude was 2,200 feet with 6/10 cloud.

The U-boat continued on course until the aircraft was about five miles on the starboard beam; it then began turning to starboard toward the Liberator and the aircraft turned to port toward the U-boat. It maintained about 2,000 feet altitude, while the U-boat continued its starboard turn as if attempting to present a beam target.

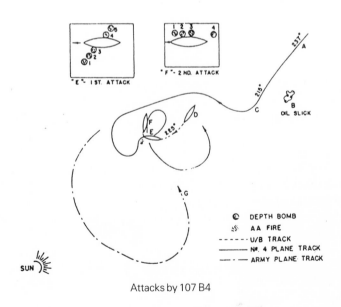

Attacks by 107 B4

The pilot applied high rpm and 44-inch manifold pressure, and began to dive. Gunfire reportedly passed over the port inner engine and cannon fire was also reported. The pilot turned sharply to the left and then straightened out to attack across the bow, dropping five 350 lb flat nose Torpex depth bombs, spaced at 60 feet from a 70 foot altitude. The stick straddled the U-boat with bombs number 3 and 4.

From half mile range, the aircraft fired continuously with its two bow guns and mid-upper turret gun, concentrating on the conning tower. After passing over the rear gunner went into action.

The Liberator immediately followed up the first drop by pulling up to 400 feet and whipping around to make a run from the U-boat's starboard bow. The four remaining depth bombs were dropped close aboard along the starboard side, from 50 feet. The target continued turning to starboard, with a starboard list, but made no headway.

After pulling out of its dive into position to observe the U-boat, those in the aircraft noted that it was settling. Suddenly, from the conning tower forward it shot up in the air, followed by a terrific cone-shaped explosion which came from and surrounded the U-boat.

A group of some twenty-five to thirty men, together with three life-rafts and a dark object which resembled a part of the submarine appeared in the middle of the oil patch. Some of the men were clinging to rafts, others were swimming in the water. One of the rafts failed to open and sank. B-4 dropped one life raft into which survivors climbed.

Soon after the attack the US Army Catalina arrived, dropped three more life rafts, some twenty men were seen to climb aboard. The Catalina stood by while the Liberator flew to notify the nearby HMS *Fort Cumberland* of the location of survivors. Returning to the scene of the kill at 1900 it was decided by both pilots that further patrol was not necessary, so in the gathering darkness they departed. Unfortunately, only one of the 63-man crew was rescued. He was found drifting in a boat by USS *Marblehead*, but died a few days later.

U-848 had proved a doughty opponent. It survived for almost eight hours against attacks by six aircraft and it took 32 depth bombs to finally finish it off.

The loss of a successful captain who had been responsible for the sinking of twenty-two enemy ships was also another blow for U-boat headquarters.

Liberator crosses the conning tower of *U-848* at 25 feet after dropping depth bombs short. Two crewmen, in white, are crouching behind the guns.

CHAPTER ELEVEN

Baby Flat-Tops

As USS *Card* had already demonstrated, auxiliary aircraft carriers soon showed their mettle in the rough, heavy seas in the Atlantic. 'Baby Flat-Top' 13 was fashioned from a freighter hull. The keel was laid down early in 1942 and in mid-May ACV13 was launched as USS *Core* from the same yard as *Card*, at Tacoma.

Core was fourth of the class of eleven sister ships and its designation was subsequently modified from ACV to CVE.

Captain Marshall R. Greer was appointed commander after its commissioning ceremony on 10 December. During the following month *Core* was engaged in the usual shakedown cruise, additions to her armament, alterations and adjustments necessary to make the ship ready for wartime duty. Composite squadron VC-13 was assigned to the ship's air group. The carrier, escorted by USS *Waters*, moved from Puget Sound Navy Yard at Bremerton, Washington, to San Diego on 6 February 1943. Flight quarters was first sounded five days later. During the qualification landings the crew and flight deck personnel became trained and indoctrinated, and by late March the vessel was ready to move to the Atlantic, passing through the Panama Canal on 3 April. *Core*, escorted by USS *James O'Hara* and USS *Gillespie*, reported to the Commander Air Force at Norfolk, Virginia for duty eight days after transiting the canal.

The duty of the ship was laid down to be the protection of Atlantic convoy lanes and taking offensive action against underseas raiders. At this time employing the carriers against the U-boat menace was a comparatively new tactic and its efficiency had yet to be proved when *Core*'s task group began its first operation. The group, including VC-13 with twenty-one aircraft and three destroyers, USS ships *Badger*, *Bulmer* and *Barker*, sailed on 27 June to provide air coverage for a Gibraltar-bound convoy.

First blood came on 13 July when Lieutenant Robert Williams flying an Avenger sank *U-487* south-east of the Azores. Three days later the same pilot sank *U-67*. The *Core*'s only personnel casualty from enemy action during the war came during the destruction of the first U-boat when a pilot was listed as missing in action after his fighter crashed during a strafing run on the U-boat.

Returning to Norfolk on 31 July, the task group received a 'Well done' for its first operation from the Commander-in-Chief, Atlantic Fleet, and later was awarded an operations star.

The same units sailed as a task group from 16 August to 2 September and struck at a U-boat refuelling rendezvous south of the Azores. In air attacks a U-boat was damaged on the 23rd and the next day Lieutenant Williams sank two more U-boats, *U-185* and *U-84*. In recognition of his feat the pilot was awarded the Navy Cross; two gold stars and three citations by C-in-C, Atlantic Fleet. The operation was cut short because of a machinery defect in *Core*. Captain James R. Dudley took over as commanding officer on 2 October, and three days later *Core*, with her task group, moved out to strike in the Central and North Atlantic. The group included USS ships *Greene*, *Belknap* and *Goldsborough* and later the *Ericsson*. The first U-boat encountered was *U-378* on 20 October, which had been active for more than eighteen months, and which only twelve days earlier had sunk *Orkan*.

U-378, a Type VIIC boat, under the command of Kapitänleutnant Erich Mäder, was launched from the Howaldts Werke at Kiel in mid-September 1941 and commissioned at the Baltic base on 30 October.

On 11 March 1942 it commenced its first patrol, rounding the North Cape, and on completion joining up with Arctic forces at Kirkenes on 1 April. At this time *Tirpitz* had been at sea, menacing Russian convoys, and itself was the target of thirty-three Halifaxes at Trondheim on 31 March. *U-378* joined a destroyer flotilla at Kirkenes and its first patrol from the northern base commenced on 7 April and a day later convoy PQ14 sailed for Russia. One ship was sunk by a U-boat, and several ships and U-boats were damaged by ice. *U-378* returned to Kirkenes in time to celebrate Hitler's birthday on 20 April. Nine days later it left the northern base for the last time, putting in to Trondheim a week later. It was given a six-week refit, then ready for sea again it headed south for Kristiansund, to complete its refit, which took a further two weeks. Back again, to Trondheim, it was another month before it was properly ready to resume battle in the Arctic Ocean.

The U-boat sailed against PQ18 on 12 September and was one of a group that co-operated with the Luftwaffe in a combined attack. The aircraft sank ten ships and the U-boats three, for the loss of forty-one aircraft and three U-boats. *U-378* returned after a fortnight at sea and was under repair from 20 October until 7 November. Four days later it was at sea for a month on another Arctic patrol. Once again *U-378* was so damaged that its refit lasted from mid-December through until the beginning of March 1943.

Conditions in the far north, with darkness twenty-four hours a day during the winter, with fog, ice and extreme cold were enough to dampen morale but the freezing temperatures caused surfaced U-boats to ice up and become top heavy, inflicting more than the usual heavy weather damage.

On 15 March the U-boat sailed again, up to the North Cape, and put in at Hammerfest on 1 April – it had been in Norwegian waters for a year. Eight days later, much to the relief of the crew, *U-378* was detailed for action in the North Atlantic. Stopping in at Trondheim on the 12th, *U-378* said farewell to their friends of the 13th Flotilla.

The conclusion of the seventh war patrol brought the boat into the 3rd Flotilla base at La Pallice and it was from the French base that *U-378* started its eighth and last patrol on 6 September. The boat was one of a group of nineteen hunting convoy ONS19. It was then switched to the *Rossbach* group seeking SC143. On 7 October *U-378* reported being attacked by aircraft while tracking convoy escorts. At dawn the next morning, Kapitänleutnant Mäder carried out a snap attack on the escort group's Polish destroyer *Orkan*, hitting its after magazine and it sank with a heavy loss of life. This was exactly the type of attack Admiral Dönitz had ordered – destroy the escorts and the rest would be easy. The last message from *U-378* was received at U-boat headquarters on 13 October. A week later, north of the Azores *U-378* was running fully surfaced, with its guns unmanned, when surprised by an Avenger and a Wildcat from *Core*.

The attacking section of an Avenger, piloted by Lieutenant R.W. Hayman, and a Wildcat, piloted by Lieutenant-Commander C.W. Brewer, was flying the second leg of an offensive search into an area reported to contain a refuelling concentration. The sky was overcast, with scattered showers, though the area immediately over the scene of the attack was clear. Visibility averaged ten miles except in rain squalls. The sea was very rough with a strong wind. The section had previously been flying at 6,000 feet searching visually, but had reduced to 4,000 feet to go under a cloud. Emerging from the cloud, the U-boat was sighted by the Avenger pilot approximately thirty degrees off his starboard bow at a distance of three miles. The U-boat was fully surfaced heading directly into the wind, and was

(Opposite) U-378 sinking after attacks by aircraft from USS Core.

making very little more than steerage way.

The Wildcat was flying close aboard and immediately caught the Avenger pilot's hand signal, located the U-boat and started a strafing run attacking *U-378* from the port quarter, thirty degrees from astern. Sun on the port quarter made this run almost directly from out of the sun. Fire was opened from a thousand yards and tracers were seen by the accompanying Avenger's crew to ricochet from the deck and conning tower. Approximately a thousand rounds of ammunition were expended. Fire was concentrated on the conning tower as the after guns appeared not to be manned. When the Wildcat was at 500 feet a violent red flame was seen to break out, which completely filled the conning tower and extended aft to the upper gun platform. No anti-aircraft fire was experienced. Pulling out of the strafing run, the Wildcat turned left and gained a position which afforded an unobstructed visibility of the forthcoming depth charge attack.

The Avenger had meanwhile turned right to lose altitude and gain a more favourable position for an attack, the angle of direct attack being too steep. The attack was made from almost directly astern in a final glide of approximately ten degrees. The pilot expended forty to fifty rounds from each gun in strafing during the approach. The bombs were released at 175 feet and entered the water 100 and 170 feet over and slightly to the left of the U-boat's course, probably due to the aircraft being in a left skid at the time. The tip of *U-378*'s bow was obscured by the water thrown up by the explosion.

The U-boat proceeded on into the depth charge disturbance. Some thirty seconds following the depth charge explosion, *U-378* suddenly rolled over sixty degrees to port. Very shortly thereafter the bow and conning tower disappeared, leaving the stern above the surface at an angle of thirty degrees. Twenty to forty feet of stern was visible for twenty to thirty seconds, the length visible being varied by the waves. The stern then slowly disappeared. During this time the Avenger had made a turn to the left to gain position for an attack with a Mark 24 mine acoustic torpedo.

Thirty seconds after the stern disappeared the Avenger made another run upwind along the course of *U-378*, dropping the homing torpedo at the centre of the disturbance left by the disappearing stern. The torpedo entered the water, ran straight ahead true and then made a sharp turn to the right. Approximately two minutes thereafter, the pilot and radioman observed a shock wave and a white flash 'as if some one had turned on a flashlight under water'. 300–400 feet forward and to starboard of the point of the mine's entrance. This shock wave developed into a symmetrically round area of green water and air bubbles. This area faded out within a minute or two in the heavy seas.

No further evidence was observed by the aircraft, which both remained on station for over two hours and kept the position marked with dye markers and smoke floats. The sea was so rough that the dye markers, which usually persist for a matter of hours, were very nearly obscured in fifteen minutes.

USS *Core* maintained a 24-hour W/T watch on the two H/F's of that and the adjacent area. The three escorting destroyers searched continually on other bands but no transmission which might possibly have emanated from *U-378* was intercepted. *Orkan* had been avenged.

The US Escort carrier *Block Island,* another baby flat-top, took its name from a small land patch situated off the coast of Rhode Island. This carrier too was constructed by the Seattle-Tacoma shipbuilding company and launched at the beginning of June 1942.

When commissioned in March 1943 Captain Logan C. Ramsey found he had fifty experienced men, survivors of USS *Lexington,* which had gone down in the Coral Sea ten months earlier. The rest of the crew of about a thousand men were ex-civilians.

After a shakedown cruise off the west coast, the carrier left San Diego and traversed the Panama Canal to Norfolk, Virginia. Delivery runs then followed, for the crew to feel their sea legs. *Block Island* made two runs from New York to Belfast ferrying Army fighter aircraft.

The carrier took on board six Wildcats and twelve Avengers and within a few days of her North Atlantic hunting career *Block Island* flushed several U-boats and one night as her escorts attacked, many of the carrier's crew topside watched in amazement as starshells and gunfire blazed in the black sky. This was their battle initiation.

A couple of days later two of the carrier's aircraft encountered two U-boats, one of which was *U-220.* This U-boat was a rare Type XB, of which only eight were built. It was a minelayer and on this occasion was also doubling as an emergency tanker. Launched from the Germania Werft in Kiel in mid-January 1943, *U-220* was under the command of Oberleutnant Bruno Barber. The initial three-day cruise took the boat up to Bergen and it was from here that it left

USS *CORE*

USS *BLOCK ISLAND*

on 8 September. The Type XB boats stowed three mines apiece in six internal shafts forward and two apiece in twenty-four external mine shafts, twelve a side. The U-boat was ordered to lay the mines off St John's, Newfoundland, on or about 8 October and then proceed to the Atlantic to refuel other U-boats. It was the mines from *U-220* that caused the loss on 19 October of two ships, the American 3,478 ton *Delise* and the British *Penolver*, 3,721 tons, and caused the serious disruption described earlier. By the time *Block Island* caught up with *U-220* it had already refuelled *U-603* and *U-256* and was seeking to replenish a third.

There was clear weather on the morning of Thursday, 28 October, as Lieutenant Franklin M. Murray lifted his three-man Avenger from the deck of *Block Island*, accompanied by Ensign Harold L. Handshuh, flying a Wildcat.

The two aircraft took off at 0845 on a U-boat search as the carrier cruised off the Newfoundland coast. The sea was very choppy with swells from the north-west.

After being airborne for twenty minutes in his Avenger, forty miles from the carrier, at an altitude of 1,500 feet Lieutenant Murray takes up the story:

I saw two dark objects in the water twenty-five degrees on my port bow at about twenty miles. I immediately headed towards them, telling my crew to standby for an attack. I zoomed to get the fighter joined up and then with my field glasses verified my first impression that the two objects were U-boats. The U-boats were about two hundred yards apart and abreast of each other travelling at about eight knots. The nearest one had its deck out of the water while only the conning tower of the other was visible. I waved the fighter out to the side so that we could make the attack from different angles. I called the carrier giving them the contact report. The radioman turned on his equipment and ran over the arming check-off list to make sure that everything pertaining to ordnance was in working order.

I made my attack from twenty degrees on the closer U-boat's starboard bow, while the Wildcat made its approach from the starboard beam. The attack took both U-boats completely by surprise until the aircraft started strafing them. The conning tower of the closest U-boat, *U-220*, was covered by gunfire from both aircraft. It wasn't until I was in my final dive to drop the depth bombs that I noticed that the U-boat farthest away was the larger of the two, but by then I was in position to drop. I did not see the depth bombs enter the water but the explosions of the charges came from underneath the conning tower. The spray from these explosions came from both sides of the U-boat so that it was out of sight momentarily until the water subsided. About this time I noticed that gunfire was coming by me on both sides so I jinked round trying to get a better view and also a picture of the bombed U-boat. My radioman called me and told me that the camera had jammed and he did not get a picture of the drop or the explosion. All of the gunfire came from the larger U-boat that I had not bombed. No fire came from the bombed U-boat. This boat that we had bombed lost all forward motion and had skidded in a turn to starboard of about 180 degrees. Gunfire from the other U-boat became rather intense, so I climbed to about 2,500 feet.

Eighty to ninety seconds after the bombing, the stern of the bombed boat suddenly rose out of the water at an angle of at least 45 degrees, hung there momentarily and then slid under the water. By this time, the radioman had the camera working, but we were too far away for the small camera to get the details.

During the attack the large U-boat had its deck out of the water, keeping up strong anti-aircraft fire with the gun forward of the conning tower and the guns on the conning tower. After the first U-boat sank, the large U-boat tried to keep its bow pointed toward me, but still moving in a south-easterly direction. I called the carrier and asked them if they had received my first message. They replied negative but other pilots in the air had re-transmitted the course and distance that Ensign Handshuh called in. The distance got mixed up so that we did not get any assistance. However, I heard the carrier sending other aircraft vectors, but I didn't pay any attention to them because I was busy jinking and watching the other U-boat. I wouldn't let the fighter make more strafing runs because I thought we could keep drawing the gunfire from the U-boat, keeping it worried so it wouldn't submerge in fear of an attack and thus enabling relief aircraft to make an attack. Once it made a pretence of diving, so I turned on my gun camera, which I had forgotten on my bombing run, and started in on a strafing run to get some pictures. On the way in my left gun jammed and the U-boat started intense fire by my nose, so I pulled out and regained altitude.

At about 0945 the U-boat crash-dived, so I immediately went

in to drop my Mark 24 mine. My course was toward the U-boat's port beam, altitude 200 feet and speed 150 knots. The mine was dropped, hitting the water 46 seconds after disappearance of the conning tower, about 100 feet beyond the swirl. The Wildcat pilot and my crew saw the mine enter the water and begin its run. Before the mine's wake disappeared from view, they observed it to turn thirty degrees to port. I dropped a sono-buoy five seconds before the mine hit, but it did not work. I told both my crew to keep their eyes open for an explosion or a shock wave, neither of which was observed.

It would appear that the aircraft interrupted what was to be a refuelling operation for the U-boats were cruising trimmed down. The decks of *U-220* were awash and the other was trimmed down a little further, with only the conning tower visible. The look-outs must have been more interested in watching each other's boat than in searching for an attacker as the aircraft that had sighted the U-boats at twenty miles were able to attack unnoticed. There were numerous cumulus clouds providing 5/10 coverage, but except in the squalls the visibility was unlimited!

No gunfire at all was experienced from *U-220* but the other U-boat, which was seen to have an insignia on its conning tower, put up a heavy barrage. Anti-aircraft fire appeared to come not only from the after platform but also from a point near the forward end of the conning tower. Both tracers and explosive shells were used, the forward fire being from a single spot at the apparent rate of 60–80 rounds per minute. The gun crew seem to have been poor deflection shots.

After the attack the aircraft circled the area for thirty minutes until ordered back to the carrier. The Avenger sank *U-220* with two Mark 47 depth bombs fused to explode at 25 feet and expended 60 rounds from its wing guns and 150 rounds from the turret. The Wildcat fired 375 rounds of ammunition during the attack.

Other units from the carrier arrived later but nothing further was seen. The second U-boat escaped the homing torpedo. The Wildcat pilot reporting on it said:

I saw it hit the water and start to turn left into the course of the U-boat. After it completed about a thirty degree arc, I could no longer see its wake. It seemed to be gaining depth as it progressed in its turn.

So, without realising it at the time, USS *Block Island* had dealt a major blow to the U-boats by sinking their auxiliary tanker *U-220*.

We left *Card*, with her seven U-boat successes, at anchor in Casablanca on 18 October. After remaining in port for two days the group put to sea to carry out U-boat search patrols. On 24 October the group sighted Santa Maria island of the Azores and the days passed without incident until the 30th, on which day, about fifty-seven miles from the Task Group, a U-boat was sighted on the surface and attacked unsuccessfully, as it was submerging.

Aircraft were up the next day on anti-U-boat sweeps and just as a patrol group were preparing to land on *Card*, from the last sweep of the day, the pilot of an Avenger sighted two surfaced U-boats, *U-91* and *U-584*.

Lieutenant W.S. Fowler had taken off from the baby flat-top at 1436 and nearly four hours later, on the return leg of the last vector of a regular sweep, he saw the enemy craft. He was flying at 2,500 feet in scattered cirrus clouds, just eighteen miles from the Task Force, where the rest of the patrol were awaiting permission to land on.

One of the boats, *U-584*, was reported as the smaller of the two. The Type VIIC boat was built by Blohm and Voss and had been launched at the end of June 1941. At this time Leutnant Heinrich Wulff, a reserve officer, was appointed 1WO. At thirty-two he was rather old for his first underwater appointment. Like the boat, he too was from Hamburg. The boat sailed from Kiel at the end of November to join the Arctic flotilla. It remained in that area for less than six months and at the beginning of May it set out from Kiel on its first Atlantic patrol and put in to Brest eleven days later. The first trip out again, at the end of May, was no ordinary patrol, for *U-584* landed agents on the coast of the United States before returning two months later. The third patrol, of seven weeks, was in the North Atlantic. Here, on 10 September, *U-584* gave the *coup de grâce* to the British tanker *Empire Oil*, which had been torpedoed by *U-659* but had not sunk. The fourth, at the beginning of 1943, was a little nearer home, for as well as the North Atlantic *U-584* was instructed to patrol off the Scilly Isles. Returning to Brest, *U-584* had six weeks in port before commencing its fifth two-month Atlantic patrol at the end of March. This was at the time when the crucial convoy battles were raging. It somehow survived the fate that accounted for forty-one other U-boats in May. Their first 1WO

Heinrich Wulff commanded one of the forty-one victims. After he left *U-584* in August he was appointed to the new *U-646* but on 17 May the U-boat was sunk by a Hudson while on its first patrol.

After a long summer break *U-584* sailed, on 2 September, under Kapitänleutnant Joachim Deecke, to the North Atlantic. The U-boat was one of nineteen in a group seeking the fully laden eastbound convoys. By the end of October all fresh provisions had long since been exhausted and fuel was running low, so *U-584* was in the designated fuelling area when seen on the Sunday evening, 31 October, by Lieutenant Fowler in his Avenger. He takes up the story:

I sighted two fully surfaced U-boats cruising in left echelon a thousand yards apart at a distance of six miles making about twelve knots. The leading U-boat was the larger of the two. At this instant my radioman reported a radar contact 'Two objects sixty degrees to starboard, six miles away.'

At first, we thought the U-boats to be part of our task force. As soon as we knew differently we dived to take up station 1,500 yards astern, ready to drop our mine as soon as the U-boats submerged. We were in perfect position to drop our 500 lb bomb, but the definite doctrine of the carrier required us to take station astern and await help before attacking, unless the last U-boat submerged.

As soon as we reached our station astern the larger U-boat submerged after firing at us. The smaller one started a tight turn to port firing continuously, pausing only at brief intervals. Its fire was not very accurate. On one occasion it ceased firing for almost a minute, even though we teased him.

Upon the arrival of two Avengers piloted by Lieutenants Balliett and McAuslan the remaining U-boat dived. I went in and dropped a mine about 125 feet ahead and slightly to starboard of the swirl, fifteen seconds after the conning tower had disappeared. Lieutenant Balliett dropped his mine about 350 feet ahead and slightly to port.

My position prevented my seeing the explosions although others on the scene did observe them.

A large circular oil slick with blotches of heavy oil and debris was observed as well as a steel coloured cylinder of about two feet in diameter. We took pictures, and were recalled to the ship, a few minutes later.

The reason the aircraft were ordered to return to the carrier was that it was getting dark, Lieutenant L.S. Balliett, who had been waiting to land at the time of the sighting, reported:

> Lieutenant McAuslan and I were vectored from the carrier to the scene of the contact, arriving on station about twelve minutes after the contact was made, but by this time one U-boat had already submerged. The surfaced U-boat was executing a circle to port, presumably to keep its guns bearing on Lieutenant Fowler, who was circling in position for his mine release in the event the U-boat were to submerge.
>
> We arrived on station at about 4,000 feet altitude. I called Lieutenant Fowler and told him I was starting my glide bombing attack. Before I had a chance to release the 500 lb bomb the U-boat began to crash-dive. I called Lieutenant Fowler and told him the U-boat was submerging.
>
> He started his attack and dropped his mine about 15 seconds after the conning tower was last seen. His drop appeared to be in excellent position, about 150 feet ahead of the swirl and about twenty feet to starboard.
>
> I had, in the meantime, dropped my wheels, cut my throttle and circled wide, arriving at the release point about ten or fifteen seconds after the other Avenger. I dropped my mine about 350 feet ahead of the swirl and about fifty feet to port in order to ensure a straddle with the other Avenger's drop.
>
> Explosions were observed by both members of my crew. My gunner observed an explosion after Lieutenant Fowler's release, and my radioman observed an explosion after our attack.
>
> There was a very large circular oil slick observed after the attack, about 75 yards in diameter, with a large amount of debris. There was also what appeared to be a steel cylinder bobbing in the water in a vertical position. This also was inside the circular oil slick.

U-584, the eighth victim of *Card*'s aircraft, was the recipient of a well co-ordinated attack of excellent teamwork by the pilots. It was the first mine attack to be delivered by the carrier's aircraft. The baby flat-tops certainly proved their worth in the Battle of the Atlantic.

After the attack *Borie* was dispatched to the scene with orders to conduct a night search and, if necessary, offensive action. The result was an epic duel.

CHAPTER TWELVE

An Epic Duel

On 24 October twenty-four U-boats, the *Siegfried* Group, were in position in the North Atlantic awaiting convoy HX262; *U-274* which was on its way to join the group had been sunk the previous day by Liberator Z-Zebra of 224 Squadron and HMS *Duncan* and *Vidette*, as recounted elsewhere. The convoy was routed south of the group and all that happened was that two U-boats were attacked and a third, *U-420*, sunk by a Canadian aircraft escorting ON207.

U-420, a Type VIIC boat was launched in August 1942 from the Danziger Werft. For some reason the Danzig boats were never popular with the U-boat crews. Oberleutnant Hans Jürgen Reese took *U-420* on its initial cruise from Kiel to Kristiansand. On its first North Atlantic patrol it was severely damaged by Canadian Liberator B-Baker, flown by Pilot Officer R.R. Stevenson of No 10 Squadron out of Gander, Newfoundland on 3 July. The boat limped back into Lorient thirteen days later. It took three months for the U-boat to be repaired, and a thorough overhaul put it back in first class condition.

Meanwhile, the boat had moved north and left Brest, with its escort, on 9 October. After the necessary preliminaries had been successfully carried out the commander dismissed the escort and his boat purred smoothly through the heavy Biscay waves on its way to the Atlantic battleground in search of the westbound convoy ON207.

The Royal Navy Second Support Group, which had been operating in the vicinity of the convoy, left in the early hours of the 25th as the convoy did not appear to be menaced. The escort was left to the Eastern Air Command, or more precisely the Liberators of No 10 Squadron at Gander. The next day eight patrols were called for; F-Freddie took off at 0330 and K-King an hour later. The third aircraft sent on convoy patrol was A-Able. Flight Lieutenant R.M. Aldwinckle took off at 0710, on a windy day with a rough sea and patches of overcast. Four hours after take-off, as the Liberator neared the convoy there was occasional rain and snow.

Bob Aldwinckle recalls:

I was flying out at 8,000 feet, which is unusually high for anti-U-boat warfare, but I was keeping in the cloud base and not using the search radar since we thought that the U-boats were picking up the radar before the radar picked them up and, as a result, warned of an approaching aircraft, the U-boats could dive and not be detected. In any event, suddenly I saw a U-boat ahead fully surfaced. It was several miles ahead so I ducked back into the cloud, I rang the bell, it's something like an old-fashioned doorbell and sounds the same, to alert the crew and increased speed. When we broke cloud again it was still fully surfaced and we started a run-in. I had one acoustic torpedo, which we called a Zombie, and eight 250lb depth charges. Since I couldn't drop the Zombie on a surfaced U-boat I called for depth charges. About half way in to the attack one of the crew shouted that the U-boat was diving and I called for the Zombie. It turned out that it did not dive and we ran over at about fifty feet, dropping a stick of six depth charges. The stick straddled the target, but unfortunately only the most distant depth charge exploded. We found out later that this was because the armament technicians had used grease when assembling the ball bearings, which retained the pistol in the hydrostatic fuse. Because of the cold at 8,000 feet the grease had congealed, the balls had not dropped out and the striker had not been released.

The look-outs on the U-boat must have seen us as we emerged from the cloud, for its guncrews were right on the job. They opened up on us with 20mm stuff. We could count about fifty bursts in the air at one time. It wasn't the kind that has to hit to explode. It bursts on time fuses. They were really working those guns. At the same time Pilot Officer Roger Beamish tried to sweep the U-boat's decks with his front machine gun, but the window was coated by frost. Sergeant Ian Jackson dusted the U-boat's decks pretty heavily with his tail guns as we roared over the conning tower.

We could not drop our Zombie while the U-boat remained surfaced, so circled it so that its flak was bursting just off our port wing tip. We reported the attack and tried to contact another aircraft that we knew was somewhere in the area. Eventually it was clear that we could not contact it and we were running short of fuel. As I felt our R/T was being monitored, I went on in plain language, and said I was low on fuel and would have to return to base, hoping to induce the U-boat to dive. We turned for home and about five miles away the tail gunner shouted, 'He's diving!' I swung around and dropped my two remaining depth charges on the periscope which was still visible. There was an explosion with a large black plume as well as the depth charge explosions. We dropped the Zombie as well, for good measure.

On the way back to base we sighted and photographed a second fully surfaced U-boat. It did not dive and almost appeared to be aware that we had no more weapons.

The elated Liberator crew arrived back safely at base in darkness after fourteen hours in the air, one of which had been spent on the attack.

After the destruction of *U-420* by 'Wink' Aldwinckle the *Siegfried* Group were then split into three sections and ordered to take up smaller patrol lines, east of Newfoundland, against convoy SC143.

On 29 October *U-405* and *U-608* of Section One drove off Fairey Swordfish biplanes from the escort carrier *Fencer*, which together with Escort Group B6 and the 8th Support Group and three destroyers was escorting the 32-ship convoy. In mid-morning next day Korvettenkapitän Rolf Hopmann fired two torpedoes from *U-405* but they exploded at the end of their run without having hit anything. The Type VIIC boat had also been built at the Danziger Werft, though a year earlier, in June 1941. The boat left Kiel for Trondheim at the beginning of March 1942 where it joined the Arctic Flotilla and carried out a number of cruises.

Returning south from Bergen in February 1943, on its first North Atlantic patrol, *U-405* sank the British 7,000 ton ship *Wade Hampton*, which had two small boats on board, on 28 February. Ten days later *U-405* sank the Norwegian ship *Bonneville* of 4,665 tons which had *LCT 2341* stowed aboard. After their recent successes it was a delighted crew that put in to St Nazaire on 23 March and stepped ashore for the first time on French soil. Their first cruise from the French port, in May, was cut short when the boat was damaged by an aircraft attack, forcing it to return to base. It was not until 10 October that *U-405* put to sea again, and on the 30th heard the detonation of two torpedoes after twelve minutes. These were end of run explosions of torpedoes that had missed their intended target.

On the same day USS *Card*, with its attendant destroyer escort of *Berry*, *Borie* and *Goff*, failed to sink a U-boat that had been located.

Flight Lieutenant Bob Aldwinckle (centre) with his Liberator crew. (l to r) W.O. C Loader, W.O. J Criggs, F/O R Beamish, Sgt I. Jackson, F/O P Hughes and F/O H Wilson. F/O Brady flew instead of F/O Wilson on the day *U-420* was sunk.

USS *BORIE*. A pre-war photograph.

However, next day *U-584* was sunk by the carrier's aircraft, though *U-91* which had also been present, escaped.

This was the general scene, when at sunset on the 31st Lieutenant-Commander Hutchins, commanding officer of *Borie*, was ordered to the position of the attack to search for the escaping U-boat, *U-91*.

USS *Borie* was a Clemson Class destroyer, launched at the end of 1919, which had been modified for escort work. Arriving on station *Borie* conducted a search and obtained a radar contact, which was closed. The contact, held by radar, was travelling at 15 knots on the surface. *Borie* approached to within 1,700 yards. Starshells were then fired and the U-boat dived. An asdic contact was made, which showed the U-boat to be travelling on a straight course at 4 knots. An immediate depth charge attack was made and a heavy underwater explosion was heard and felt. The attack also damaged the 1,200 ton destroyer, blowing fuses and knocked some brickwork out of one boiler, but repairs were effected within ten minutes and the area again closed.

During the second approach, sound contact was obtained at about 300-400 yards, but before the attack was launched a heavy odour of diesel oil was noticed by personnel in many parts of the ship. The second attack was delivered and procedure to regain contact was instituted.

As *Borie* turned to attack again the U-boat was seen to rise to the surface, silhouetted by the float light dropped by *Borie*. Radar contact was simultaneously obtained. The U-boat appeared to lift out of the water, bow high, then after three appearances on the radar screen, it was observed to submerge, stern first, and radar contact disappeared.

The U-boat was picked up by asdic and a third attack delivered but after this contact was lost and further efforts to regain contact were without success, despite the area being searched for three and a half hours for the target or any evidence of destruction. No target was found, but upon returning to the point of the attacks. *Borie* observed that the surface of the sea was profusely covered with diesel oil, the extent of the slick being estimated at a thousand yards.

In the early hours of the next day, while still conducting a search, now twenty-six miles from the point of action another radar contact was made. The destroyer increased speed to 27 knots, holding radar contact until it was lost at 2,800 yards. *Borie* slowed down and conducted a depth charge attack. As *Borie* drew away from the point

↗ What's it ?
a cruiser

of the attack the U-boat was seen to emerge from the depth charge disturbance. Radar contact was simultaneously obtained, range 400 yards. The 24-inch searchlight was immediately trained on the U-boat. The destroyer changed course to close and increased speed to 25 knots, range was opened to about 1,400 yards before the turn was completed. *Borie* opened fire with all main battery guns and 20mm machine guns as they came to bear during the turn.

The U-boat returned fire from its six guns shortly thereafter and scored hits in the forward engine room, as well as scattered and harmless hits near the bridge area. However, *Borie*'s 20mm battery was extremely effective and in a matter of seconds wiped out every exposed member of its opponent's crew topside. The U-boat crew made continuous efforts to man their guns, but as each man emerged from the conning tower hatch, to the bridge, he was immediately met by a hail of 20mm projectiles.

As *Borie* completed its turn to close and all the port main battery could bear, control was shifted from local to centralized control. Thence depending on the situation, this method and director control were used almost entirely. Either the second or third salvo saw all three shells strike the U-boat's fo'c's'le apparently under the forward deck gun. When the smoke and fire subsided, the deck gun was gone without having fired a shot.

The U-boat captain manoeuvred on extremely evasive courses at about 15 knots, trying to escape on the surface as *Borie* steamed in, firing all guns, and closing to ram.

As *Borie* came up on the U-boat's starboard quarter at 25 knots, range closed rapidly, and *Borie* turned in to ram. Just a few seconds before the crash, the U-boat turned hard left attempting to parallel *Borie*. However, *Borie* struck about 30 feet abaft the bow and rode up over the U-boat's fo'c's'le, pinning it under. The two ships remained in this position for about ten minutes, with angle between centrelines about 25-30 degrees from parallel headings.

During this part of the action the destroyer's main battery guns and 20mm guns kept up a continual fire, battering the conning tower, the guns and leaving the after end of the U-boat a flaming wreck.

The action then became bloody. Several attempts were made to man the U-boat's guns but no one got near them. Those that attempted to leave the conning tower were met by murderous fire. From just 40 feet the 4-inch and 20mm guns fired at point-blank range. The executive officer on the bridge was raking the U-boat with Tommy Gun fire; others were firing with pistols, a rifle and shotgun fire. One man was killed when a sheath knife was thrown from *Borie*'s deck and buried itself in the man's stomach; another was knocked overboard by an empty 4-inch shell case thrown by the gun captain of a gun which could not depress itself enough.

When the U-boat was thoroughly examined it could be seen that the bow had been badly damaged. It was during this period that *Borie* received severe underwater damage along the entire port side, including both engine rooms, as the ships pounded together in the sea, before separating.

The U-boat, which had a polar bear emblem on the conning tower, and was identified as *U-405*, then got underway. *Borie* followed in pursuit, firing main and 20mm battery effectively, one 4-inch shell exploding in the starboard diesel exhaust. The U-boat took advantage of its short turning circle to open range to about 400-500 yards. At this time *Borie* brought its port torpedo battery on target, but as the first torpedo of the salvo was fired the target turned radically. The balance of the spread was not fired and no hit was made.

The U-boat then went into a tight circle to port and because of its larger turning circle *Borie* could not close. By this time also the forward engine room had flooded hampering the ship's movements. However, the U-boat was held under continuous fire, hits being registered regularly. Many of the U-boat crew had been killed.

The destroyer's searchlight was then doused and the U-boat, trying to escape in the darkness, turned to starboard. Radar was used to follow its passage until the position was advantageous to use the light again. The U-boat was then illuminated.

The U-boat now came on the starboard bow under fire of the destroyer's starboard battery. *Borie* closed in to ram again, but just before contact, the U-boat slowed and turned into *Borie*'s starboard quarter. *Borie* immediately turned hard to port, backing full on port engine, throwing its stern toward the U-boat, to bring it in range of projectiles and fired depth charges from the starboard battery. Three charges, set at thirty feet, gave a perfect straddle, grouped around the conning tower, one over and two short. All exploded and *U-405* was lifted bodily and stopped short of *Borie*. Being nearly dead in the water the destroyer was well shaken by the charge explosions. During this entire time all guns that would bear had been firing and registering hits.

The U-boat then turned astern of *Borie*, at reduced speed. *Borie*

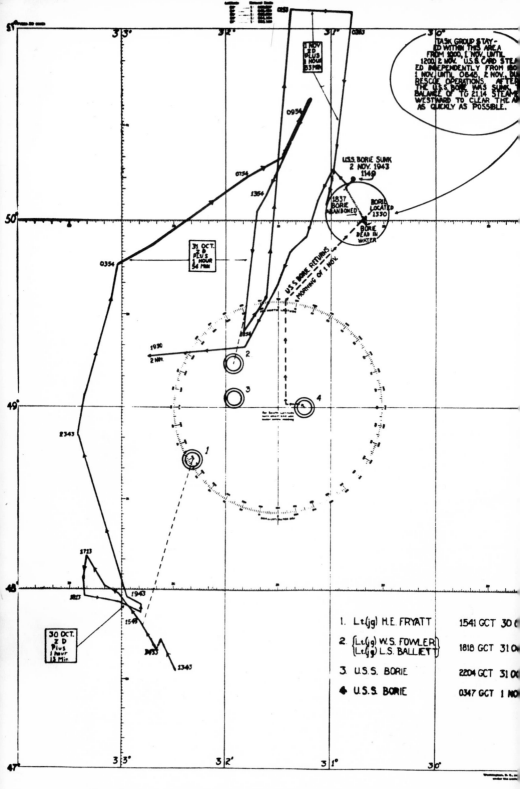

Track Chart, showing anti-U-boat attacks by VP-9 from USS *Card* and by USS *Borie* 30 October – 2 November 1943 (All times GMT)

turned to port to close again and range opened out to about 600-700 yards. The remaining two torpedoes in the port battery were made ready and the tubes turned on to the target. Just prior to firing, with tubes ten degrees from the bearing, the main battery fired a full salvo which knocked an engine room hatch open catching the underside of the tube, jamming it. One torpedo was fired and seen to pass within ten feet of *U-405*'s bow, but did not hit.

However, a main battery salvo again struck the U-boat's starboard diesel exhaust and *U-405* immediately slowed, stopped and surrendered, firing white Very lights. Several were fired with a few red and green, apparently a shower.

About fifteen members of the crew abandoned the boat into yellow rubber rafts. Within two to three minutes *U-405* sank stern first at a steep angle and exploded.

As *Borie* manoeuvred to pick up the first survivors, the crew in the rafts continued to fire Very pistols, apparently signalling to another U-boat, or so the destroyer captain thought. The entire group of survivors were in a group only fifty to sixty yards from *Borie* and were held in the beam of the searchlight. An answering light was observed on a bearing of 220 degrees.

At this time, with the survivors just off the bow, and *Borie* heading 240 degrees, the radar operator heard a torpedo, bearing 220 degrees. The destroyer immediately surged ahead with all available speed, turning to port. The torpedo was followed down the port side by sound gear and a slight phosphorescent wake was apparent.

Unfortunately, these evasive tactics forced *Borie* to run directly over a group of survivors. They were not seen again as *Borie* cleared the area, using a radical zigzag as it made to the north-west.

The entire action, from the initial contact until *U-405* sank, lasted just sixty-four minutes.

The destroyer was badly damaged; three-quarters of the port side, back from the bow, was badly crushed and holed. The forward engine room flooded completely in spite of all efforts to prevent it. Just before 1100 *Borie* reported that her engines would last only about another two hours and that she was in a sinking condition. The task group changed course immediately and churned towards the stricken ship, sighting her at noon. In the late afternoon the crew abandoned ship, while the other destroyers circled round the area picking up survivors. Early the following day, *Borie* was destroyed by shell fire and depth charges from her sister ships to hasten the death of a gallant ship whose end was inevitable. Twenty-seven of the crew had been lost.

There were no survivors from *U-405*; 37-year-old Korvettenkapitän Rolf Hopmann and the other forty-eight crew members all perished.

It had been an epic and bloodthirsty duel.

CHAPTER THIRTEEN

Rock Wellingtons

During the war the Germans had infiltrated many U-boats through the Strait of Gibraltar, with its strong currents, into the Mediterranean. These boats, hugging the coast of neutral Spain and Portugal, after leaving their Biscay bases, came under heavy attack from the sea and air forces on the Rock if they were discovered.

During mid-1943 the German U-boat strength inside the Mediterranean had been steadily declining. No reinforcements had arrived since the end of May. By the autumn only thirteen U-boats were left in the Mediterranean. The Italian surrender, and the loss of their thirty-four remaining boats, meant that Admiral Dönitz had to reinforce the Mediterranean U-boat flotillas. The immediate need was for more U-boats to stop Allied seaborne supplies reaching the invading forces on the European mainland pushing up through Italy.

The Rock had always boasted a strong naval presence but the airfield was not fully developed until 1942. Before the war the Bay had been used for RAF flying boats and discussions about the construction of a military airstrip had been going on between the services and the Foreign Office during the thirties. The only possible place to construct an airfield was at the base of the Rock, at almost sea level and hard against the Spanish border.

At the time the belief was that France would be Britain's ally, and the use of airfields in France would be sufficient to obtain air mastery over the Mediterranean. The strip of land that was required for the airstrip covered the old neutral ground between Spain and Gibraltar; this had been converted to a racecourse and a military training ground. Prior to the war only light civilian aircraft had landed at Gibraltar, with the military flying boats landing in the Bay.

After the fall of France a good deal more thought was given to the construction of a large scale military airfield near the Rock. During the early part of the century thousands of tons of rock were blasted from Sandy Bay to construct the harbour. Now thousands more tons of rock, stone and rubble were being excavated as tunnels were constructed to provide accommodation for living, sleeping and hospital facilities for the garrison as well as communication tunnels. With the surplus rock being excavated a decision was required on where to dump it; the obvious answer was in the Bay of Algeciras, and this formed the base for the airstrip that was to extend half-a-mile into the Bay. This was a major engineering feat and while sappers were busy at their work their opposite numbers on the diplomatic side were busy talking with Franco's Spanish Government whose sympathies at this time were strongly pro-German although officially neutral.

The work on the airfield construction continued apace; the runway continued with stone being rolled into the ground at an astonishing rate, so much so that it was lengthened to 1,150 yards in April 1942. Twin-engined aircraft from the United Kingdom were able to fly out and land there while the runway was still being extended out to sea. Then, as now, there was always a danger of being blown against the face of the Rock when landing in a cross wind.

A major difficulty in operating the airfield was that the labour force of Spanish workers from La Linea had to cross the airfield twice each day on their way to work in Gibraltar. In early 1943 the length of the runway was further extended.

Leigh light Wellingtons of No 179 Squadron were amongst aircraft flying from the airstrip. In fact Vickers Wellington aircraft had used the strip in 1941 as a staging post before flying on to the Middle East. Squadron Leader Humphrey de Vere Leigh gave his name to the light of his invention. It had been developed from an idea he had for illuminating U-boats at night which was first put forward in 1940: simply a searchlight fitted to an aircraft which would be used once the U-boat had been located. Wellingtons were initially used, as they were being phased out as night bombers but many of them still had an extra motor and generator that could supply the current necessary to power the light. The standard installation consisted of a 24-inch naval searchlight mounted in a Frazer Nash FN77 hydraulically operated turret. The turret enabled the Leigh light to be rotated in azimuth, elevated and depressed into or extended from the Wellington's fuselage. It was controlled by an operator in the aircraft's front gun turret.

Thus, by the autumn of 1943 Wellington crews were proficient in using the light. Illumination at night produced an element of

Vickers Wellington of Coastal Command

The airstrip at Gibraltar. On the near side can be seen the water catchment area. The harbour is on the far side. Gibraltar is to the left of the airstrip, the rest is Spain. A wartime photograph.

strategical and tactical surprise which had far reaching effects. U-boats found themselves unable to detect the presence of aircraft until they were illuminated. They had no time to dive before an attack developed.

The Germans selected a moonless period towards the end of October as the best chance of slipping U-boats through the Strait unobserved. From information received it was appreciated on 23 October that a number of U-boats were moving down the Portuguese coast, probably with the intention of passing through the Strait of Gibraltar. Patrols of Leigh light Wellingtons were therefore laid on to cover the area. The aircraft carried the ASV Mark III radar, of whose emissions would not register on the German U-boat receivers.

In the early hours of 24 October Sergeant D.M. Cornish, a Canadian pilot flying Wellington A-Able of 179 Squadron, was carrying out an anti-U-boat patrol off the Portuguese coast when a radar contact was obtained at six miles range from 2,000 feet. The position was a few miles north-west of Oporto. The aircraft immediately altered course and began homing, and at a range of one mile a large phosphorescent wake was seen. This was at first thought to be the lights of a neutral vessel and consequently the Leigh light was not switched on, but as the aircraft passed over, a fully surfaced U-boat was seen travelling at high speed. The aircraft immediately circled and homed again until the wake was sighted at one mile range. At three-quarters of a mile the Leigh light was switched on and the fully surfaced U-boat travelling due south, was illuminated. It was *U-566*.

The Type VIIC Hamburg-built boat from the Blohm and Voss yard had been launched in February 1941. In its two years at sea it had led a varied and interesting life. It left Kiel at the beginning of December 1941 and arrived in Lorient just in time for Christmas. Its second two-month patrol took it to the Canadian seaboard and back to Brest, which became its permanent base. The third ten-week patrol, to the end of June, was to the same destination. The fourth, a four-week patrol, was off Spain and the Azores. Next time out *U-566* had been on patrol for nearly five weeks when it was damaged by aircraft of 232 Squadron west of Gibraltar; it limped home, arriving in Brest on 1 December. After repairs *U-566* sailed for the North Atlantic on 6 February. A month later, when acting as contact keeper for a U-boat pack hunting convoy SC121, it was driven off by Liberators of 120 Squadron on 9 March and arrived back at its

Biscay base sixteen days later. Exactly a month later *U-566* set out on its seventh patrol but was soon damaged by R-Rodger of 172 Squadron and had to return to base. This was its third aircraft attack in its last three patrols. It was nine weeks before it was fit for further service and on 5 July was sent to the American seaboard and laid mines off Norfolk Virginia at the end of the month. It had a mixed complement of mines and torpedoes for on 5 August Kapitänleutnant Hans Hornkohl torpedoed and sank APY *Plymouth*, a 2,256 ton ship. The U-boat arrived back at Brest on 1 September. Some six weeks later *U-566* left Brest, for the last time, on its ninth patrol, destination Toulon to link up with the 29th Flotilla U-boats. The boat slipped from the concrete bunker on 18 October, was escorted half way across the Bay of Biscay, the deep diving trial was successfully carried out and the torpedo boat escort sent back. The captain conned his boat round Cape Finisterre and then proceeded down the Portuguese coast, where it was attacked.

The experienced, now illuminated *U-566* that had survived previous aircraft attacks, immediately opened fire hitting the aircraft's tailplane, and the Wellington replied with the front guns. The attack was made from the U-boat's starboard quarter and six depth charges, spaced 60 feet, straddled it roughly midway between the stern and conning tower, three depth charges falling on each side. As the explosion plumes subsided, an orange light shot vertically into the air to a height of about 200 feet. It looked rather like a rocket, but it left no trace on its upward flight and appeared to go out on the way. As soon as the depth charges exploded the U-boat ceased fire and lay stationary on the surface. The Wellington shadowed by radar for over two hours and then set course to the nearest land to check position as its prudent limit of endurance had almost been reached. Returning twenty-two minutes later no radar contact was obtained although a flame float which had been dropped, was seen. What actually happened was that the attack by the Wellington so damaged *U-566* that it was unable to dive and about three hours after the attack, that is after the Wellington had returned to base, the U-boat crew took to their dinghies. Forty-nine survivors were picked up by the Spanish trawler *Fina* and landed at Vigo the same evening.

Of the attack Sergeant Cornish, from Scout Lake Saskatchewan, said:

It was like a disappearing act; one minute it was there; the next it wasn't. We searched high and low for it without seeing a trace. The survivors didn't show up in the swell that was running and in the darkness. But we knew we'd damaged it pretty badly and we didn't think they could have repaired it and crash-dived to safety. The burst of flame was pretty conclusive evidence. It rose somewhat like a rocket, but without the tail of fire – almost like an outsize shooting star in reverse.

Once it became known that the survivors had been picked up and landed Sergeant D. M. Cornish was awarded an immediate Distinguished Flying Medal.

The next sighting was of *U-642*, again a Type VIIC Blohm and Voss Hamburg-built boat, launched fourteen months earlier. It had left Brest on 17 October under the command of Kapitänleutnant Herbert Brünning. This U-boat remained undetected for a week until sighted by a Mosquito of 814 Squadron on a transit flight from the United Kingdom to Gibraltar, some thirty-five miles north-west of Cape St Vincent, at about noon on 24 October.

Almost certainly *U-642* passed through the Strait during the night of the 27/28th and remained undetected until the early hours of 1 November when seen by a Wellington just east of the Greenwich Meridian. *U-642* was the first of the reinforcements to join the 29th U-boat Flotilla at Toulon.

We will continue with the story after the next chapter, which deals with events inside the Mediterranean to show why reinforcements were needed.

CHAPTER FOURTEEN

Ultimatum

During the bright summer evening of Friday 20 August 1943 HM s/m *Ultimatum* slipped from HMS *Wolfe* and left Holy Loch in company with HM s/m *Truant* and Free French submarines *Curie* and *Minerve*. The submarine convoy was escorted from the Clyde by the armed trawler *Kingston Amber*.

Ultimatum, commanded by Lieutenant W. Hedley Kett DSC RNR, was returning to service in the Mediterranean. The submarine was one of the second group of 'U' Class submarines; when designed pre-war they had been intended to replace the old 'H' Class for anti-submarine training. The boats were of single hull construction. Once hostilities had commenced it was quickly realised that these small submarines would be particularly useful for service in the shallow waters of the North Sea and the Mediterranean so they were put into war production.

As *P.34* the submarine was built by Vickers-Armstrong at their Barrow Yard and launched, unnamed, on 11 February 1941. At this time the yard was turning out a submarine a month.

After a successful work-up, under the command of Lieutenant P. R. H. Harrison RNR, *P.34* was sent to strengthen the Mediterranean submarine force during October 1941. At the time Malta was hard-pressed and the Axis were shipping supplies from Italy to their desert army Afrika Korps in Libya.

P.34 carried out a number of patrols from Gibraltar, Malta, Alexandria and Haifa. During these patrols the fully laden 3,320 ton ship *Dalmatia L.* was torpedoed in the Messina Strait in January 1942. In March the conning tower of an enemy submarine was sighted, at four miles range, close inshore. The Italian submarine *Millo* remained on the surface long enough for Lieutenant Harrison to get within range and hit it with two torpedoes. *P.34* then surfaced and rescued fourteen survivors before being forced under by machine-gun fire from the shore. In a later patrol *P.34* was lucky to escape with just her torpedo tubes damaged when she struck a mine in the Gulf of Taranto.

Operation *Pedestal*, to bring much needed supplies and fuel to Malta, was the big Mediterranean naval operation of August 1942 and *P.34* was one of eight submarines taking part, being stationed off Pantelleria to cover against an attack by surface ships.

On its next patrol, while attacking a convoy, *P.34* suffered a premature explosion while firing a torpedo. The counter-attack was heavy enough to cause the submarine to break off the patrol and return to base. At the end of September *P.34* carried out a patrol off the west coast of Sardinia on passage from Malta to Gibraltar on her way home to refit.

The refit was carried out at Devonport dockyard and in the meantime *P.34* became *Ultimatum* as Winston Churchill said he thought it better that submarines had names instead of numbers.

Following the refit Lieutenant W. H. Kett DSC was appointed to command *Ultimatum* with Sub-Lieutenant Peter Harvey as his first lieutenant.

Hedley Kett began his sea-going career with the Merchant Navy in 1929, joining the RNR in 1938. He was second officer in the RFA tanker *Arndale* when war broke out. He volunteered for submarine service and was appointed navigator of HM s/m *Oberon*. Later with *H.32* he had the extreme good fortune to serve for a short spell with David Wanklyn, the most successful British submarine commander of all time who subsequently received the Victoria Cross. Progressively Hedley Kett was appointed as first lieutenant to the fleet submarine *Clyde*, then the largest submarine in the Royal Navy. In June 1943 Hedley Kett was awarded the Distinguished Service Cross for 'bravery, skill and outstanding devotion to duty while serving in *Clyde* in five hazardous patrols to Malta carrying vital supplies'. The 'vital supplies' were stores and fuel from Gibraltar.

It was therefore a submariner, experienced in Mediterranean conditions, that was taking the newly refitted *Ultimatum* back to Gibraltar after six gruelling weeks of exercises to train her crew of four officers and twenty-eight ratings.

The small convoy, with the submarines surfaced, proceeded through the Irish Sea during the weekend, on to the South West Approaches where *Ultimatum* flashed goodbye to HMS *Kingston Amber*, off Bishop's Rock, in the early hours of Monday.

A patrol was carried out in the Bay of Biscay, which consisted of investigating and dodging Spanish fishing vessels. Allied submarines on passage were routed to steer a large detour out into the Atlantic, within a twenty-mile band, to prevent attacks by

Lieutenant W. Hedley Kett, Captain HMs/m *Ultimatum*

friendly aircraft. Despite this precaution *Ultimatum* was illuminated by an aircraft burning a blue searchlight six nights later. Taking no chances *Ultimatum* crashed to ninety feet. Half-an-hour later *Ultimatum* surfaced and continued passage having previously set radar watch. Ninety minutes later an aircraft circled the submarine at three miles before departing. The ASV identified it as a British aircraft. This was confirmed when a signal from a No 179 Squadron Leigh light Wellington was intercepted giving the position, course and 14 knot speed of the submarine and saying, 'most probably *Ultimatum*'.

The following Wednesday, Cape St Vincent light was identified at fourteen miles when *Ultimatum* charged her batteries in the early hours. Next afternoon saw *Ultimatum* in the narrow configuration of the Straits, and as the huge mass of the Rock of Gibraltar was approached Telegraphist Wade established contact with Europa Point signal station. *Ultimatum* was escorted into the Bay, entered harbour and secured alongside.

Ultimatum remained in Gibraltar for nine days before leaving on 18 September for a working-up patrol in the Gulf of Lions. The submarine headed for the Marseilles-Toulon area to share in the job with other submarines of preventing any shipping passing along the coast to supply the German armies in Italy.

On the bridge, the officer of the watch, twenty-year-old Sub-Lieutenant David Walters, with two look-outs, ceaselessly scanned the sky through binoculars for the first sign of aircraft, at which the submarine would dive without a moment's hesitation. Inside the 545 ton submarine, in the tiny wardroom, the size of a railway compartment, where the officers slept and ate, the captain studied the reports of enemy shipping in the Gulf of Lions and the charts of the area. In the forepart of the vessel, the torpedo officer, Lieutenant Tom Alison RNVR, was checking up on the final adjustments to the four torpedoes all ready to fire, and the four spare torpedoes lying in the racks ready to be loaded into the tubes when the first ones had been fired. The first lieutenent was going round the submarine checking up on everything: that the machinery was in good working order; that there was the right amount of water in the tanks; that all the food and stores were properly stowed and that everyone was happy.

Ultimatum arrived at her billet on the 22nd. During the day the submarine was submerged at periscope depth just below the surface so that when the periscope was raised to its full extent the top of it was about two feet above the surface. *Ultimatum* patrolled submerged going as slowly as possible at about one knot in order to conserve the electrical power in her batteries and so that the periscope, when it was sticking up, did not make any wash or feather.

Below, the OOW in the control room kept an eye on the machinery and the depth of the submarine, which was kept within a few inches of 27 feet. Every two minutes he gave the order, 'Up periscope,' whereupon the engineer rating pushed a lever which operated the machinery which raised the periscope. The officer had a quick look round to make sure that there was no aircraft about, and then had a more careful look to spot the tips of any masts on the horizon; but he never left the periscope up for more than a minute in case an observant watcher on the coast, only about two or three miles away, sighted it.

As it grew dark the submarine headed out to sea and when it was about ten miles off the coast, surfaced. This was always an anxious time in case there was an enemy destroyer waiting, but as soon as the captain had made sure that there was no enemy about, the diesels were started up, and the submarine cruised slowly up and down charging the electric batteries, with the OOW and lookouts on the bridge peering into the darkness through binoculars making sure they saw any potential enemies before they saw the now vulnerable submarine.

An armed trawler passed out of range on the 27th, and a drifter towing a target was also seen that day. Bad weather was encountered during most of the patrol, but on the 30th the vigilance of the OOW was rewarded when, in the afternoon, he spotted some dots on the horizon. He called the captain to the periscope and the crew were summoned to action stations. The petty officer in the fore-end had his hand on the firing lever of the torpedoes. David Walters was at the chart table keeping a record of all the information and plotting all the movements on the chart. Tom Alison was at the instrument which worked out courses and speeds from information given by the captain who was watching the target through the periscope. Peter Harvey was responsible for keeping the submarine at the right depth.

As the target approached it could be seen to be four large self-propelled supply barges, escorted by seven armed patrol vessels. The captain manoeuvred the submarine into the best position from which to fire torpedoes all the time keeping an eye on the escort vessels which so far had not spotted the periscope. He wanted to get as close as possible and then fire more than one torpedo in the hope that they would sink several barges.

All went well and then the moment came. The captain gave the order: 'Fire one', and the first torpedo of the commission was fired. The submarine gave a lurch as the torpedo left its tube and sped on its way to the target. A few seconds later the order was given: 'Fire two', and *Ultimatum* lurched again as the second torpedo started on its run. Then came a shattering explosion. The lights went out and broken glass tinkled everywhere.

One torpedo had found its mark and the resultant explosion severely shaking the submarine causing it to lose trim and plunge downwards. The nose dropped and *Ultimatum* dived steeply. The luminous dials of the depth gauges showed that she was descending rapidly. Orders were rapped out. Pumps were started. The depth gauge needle passed the 100 feet mark going faster. Then came a jolt. The submarine had hit bottom. Fortunately it was not too severe, the sea bed being soft mud. The motors were stopped and the submarine just stayed there as the lights were replaced and work on repairs started.

Due to the listening gear being out of action the crew waited anxiously for several hours wondering what was happening above. The escort chasseurs were hunting *Ultimatum* but were unable to locate her. Only one depth charge was dropped, and that some seven hours after the attack.

As it was all quiet at midnight the captain decided to make a move; so all the crew who had been lying on their bunks meantime closed up at their action stations, and set about bringing the submarine up. It was far from easy. She was well and truly stuck in the mud. All the water was ejected from the main ballast tanks, which are full of air on the surface, and the propellers went full speed astern. Then with a loud squelching sound *Ultimatum* broke free and rose rapidly. The captain did not want to break surface too close to the shore, so the main ballast tanks were flooded again with water and the submarine started sinking again. There followed rather a topsy-turvy existence as the submarine regained its proper trim and headed out to sea still submerged. When well clear of land she surfaced to find that there was no enemy about. For the crew it was nice to breathe fresh air again after being so long submerged.

No further targets had been sighted when *Ultimatum* was ordered by wireless to leave patrol and proceed to Algiers, where the submarine depot ship, HMS *Maidstone*, was berthed.

On arrival it was learned that the target attacked was a string of ammunition barges, and it was these blowing up that caused the explosion that grounded *Ultimatum*. After a thorough inspection the submarine was dry docked to make good propeller and asdic dome defects. Oil leaks on the port shaft were attended to at the same time and after ten days both submarine and crew were ready for sea again.

Ultimatum left the 5th Submarine Flotilla base at Algiers in the early evening of 19 October to patrol off the south coast of France, arriving in the area two days later. On the morning of the 22nd *Ultimatum* dived when a low flying aircraft was spotted; later, when at periscope depth, seven or eight Ju87's were seen dive bombing. These Stukas continued to inflict casualties on the British Mediterranean Fleet throughout 1943. Two mornings later *Ultimatum* was again taken down to 70 feet when a Blohm and Voss flying boat was sighted on patrol in Toulon Bay. In the dark hours two days later the captain was called when a brightly illuminated ship was seen approaching from Cape Sicie. *Ultimatum* closed but the ship was identified as a safe conduct German repatriation vessel and so the crew were stood down and *Ultimatum* dived to continue patrol. That same afternoon Hedley Kett took a close look at Toulon Harbour.

The Germans had taken over the French naval base in mid-1940 when an armistice was signed between the two countries. The terms were that Germany was to occupy two-thirds of France, including the entire Channel and Atlantic coastlines, and the French Fleet was to be disarmed and demobilized under German and Italian supervision. So now, in 1943, Toulon housed part of the demilitarised French Fleet with the German 29th Submarine Flotilla based there also. There were usually five or six U-boats there at any one time, in a dock large enough to house a battleship. There was, unlike the Atlantic bases, no shelter for the U-boats but there was one for the crews.

Against the background of green hills and the red and green topped roofs of whitewashed houses the *Ultimatum*'s captain identified a battleship and three cruisers or large destroyers. A large merchant ship was observed alongside the coal depot.

At dusk that same day hands were called to action stations when what was thought to be the conning tower of a U-boat was seen leaving Toulon at a range of seven miles. A few minutes later nothing

could be seen of the target against the land background and due to
the fading daylight, but HE picked up the correct bearing. After 18
minutes the captain decided the chances of success firing by Asdics
at a range of five miles did not justify firing torpedoes and so he broke
off the attack.

Already in the war there had been many encounters between
submarines and U-boats and it was a great ambition of any captain
to sink one of his own kind. The vast majority of such encounters
had occurred by day when the enemy was unwise enough to be on
the surface in areas patrolled by submarines at periscope depth. The
U-boat was a very small torpedo target, and thus seldom sighted
until very close on account of its low bridge. This view made it
difficult for the attacker to estimate the course which the enemy was
steering. Accurate estimation of course and speed were essential to
determine the direction in which to aim the torpedoes in order to hit.
The actual range of the enemy at the moment of firing did not
matter, provided the course and speed were assessed correctly as
long as the U-boat was within the effective range of the torpedoes,
which was about five miles. The ideal range, though, which a
submarine captain always tried to achieve by manoeuvring his craft,
was about half a mile.

Quite coincidentally just four days earlier, on 22 October, an
article in the *Deutsche Allgemeine Zeitung* dealt with Mediterranean U-
boats; part of it read:

It is well known that the Mediterranean, where for two years past
U-boats have carried on a successful and active campaign against
a very strong enemy, is a particularly difficult operational area for
our brave U-boat commanders and their well-tried crews. The
relatively limited sea area and the nearness of enemy bases,
particularly air bases, forces the boats into almost continuous
contact with the enemy. The highest degree of watchfulness is
necessary in order not to offer any target to the fairly close-meshed
aerial reconnaissance of the enemy, which tries with all technical
means to find out the position of the U-boats, day and night.

Every U-boat commanding officer tries to remain as long as
possible in his operational area without being discovered, and in
some cases this is half the reason for success. This makes it
necessary for the U-boats operating in the Mediterranean to
proceed mostly submerged during their long patrols. What this
means physically and spiritually for the U-boat man has often

been described and may be assumed to be well known. The heat in the boat and the lack of fresh air tell on the men, who do not see the sun for weeks, particularly as the increased necessity of being ready at any moment to dive rarely allows any of the men apart from the bridge watch to go aloft for a breather.

Unlike the U-boats in the Atlantic, those in the Mediterranean often stay close inshore in order to meet the enemy. Even today when the situation in the Mediterranean has altered so much in his favour, the enemy prefers this coastal route for particularly valuable transports. For the same reason the battle has become increasingly difficult for our U-boats. Because of this increased difficulty the sinkings are all the more creditable, particularly those scored recently.

When we compare the difficulties that our U-boats have had to overcome since the beginning of the war with those that they meet today, it can be said that every ton sunk equals perhaps four times as much as formerly.

Shortly after noon the next day, 27 October, when off Cape Sicie *Ultimatum* sighted a convoy of two westbound merchant vessels, escorted by two trawlers. Four torpedoes were fired at the rear ship, of 3,000 tons, range 7,000 yards spread two lengths, and individually aimed. One torpedo explosion was heard at the target's range, followed by three more, two minutes later, the latter evidently being torpedoes going off against the land. *Ultimatum* wisely took avoiding action on firing, but since no depth charge attack took place, came to periscope depth twenty minutes after firing. The leading ship and the two trawlers only were in sight, the other was sunk. It was later found that No 4 tube top stop was defective and the torpedo was withdrawn in order to examine the top stop. The nut holding down the top stop guard cover proved immovable and attempts to remedy the defect had to be abandoned. Effectively the submarine now had only three tubes with which to see out the patrol.

While contemplating this mishap a signal was received saying a U-boat had been reported 120 miles to the east, steering west. As the Germans were using Toulon as a base it was reasonable to assume this was its destination.

The boat was *U-431*, a Type VIIC U-boat, built at the Schichau works in Danzig and launched early in February 1941. It commenced its first war patrol, in the North Atlantic, from Trondheim in July 1941 and on completion joined the flotilla at St

Nazaire a month later. The next patrol lasted from mid-September until mid-October and *U-431* finally departed from the French Biscay base on 16 November and entered the Mediterranean during the night of 24/25 November 1941, and had been operating in that theatre of operations for nearly two years.

Under the command of Kapitänleutnant Dommes, *U-431* sank the 4,000 ton British ship *Eocene* on 20 May 1942 and two other 2,000 ton ships, *Havre* and *Martin*, on 10 June. Five months later the Dutch warship *Isaac Sweers* was torpedoed. Wilhelm Dommes, an older man than most U-boat commanders, was a Knight's Cross holder and an East Prussian farmowner, he left the boat in December. Oberleutnant Dietrich Schöneboom took his place and quickly showed his aggressive intentions when he gunned, and sank, the small boat *Alexandria* running between Cyprus and Palestine on 23 January. Two months later, on 26 March 1943, the 6,415 ton ship *City of Perth* was torpedoed and sunk.

As Oberleutnant Schöneboom and his crew were running westwards toward Toulon on the 29th, no doubt looking forward to some time ashore with the delights of the French Riviera, we will let Hedley Kett, captain of *Ultimatum*, take us through the next few hours:

> It seemed certain that the U-boat was returning to Toulon and would arrive to enter harbour early next morning.
>
> The likely course and speed was therefore plotted on the chart and as the expected time of arrival was soon after daylight I decided to be off the entrance to Toulon and on its track by daybreak next day.
>
> When darkness descended that evening we surfaced as usual and retired ten miles off the coast to charge our batteries. This was completed about 0200 and course was set to close the entrance to Toulon. At 0400 we dived to 100 feet so as to make our approach unobserved. There was a coastal radar sweep off Toulon and a regular A/S patrol. About 0700 when it was estimated that there was sufficient daylight to get a fix, we came to periscope depth.
>
> The first lieutenant who was in charge of diving slowly brought the submarine to 36 feet and I gave the order 'Up periscope'. Before the outside ERA could raise it sufficiently for me to look through the Asdic operator, John Oliver, reported loud HE on the starboard bow at 093 degrees adding 'It sounds

like a diesel, could be a U-boat.'

We were already at 'diving stations' so I gave the order 'Bring all torpedoes to the ready' and raised the periscope with the help of the signalman, my right hand man, sweeping the periscope on the bearing.

I could immediately see the conning tower of a U-boat. I could see officers on the bridge, crew lined up on the fore casing and a large red Kriegsmarine ensign flying abaft the bridge.

It was difficult to gauge the exact course in the moderate swell but by comparison with plotted expected course and my periscope estimation of the angle of bow, the navigator, Lieutenant Walter, who was running the plot concluded it was 320 degrees, We counted the revolutions by asdics and estimated 12 knots. The time was now 0705. In order to close the range I again went deep and ran in at 5 knots on a 120 degree track.

0713: Ordering a depth setting of 8 feet to be set on my three effective torpedoes and a running speed of 40 knots, we came to periscope depth. The signalman swung me on to the bearing. A quick look suggested the U-boat had altered course, so I corrected it to 330 degrees and confirmed its speed as 12 knots. I had decided to aim my three torpedoes, one-sixth ahead, one on target and one-sixth astern so as to achieve the best possible spread.

0714: Lieutenant Alison, the torpedo officer, reported 'all torpedoes ready'

0715: Stand by to fire individually

0716: 16 seconds. DA on. Fire one aimed one-sixth ahead

0716: 23 seconds. Fire two at conning tower

0716: 30 seconds. Fire three one-sixth astern

'Down periscope.' Almost immediately came the report 'All torpedoes gone', and we settled down to wait. The navigator with his stop watch. I had a quick look with the periscope and had just lowered it when there was an unmistakable explosion. A cheer rang through the boat. I gave the order 'Up periscope'. All I could see was a tall column of black smoke billowing up into the sky. The Asdic operator reported all HE stopped abruptly followed by breaking up noises. I put the periscope up further and as the smoke climbed into the sky I could just make out the conning tower before it disappeared beneath the sea.

Fifteen minutes later an armed anti-submarine patrol vessel was observed leaving Toulon, later followed by three E-boats, painted white. They came very close but failed to detect us. They were soon joined by a Dornier flying boat with an aerial-like ring underneath, which searched the area all day but also failed to detect us. We eventually dived to 130 feet and retired from the scene, all torpedoes expended.

It was not until just before midday that the first depth charges were dropped and these some distance away. The last pattern, of four, were dropped two and a quarter hours later. Well out to sea *Ultimatum* surfaced in darkness to charge the batteries before setting course for base as ordered.

At 1216 the next day *Ultimatum*'s diary records 'Underwater explosion' and at 1318 'Distant underwater explosion'. This just shows the sensitivity of the listening gear and the long ranges that the sound of depth charges could be heard for these were the attacks on *U-732* by HMS *Imperialist*, recorded later in this book.

Before reaching port a small U-boat had been added to the Jolly Roger, the skull and crossbones flag on which all successes were recorded, and was flown by every submarine while entering harbour after a successful patrol and on other special occasions.

The success also earned the captain the sobriquet 'Deadly Hedley'. On reaching port the spirit of the crew was rather dampened by the news that no confirmation of the sinking had come through from French Intelligence sources. This was a bitter disappointment as it could only be recorded as a 'probable'. At the same time they were unable to confirm that it had been missed and not sunk, which sometimes happened, and so the crew had to just hope for the best.

Further bad news for the crew was that they would be spending no time at all in Algiers as *Maidstone* was sailing for the Far East and next day they would proceed to join the 1st Flotilla at Beirut, via Malta.

In all *Ultimatum* completed ten patrols in the Mediterranean from Gibraltar, Algiers, Beirut, Malta and Maddalena. Only one patrol was blank.

During one patrol *Ultimatum* was counter-attacked for three hours and depth-charged, causing a great deal of damage to instruments and electrical gear. At one period she was forced down to 400 feet, an outboard vent having been forced open. The descent was only checked by using full speed going up. However, *Ultimatum* remained perfectly watertight and showed no sign of straining.

U-boat crew ready to enter harbour.

It was from Maddalena, the former Italian base in northern Sardinia, that *Ultimatum* carried out her tenth and final patrol on 17 July 1944. It was back to the happy hunting grounds off Toulon. The situation was getting desperate for the Germans. The Allied landings had been made in Normandy and it was obviously only a question of time before the South of France would fall into Allied hands. One of the functions of the last patrol was to patrol minefields in the area. The success of this venture can be gauged from the signal made to the Admiralty, which said: 'The information gained from the Mine Detection Unit sweeps carried out on this patrol was most valuable.'

So after sinking sixteen vessels and damaging another, taking prisoners and carrying out a land bombardment *Ultimatum* left the Mediterranean and arrived at Rothesay in the Clyde during August and secured alongside HMS *Cyclops*, the depot ship for the 7th Flotilla.

Thus ended a happy commission; there had been hardly any changes in the crew during the twelve months *Ultimatum* had been away.

The record of *Ultimatum* was probably unique; she had never missed a target. Every target that was attacked was sunk or damaged, six victims by torpedo, ten by gunfire and another damaged by gunfire – a total of 6,480 tons of enemy shipping sunk.

After *Ultimatum* had her wounds patched up she spent some time at Fishguard co-operating with the Fleet Air Arm. Shortly before the end of the war, while on route to carry out a patrol around the north of Scotland, the battery tanks started to disintegrate and she was actually alongside the wall in Dundee on VE Day.

Finally, two months later, the news all the crew were waiting for was confirmed on 6 July 1945. An examination of German records disclosed that *U-431* had been sunk by torpedo at the entrance to Toulon harbour on 30 October 1943 and at long last HMS *Ultimatum* was officially credited with the sinking.

Lieutenant Hedley Kett who had been in command throughout was awarded a Bar to his Distinguished Service Cross, the first lieutenant and six ratings were Mentioned in Despatches.

It is interesting to speculate that had the sinking been confirmed at the time whether the commander might have been awarded the Distinguished Service Order. Others who had achieved much less had received this higher award.

Crew of the succesful HMs/m *Ultimatum* with their Jolly Roger

CHAPTER FIFTEEN

The Battle of the Strait

Two chapters ago, five U-boats were proceeding south to reinforce the 29th U-boat Flotilla at Toulon; *U-566* had been sunk and *U-642* had safely negotiated the Strait of Gibraltar. This left *U-450*, *U-732* and *U-340* to be accounted for.

Air patrols were maintained concurrently night and day in the western approaches to the Strait as far out as the longitude of Cape St Vincent.

Five groups of surface craft were instituted:

Group A – *Witherington, Velox, Wishart* and *Anthony*.
Group B – *Thalassa, Spirea, Alisma* and *Commandant Detroyat*.
Group C – *Imperialist, Loch Oskaig, Scottish, Lady Hogarth* and
Man O'War.
Group D – *ML's 175, 170* and *172*.
Group E – *Boadicea, Bulldog* and *Beagle*.

Other ships were also to join in the hunt, including *Active* and *Fleetwood*. A rating on each ship remembers conditions at this time. A. R. 'Taffy' Davies was one of five ERA's aboard *Active*:

We were working out of Gibraltar and life was pretty grim as you can imagine. Too many service personnel, no women, dreadful Spanish bars, plenty of Jungle Juice and Merrie Merries which resulted in some hectic nights ashore.

We were working three straight watches. The morning watchkeeper always turned to until noon, doing odd jobs. During action stations, if on watch one completed that watch then went to the After Damage Control station. If events still persisted at the change of watch one changed to Forward Damage Control station and so on until it was time to turn to on watch again.

Leonard Silvester was an asdic operator in *Fleetwood*:

The crew were in two watches, four hours on and four off, changed over daily by the dog watches which were only two hour stints.

After five days at sea fresh supplies ran out. When the bread was found to be green in the middle, hard biscuits were issued, these were quite palatable. The cook baked each afternoon but in the small ships galley only a few loaves could be produced. There was no flour sieve so the weevils and maggots were baked into the bread so it resembled seed cake, but it smelled delicious.

Sleep was the most important thing in life. No hammocks were allowed to be slung at sea, so one kipped wherever possible, on the deck, table, lockers, wherever there was room to lay your head. There was no such thing as undressing and a lifebelt was always round the body.

The North Atlantic in winter was atrocious, we were always wet through. There was water sloshing about the messdecks caused by condensation from the steel sides of the ship. There was no heating so gear was always damp.

Being a small ship *Fleetwood* was on canteen messing which meant two meals a day, dinner and supper. For breakfast, just a cup of tea and a fag. If all the crockery had been smashed the tea was drunk out of a soup ladle from the tea urn hung on the hammock bar.

After the 0400-0800 Morning Watch there was one hour's break for washing and breakfast and then one had to work part of ship until dinner then turn to again for the Afternoon Watch 1230-1600-

Recreation, during the dog-watches, consisted of cards, uckers, darts, dominoes and reading. Dhobying had to be done and the rest of the time was spent trying to catch up on lost sleep.

While operating out of Gibraltar we had a change of first lieutenant and the new No 1 was intent on bringing in some peacetime routine; evening quarters and rig of the day.

In harbour and being duty watch we were mustered on the upper deck for evening quarters at 1600 dressed in No 2 rig, blue suit no collar. The gunner's mate was PO of the watch and we were to have fire drill practice. Out came the hoses and foam with plenty of shouting and bawling and not too much effort from the fire party. We were still busy filling the harbour with foam when the captain came back on board. He saluted the quarterdeck then stood looking at our performance before strolling off to his sea cabin with a look of disgust on his face.

Ten minutes later the Bosun's Mate came along, saluted the first lieutenant and asked him to report to the Captain's cabin. He returned five minutes later and gave orders for everyone to fall out and clear up the mess. That was the last episode of our pusser No 1's attempt to follow peacetime routine.

The crew of *U-450* bade *Auf Wiedersehen* to their colleagues at the pleasant coastal town of La Baule before setting off to join their boat at St Nazaire.

At La Baule the quarters were remarkably good, with two or four to a room depending on rank. The town was popular with U-boat men as they were the only Kriegsmarine personnel there. A leisurely thirty-minute drive took them to their boat, well protected in the bunkers beneath hundreds of tons of concrete.

Their boat had been built at the Schichau yard at Danzig, once more famous for building locomotives and destroyers. A Type VIIC boat it had been launched in July 1942. Oberleutnant Kurt Böhme commanded *U-450*. When the basin trials were carried out, *U-450* was on its way with a torpedo boat escort, on 20 October. The escort returned to harbour after deep diving trials had been carried out and the U-boat kept out of sight until the evening of 23 October. The Bay of Biscay had been successfully negotiated, Cape Ortegal rounded, but before Cape Finisterre was reached a Wellington detected *U-450* on the surface. B-Baker of 179 Squadron dropped six Torpex filled depth charges. The Germans did not fire but promptly dived as the Wellington ran in again to rake the U-boat with gunfire.

The U-boat, undamaged, proceeded down the coast of Portugal but shortly after rounding Cape St Vincent, six days later, again ran into trouble once more its adversary was a Wellington from 179 Squadron. As well as the usual RAF aircrew there was a 'guest artist' aboard, an Army officer. This may sound unusual but it was all for the good of inter-service co-operation. It will be remembered that in the last chapter HMS *Ultimatum* had been illuminated by a 179 Squadron Wellington. Later Hedley Kett, captain of the submarine, was afforded the opportunity to fly on a long patrol over the Bay of Biscay with the Rock-based squadron and says he found their navigation spot on.

Besides the army officer the usual crew of Canadian Squadron Leader D. B. Hodgkinson, Sergeant Wilson, Flying Officer Price, Flight Lieutenant Birnie, Sergeants Mitchell and Chew were flying in P-Peter when *U-450* found itself illuminated on the surface. Less

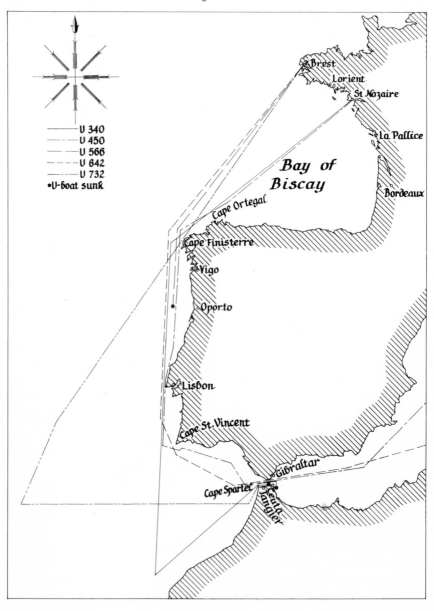

Approximate routes of five U-boats attempting to join the Mediterranean flotilla at the end of October 1943.

cautious than on the previous occasion the U-boat replied to the aircraft's fire scoring several hits which doused the Leigh light. This did not deter the pilot from pressing home the attack. Six 250 lb Torpex depth charges were dropped straddling the U-boat, four to starboard and two to port, sufficiently close to the conning tower to shake up the crew before they gathered themselves up and continued their passage south.

As contact with *U-450* was lost the Canadian pilot nursed his damaged Wellington back to Gibraltar. The aircraft was only slightly damaged and none of the crew was injured. The passenger, however, was very impressed and subsequently recorded his recollection of the patrol:

There is no moon, but the stars are bright and if you look down you can see occasional white patches on the water. In the distance a few lighthouses glow at regular intervals. Except for the roar of the motors, which you don't notice, and infrequent remarks on the intercom, which you don't understand, everything is still and silent.

The pilot is lying in the nose of the machine and the second pilot is at the controls. I am standing beside him, with one foot on the step leading from the wireless room and the other on the bracket sticking out from the pilot's platform. The luminous dials on the instrument board give off a faint light. We have been out for four hours and a half and I am wondering when they will unpack the coffee.

The little Scotsman speaks over the intercom, but I don't get it. The first pilot starts to crawl back and I squeeze myself up against the door behind me in order to let him slide under the controls while the second pilot is worming himself out. The second pilot goes into the nose and lies flat on his belly. The first pilot checks over the instrument board with the aid of a tiny beam from his flash-lamp. I make a mental note to bring a torch on my next trip.

It's been arranged that if we go into action I will man the front gun, but I hesitate to go in now because I don't want to appear too dramatic. Perhaps it's just a routine change-over – but the second pilot is pulling at my leg so I crawl forward and take up my position behind the gun. I am crouching with one foot on either side of him, both hands are in the grips and my thumbs are on the control. I can't see a thing ahead, but a lighthouse is flashing way off to the right. We are gathering speed and I wonder what we are after. How will I know whether or not to shoot? I don't want to speak over the intercom as they may need it for more important things, so I lean down, pull the earphone away from the second pilot's left ear and shout as loud as I can: 'Hit my leg when you want me to shoot.' I try this twice, but he keeps looking straight ahead, so I give up and get back to the gun.

We seem to be gaining more speed, and I peer out trying to see beyond the black wall. What are we going to meet? A sail boat? A plane? Whatever it is I am sure it is going to be friendly, but how am I going to know? I wonder if it is worth while trying to arrange another signal with the second pilot. Next time I will fix this up before we take off.

What the hell? We are in a thick white fog and all I see is the rivets holding the glass stuff together. I suppose they have turned on the light. Damn it. I can't see a bloody thing. Yes, I can. I can see a low, grey, wide house with a veranda running almost from end to end, and a very wide front door with a little platform and a railing on top.

Someone is yelling in the intercom. I press my thumbs and a line of red golf balls sails down towards the front door. What a funny thing to be shooting at. Someone will get hell for this; probably me. We keep on the dive and the first few golf balls are now the size of cigarette-ends. They take a long time to get there. Christ, it's a submarine! Probably British. I should have got this signal business worked out before.

We are going faster than ever now, and I can see quite a few cigarette-ends to the right of the tower. Now there are some to the left. They are all mixed up with mine. They seem to get bigger, and dull red tennis balls start to float past us. Jesus, they're shooting at us. It's a U-boat. Thank God!

I press my thumbs as hard as I can and try to follow the course of my golf balls. Those tennis balls are going to come right into the nose. No. They go over. We are in a sort of funnel of slow-moving red tennis balls. I can't follow them. We're going to hit the conning tower. I hope we knock the damn thing off. No. We're over it. The light has gone out. I look down to the left and can only see stars. On the right there is a flashing in the sky. Another plane. No. It's a lighthouse. How did it get up there?

The pilot is hollering in the intercom: 'We got the bastards! We got the bastards!'

There seems to be a lot of fresh air around and a slight smell of oil. The pilot calls out each man's name:

'Bill. Are you all right, Bill?'

'Yes, sir'

'Wilson? Are you there, Wilson?'

'Yes, sir, but the light has been shot out.'

'Tommy, are you OK?'

'Yes, sir'

'Scotty?'

He calls Scotty three times, each time with more urgency in his voice. Then Scotty answers. We are all alright.

The second pilot has crawled out from between my legs and is probing around under the pilot's platform. He has a little light and I look over his shoulder. There is a tangle of pipes with oil oozing out of some and squirting out of others. There is a hole in the side of the ship that you could put your hand through. After a bit we start for our base.

After the attack on *U-450*, south-east of Cape St Vincent, *Witherington* and *Velox*, from Group A, and *Highlander*, who was proceeding to rejoin convoy KMS30, were immediately ordered to the area of the aircraft's attack, but no further contact was made.

Undetected, undamaged and undeterred, *U-450* continued to take the shortest route to the Strait and all went well until the early hours of 31 October when it was picked up twenty miles from Cape Spartel. *Velox*, after obtaining a radar contact, sighted its wake just before it dived. Fortunately, for *U-450*, no asdic contact could be obtained although one attack was carried out by eye.

Oberleutnant Kurt Böhme successfully conned *U-450* unobserved through the Strait and went undetected until midnight on 2 November when it was picked up on radar by H-Harry of 179 Squadron, just west of the Greenwich Meridian well into the Mediterranean. The U-boat was able to dive before the Wellington pilot could make his attack. The second of the five U-boats was well on the way to joining the 29th Flotilla at Toulon.

We now come to the stories of the other two U-boats who were less fortunate:

U-732 was a Brest-based boat. For the crew the Biscay port was considered quite pleasant, one drawback, however, was its vulnerability to Allied bombing. For this reason many small vessels were anchored off shore to make artificial fog when the alert sounded.

The submariners attracted enhanced pay and for senior men, with their high wages and a good exchange rate France was the place to be; practically everything could be obtained, for the right price, even in the fifth year of war. The chief stoker bought two coats for his wife – antelope and pony skin, and ten sets of underwear, with four garments in each set. For himself he bought two overcoats, riding boots and ordered his tailor to make riding breeches.

On *U-732*'s first patrol the captain had the technicians change duties with ordinary ratings for one watch. The seamen went on the electric motor watch; the technicians sat in the W/T compartment, the radio man performed on the tubes, or was meant to prepare them. The engineers went up on deck. It was for only one watch so that each had an idea what the other did. Returning to *U-732* one night from ashore, the chief engineer was not allowed on board as he had no identity photograph in his paybook!

The Type VIIC *U-732* had been built by the Schichau concern at Danzig and launched the previous year. Under the command of Oberleutnant Klaus Peter Carlsen, it had been credited with sinking 25,000 tons of Allied shipping; a 5,000 and a 6,000 ton ship on one patrol and on a Caribbean patrol two 7,000 ton steamers had been sunk. The crew thought that Carlsen 'was damned good at his job'.

For the next sailing nineteen new crewmen joined *U-732* at Brest. The U-boat was to reinforce the 29th Flotilla at Toulon, but the patrol would not start officially until it was in the Mediterranean. The battle-seasoned U-boat was originally scheduled to sail on 16 October, but owing to intense Allied aircraft patrols in the Bay of Biscay the time of sailing was put back until the afternoon of the following day. The Brittany cliffs were in sight until the onset of darkness and *U-732* did not have to dive until dawn of the next day when the escort left. Course was shaped across the Bay, passing fairly close to Cape Finisterre and then a wide sweep was made before turning to the east towards the coast of Morocco. There were ominous signs on the night of 30th when the sound of *U-340* being depth-charged was heard.

After reaching a point off the Moroccan coast *U-732* made for Cape Spartel. In the early hours of 31st the depth charge attack by *Velox* on *U-450* was heard.

Shortly after noon screw noises were heard in the vicinity. Up above units of Group C were escorting six merchant ships, from Lisbon.

Asdic operator William Jeffrey obtained a good contact ahead as his trawler HMS *Imperialist* approached the searched channel. He called his captain, Lieutenant-Commander Bryan Rodgers, who immediately rang for action stations and ordered Lieutenant George Clampitt, captain of the accompanying *Loch Oskaig*, to take charge of the convoy.

As *Imperialist* homed on the target, some thousand yards distant, the depth charge settings were made and the charges primed. The order to fire was given and the first salvo released barely four minutes after the first contact – the aim was good, the pattern landed close to *U-732* almost two hundred feet below.

This accurate attack of just ten depth charges brought *U-732* to the surface on *Imperialist*'s starboard quarter and it was this attack that *Ultimatum* heard, described in the last chapter.

In *U-732* the lights had gone out, water came in in two places, by the control room and near the electric motor compartment, but both leaks were soon plugged.

For a U-boat hunter the sight of a surfaced, apparently helpless U-boat was the highlight of his career, and now all the previous hours of training and exercising could be put into practice.

Imperialist mounted a 4-inch gun forward, a Bofors and twin .5 guns abaft the funnel and two Oerlikons mounted on sponsons amidships each side of the bridge structure.

Calling for more revolutions the captain conned his trawler round so that the 4-inch gun could be brought into action to supplement the lighter armament which was already pounding *U-732*. For ten minutes *Imperialist*'s guns hammered the U-boat, there was no return of fire, in fact one of the U-boat's guns was blown clean out of the bridge structure as a result of a direct hit from the Bofors. *Imperialist* then came under fire! A steamer from a passing convoy started machine-gunning the U-boat, but was off target and the trawler crew were in more danger than the enemy. The third round from the 4-inch gun scored a direct hit at the base of the conning tower and the gunners were rewarded with the sight of a yellowish green puff of smoke.

The lifeless *U-732* then began to submerge. *Imperialist* ceased fire as she hurried to the spot and immediately threw off a second salvo of ten depth charges set to shallow depth. The subsequent explosions put the dynamo out of action in the trawler. Tracking back over the spot Bryan Rodgers ordered another pattern of eight depth charges, set deep, to be dropped.

HMS *IMPERIALIST*

With the convoy out of immediate danger *Loch Oskaig* now joined, but was unable to obtain an asdic contact. After half an hour her skipper was ordered to drop a further pattern of depth charges and remain in the area until dusk. *Imperialist* put into Gibraltar, feeling confident that *U-732* was in no state to constitute any danger; the captain claimed a 'probable'.

The workers at Schichau had built ships for decades and when they switched to U-boats exactly the same skill and expertise went into their construction. As a result *U-732* withstood all the hammering it had taken and was not torn apart. The compass was smashed, the wireless wrecked, the lighting blown and the periscope badly damaged but the boat and the men survived.

When *U-732* submerged under *Imperialist*'s attacks it was barely under control. Fortunately it bottomed at 585 feet. Motors were switched off and silent routine observed.

The combined depth charge and gunfire attacks caused such serious damage that the U-boat captain decided to remain submerged with both motors stopped and to drift along with the current. After some eight hours the air became so foul that the U-boat had to surface. On breaking surface no enemy ships were seen

HMS *FLEETWOOD*

so *U-732* made off, still surfaced, at its best possible speed, but listing badly to starboard. Destroyers were known to be in the area and about twenty radar decoy balloons were released in an attempt to mislead them.

Once Lieutenant-Commander Bryan Rodgers had given details of his attack all available suitable ships were alerted and that night a force of nine destroyers, two sloops, two corvettes, three trawlers, and five motor launches was achieved.

U-732 escaped detection for some time but then, suddenly, it was fully illuminated by a searchlight. About ten minutes later the shadow of a destroyer was seen in the U-boat's wake. *Douglas* immediately opened fire, killing several members of the U-boat's crew; some started jumping over the side. Oberleutnant Carlsen then gave the order to abandon ship and scuttle, while *Douglas* fired a ten-charge pattern to hasten its end. When *U-732* sank, several survivors were seen in the water and eventually the captain and eighteen of his men were picked up by *Douglas* and *Witherington*.

U-732 was sunk, *U-450* slipped through, which leaves the last of the five, *U-340* to be accounted for.

The Type VIIC *U-340* had been launched from the Nordsee Werke at Emden in August 1942. The first patrol was out of Kiel at the end of April. From the Baltic port to Kristiansand and then away, no tactical exercises; through the *Rosengarten* for an Iceland and Greenland patrol before putting into Bordeaux at the end of May. The next patrol was off the West African coast from which *U-340* returned to St Nazaire. The next patrol was only a short one and after carrying out diving trials Oberleutnant Hans Klaus conned the U-boat from the bomb-damaged St Nazaire at 1400 on 18 October, for its fourth patrol. Four hours later it submerged until shortly before dawn the following day.

During passage to the Gibraltar area the routine was to dive at dawn and to remain submerged for about fourteen hours, only surfacing for two periods of three hours during darkness. The course followed was a straight line from St Nazaire to Cape Finisterre and then due south to a point off the African coast in roughly the latitude of Madeira. Only twice during the passage to the Strait was *U-340* compelled to dive as a result of receiving radar aircraft contact. As the U-boat proceeded from the African coast to Gibraltar night surfacing was reduced, seldom exceeding three hours per night.

The first attack on the U-boat took place in the evening of 30 October, some thirty-seven miles south-west of Cape Spartel. Flying Officer Pickering was airborne in Wellington W-William of 179 Squadron from Gibraltar at 2126 in good but 'bumpy' conditions and thirty-three minutes later, while flying at 800 feet a radar contact was made at 40 degrees to port at a range of six miles. The pilot turned to port, homing on to the contact, losing height, and at slightly less than half mile range the Leigh light was switched on and illuminated *U-340*, travelling at an estimated 15 knots. The U-boat immediately opened fire on the Mark XIV Wellington. Red flashes were seen by the front and rear gunners. No tracer was observed and the aircraft gunners did not open fire.

Six Torpex filled depth charges were dropped as an attack was carried out 80 degrees to port of the U-boat's track. The charges were spaced at sixty feet, shallow setting, and released from 75 feet, falling across the track at 100-150 feet astern of *U-340*.

The Leigh light was switched off as the Wellington crossed the wake, turned to port and circled the two flame floats it had dropped earlier. Nothing was seen, no further radar contact was made. The pilot was ordered to drop a sea marker and home a flotilla of boats to the position by W/T, with communication by R/T.

The depth charges caused no material damage to *U-340* but the compressed air bottles flew off the bulkhead; this made more noise than the exploding charges! The attack had a harassing effect on some new members of the crew. The Wellington landed safely at Gibraltar at the conclusion of its six-hour patrol. The U-boat continued on its course toward the Strait and the next night, while just west of Tangiers, was caught unawares on the surface.

Flying Officer Ellis had taken off from Gibraltar in Wellington R-Rodger of 179 Squadron at 2059 on an anti-submarine patrol to the west of the Strait. Shortly after midnight a radar contact was made, on *U-340* at two-and-a-half miles range from 1,000 feet. After a few minutes manoeuvring to get into an attacking position the Leigh light was switched on and the fully surfaced U-boat was illuminated. The U-boat was on an east-north-east course. Intense but inaccurate flak was at once encountered as the aircraft attacked from fine on the starboard quarter, releasing six depth charges, spaced 60-70 feet. The last depth charge was reported by the rear gunner to have entered the water close to the port bow and the U-boat disappeared under the explosion plumes. After the attack the aircraft searched the area, illuminating the position with flame floats and with the Leigh light, but no results were seen. Surface vessels arrived on the scene of the attack just after 0200, after being homed on to the aircraft by W/T.

The depth charges put the starboard main motor out of action besides causing other damage of a less serious nature. The U-boat dived immediately and after about two hours struck the bottom at about 280 feet. The crew feared that this might have betrayed their position, but no attack developed.

The commanding officer then decided to drift with the strong current, using the remaining motor at silent speed. The damage, however, proved less serious than was at first feared and after two hours' hard labour, the starboard motor was again working.

At 0545 *Witherington* obtained an asdic contact just off Malabata Light. *Active* and *Wishart* joined in the hunt and several attacks were carried out. The prompt ejection of SBT's seem to have misled the attacking craft and no damage was sustained.

During the day *U-340* proceeded at a depth of about 260 feet, releasing SBT's at various intervals. In the late afternoon the captain bought *U-340* to periscope depth, he was in some doubt as to whether he was clear of the Strait and spent two-and-a-half hours looking round before finally deciding to surface. The batteries were by now very low and he therefore gave the order to proceed at full speed in a southerly direction.

The U-boat had been on the surface for two hours when enemy craft were seen approaching. At 2140 *Fleetwood*, with *Bluebell* and *Poppy* in company, was patrolling south of Ceuta between Cabo Negro and Pta Almina, when *U-340* was sighted.

When *Fleetwood* was within range the U-boat commander decided to fire his stern torpedo. He changed his mind, however, at the last moment and instead he gave the order to crash-dive. This was the moment for *Fleetwood* to make a depth charge attack. Leonard Silvester was the asdic operator in *Fleetwood*; he says:

> We were patrolling in the Strait when we made contact with a U-boat trying to enter the Mediterranean by sheltering in the lee of the coast, which made asdic operating quite difficult, owing to picking up false echoes off the land mass. However, we confirmed a contact and roused the crew to action stations, with the usual moans and groans about bloody asdics and their false echoes.
>
> We dropped a number of depth charges at the target and then I reported to the bridge that a torpedo was approaching and evasive action was immediately taken. The hissing sound was so intense that I had to lift the earphones from my ears. It wasn't a torpedo it must have been the U-boat trying to blow tanks to surface.
>
> I then lost contact and all was quiet and it was presumed to be another false alarm as we were unable to regain contact. We didn't realise at the time we had blown the U-boat to the bottom. Being very dark and there being no sign of wreckage or survivors we resumed on patrol after a time.

The depth charges dropped did no material damage to *U-340* but drove it to the bottom where it remained for five hours. By this time the supply of air was reduced to a minimum. The man at the helm was trembling and moaning, 'My God, my God'. Klaus summoned his officers and men to tell them that, as they could neither remain submerged any longer nor surface during the day to recharge the batteries, he had decided to scuttle the boat and give them a chance to save their lives by swimming to the nearby Spanish Moroccan coast. Tanks were blown for the last time and, in the absence of any attacking ships, the boat was abandoned in a leisurely and orderly manner. Shortly afterwards the scuttling charges exploded and *U-340* sank. One of the senior German ratings said:

The captain came along and we all assembled in the control room; we were to scuttle the boat. We prepared ourselves, dressing accordingly, life saving apparatus, rubber dinghies, everything was prepared, but the boat had to surface. This was a peculiar sensation. We shot up to the surface. We came up right from the bottom. To begin with, the boat wouldn't move, then it shot straight up. The captain had to hold on to the bridge to avoid being carried away. The movement of the boat swept him off his feet. We thought we would be rammed and were all ready to scramble out. We all got out, the boat was already settling down nicely when all of a sudden there was a noise and it disappeared. We then swam for it. To begin with I was in the dinghy and had to paddle with my arms, we had nothing with us to propel it. Afterwards it became too tiring so I held on to a sort of rock and thought, 'Damn it all, the men swimming are making better progress'. So I let the dinghy go, got out of it and swam.

Later the U-boat crew were rescued by some Spanish trawlers.

Fleetwood had lost contact but believing, wrongly, that it had seriously damaged *U-340* felt confident that the U-boat would probably make for territorial waters.

When, in daylight, *Fleetwood* approached the Spanish trawlers the commanding officer decided for humanitarian reasons to take the U-boat men on board. He thought they looked in an exhausted condition and took them on his ship to ensure that they received dry clothing and medical assistance.

The information in this last paragraph was as signalled to the Anti-U-boat Division in London and has been published in books ever since as what happened.

However Leonard Silvester was in *Fleetwood* at the time, and these are his recollections of 2 November:

As dawn broke the duty bunting tosser on the bridge shouted to the officer of the morning watch that there were three suspicious fishing vessels making for harbour with some rather dubious nets hung drying on their decks. He took a good look through his glasses and decided to seek the captain's advice. He was soon on the bridge and rang for 'Action stations'. The vessels were signalled to stop but failed to do so. At this the skipper was quite annoyed and ordered a shot across the bows which was fired from

Within sight of Spanish Morocco, fishing vessels close HMS *Fleetwood* to hand over the crew of *U-340*.

the Oerlikon gun, with a remark from the skipper, in his broad Irish accent, 'If they don't stop I will blow them out of the water with the 4-inch guns'.

The boats slowed and made towards us, eventually coming alongside and a search party went aboard all three vessels, rounding up 48 survivors. The give away had been the U-boat crew's gear hung up to dry.

The fishermen were compensated with cigarettes and tobacco. We finished up with a quantity of freshly caught sardines; we duly dispatched our prisoners at Gibraltar.

There ended the saga of *U-340*. Most sources stemming from the official record give the date that *U-340* was sunk as 1 November. As we have seen, however, it was the 2nd.

The story of the U-boats attempting to enter the Mediterranean was not released by the censor to the press for three months – it was then described as 'recent'.

Reproduced here is the version given by the wartime censor, of a typical contemporary release, with the names of commanding officers well in evidence, but rarely a mention of those at the sharp end of events.

In a battle which raged for eleven days and nights the Royal Navy and Coastal Command aircraft recently sank three U-boats, which tried to sneak through the Strait of Gibraltar, and damaged several others.

At least twelve separate attacks were made during the combined operations, in which seven destroyers, a sloop and a trawler, besides Leigh light Wellingtons, played a notable part.

During two nights of decisive engagement, three large Allied convoys passed through the Strait, and so completely smashed was the U-pack that they went on their way without interference. Our ships picked up sixty-seven survivors from two U-boats. There were others from a third.

The first sighting of the enemy force was made shortly after midnight by a Leigh light Wellington of Coastal Command operating under the orders of Air Vice Marshal S. P. Simpson, CBE MC.

This aircraft, which was from a squadron commanded by Wing Commander J. H. Gresswell, DFC, engaged a U-boat in the approaches to the Strait – the enemy replied with intense anti-aircraft fire, but depth charges dropped by the Wellingtons straddled the U-boat, and a burst of orange coloured flames rose to a height of about 200 feet. The vessel later sank, forty-nine survivors being picked up.

The aircraft sustained slight damage during the attack, but it returned safely to base.

Later a Leigh light Wellington from the same squadron illuminated and attacked a fully surfaced U-boat, which was forced to submerge apparently in a damaged condition.

Shortly afterwards the trawler *Imperialist* (Lieutenant-Commander B. H. Craig Rodgers RNVR) detected a U-boat in the vicinity of a convoy which was passing through the Strait. The trawler immediately attacked with depth charges and later a U-boat slowly broke surface in the centre of the disturbed waters.

Imperialist opened fire with all guns that could be brought to bear, scoring hits on the conning tower, and on the hull, which apparently further damaged the U-boat. No further contact was made.

The destroyer *Douglas* (Lieutenant-Commander K. H. J. L. Phibbs, RN) illuminated a U-boat on the surface and opened fire on the enemy. Several hits were observed, and the U-boat crew were seen abandoning ship by jumping into the sea. Soon afterwards the enemy sank. Eighteen survivors were picked up by our destroyers and made prisoners of war.

During the day strong forces of our ships maintained widespread patrols in the vicinity of the Strait. A few hours before midnight the sloop *Fleetwood* (Commander W. B. Piggott, OBE DSC RNR) encountered a U-boat on the surface and illuminated it by means of starshell.

The enemy submerged in a crash-dive and *Fleetwood* carried out four depth charge attacks over the U-boat's diving position and continued to sweep the area throughout the night.

Lieutenant-Commander Bryan Rodgers, commanding officer of HMS *Imperialist*, was awarded the Distinguished Service Cross for his part in the destruction of *U-732*.

CHAPTER SIXTEEN

Captain Walker and the Second Support Group

After taking part in the destruction of five U-boats during the summer of 1943, the Second Support Group, under the command of Captain F. J. Walker in *Starling*, started their autumn season in the afternoon of 19 October.

There were leaden skies as the sloops *Starling*, *Wild Goose*, *Woodcock* and *Magpie* swept into the Atlantic. A south-easterly gale, that had already been blowing for twenty-four hours, was producing rain, hail and sleet as the escort carrier *Tracker* joined in the evening. The gale continued throughout the next day.

On the following day, however, the weather improved sufficiently to enable a A/S search of three aircraft to be flown off *Tracker* at noon. From 1700 the group operated in the vicinity of Convoy ON207. *Tracker* was stationed within the convoy to give the support group more freedom of movement and to hide the air striking force from the enemy until more U-boats should concentrate.

The next few days were uneventful and no contacts were obtained by the group. Escort Group B7, who were also acting in support of the convoy, as already recorded, attacked and sank *U-274* some ninety miles away from the convoy in the early afternoon of the 23rd.

In the early hours of the 25th, as the convoy did not appear to be menaced, the group closed to collect *Tracker* and, at 0800, set a course to the south in the direction of convoy HX262.

In the early afternoon, while *Woodcock* was oiling from *Tracker*, the latter obtained a radar contact 6,000 yards to the northward. *Wild Goose* was ordered to search back but found nothing. It is probable that the group was being observed by a U-boat astern at periscope depth. This was later substantiated by a U-boat sighting reported from the Admiralty. It was *U-413*.

There then followed a period of searching by ships and aircraft for an enemy who seemed reluctant to put in an appearance. At 2240 on the next evening an HF/DF bearing was obtained of a U-boat estimated to be forty miles away. Course was altered and a thorough search carried out but nothing was found.

Convoy HX262, with Escort Group C5, was sighted by *Tracker*'s aircraft in the late morning of the 28th. The group met this convoy about two-and-a-half hours later and commenced to refuel from *Tracker* and the escort oiler *Fjordaas*. The sloops had all oiled by 1900 on the 29th and proceeded to the westward, where HF/DF transmissions had indicated that a group of U-boats were operating.

Regular flying by the carrier's aircraft was possible for the next two days but November opened with a full gale and the group was, therefore ordered to proceed about 300 miles to the south where better flying conditions might be expected. Later it was found necessary to heave to for some hours, mainly on account of *Tracker*. The maximum roll experienced in the carrier was 52 degrees which caused considerable damage in the hangar, putting more aircraft out of action in five minutes than in two weeks of flying at sea. *Kite* joined the group on the same day. The sloop had been delayed at Londonderry after a minor collision with a tug. However, in its frantic efforts, through the gale, to catch the group it was further damaged by the heavy weather.

An interlude of twelve hours' fine weather followed on the 2nd, during which several HF/DF transmissions were picked up varying between twenty and one hundred miles distant. Some of these were investigated, one during daylight, with the assistance of three aircraft from *Tracker*, but no results were obtained.

The senior officer intended to return to the area on the next day but was warned by the C-in-C Western Approaches that a meteorological report suggested the approach of another gale and the group withdrew to the south-west in the direction of better weather.

On the following day they turned back to the north-east, as the gale showed signs of moderating and fine weather was expected later. On the 5th one of *Tracker*'s aircraft forced *U-967* to submerge. During the night the group steered a mean course of 180 degrees at a speed of 12 knots, the five sloops in line abreast two-and-a-half miles apart, with *Tracker* one to two miles astern and all ships zig-zagging independently.

Midway through the middle watch on the 6th, *Kite*, the port wing ship of the line, under the command of Lieutenant-Commander Rysegrave, obtained a radar contact at 3,800 yards. The target was illuminated with starshell and, shortly afterwards a U-boat was sighted which dived when the range had closed to 700 yards. *Kite* immediately attacked by eye, firing a shallow pattern at 0215.

On receipt of *Kite*'s enemy report, Captain Walker ordered his second-in-command, Commander D. E. G. Wemyss in *Wild Goose*, to take *Magpie* with him to starboard to escort *Tracker* to the westward, while he, together with *Woodcock*, proceeded at full speed to join *Kite*.

The U-boat located by *Kite* was *U-226*. The Type VIIC boat, launched sixteen months earlier from the Germania Werft at Kiel, commenced its first Atlantic patrol on New Year's Eve from its shipyard base and joined the 12th Flotilla at Lorient early in March. It was exactly a month later that it started its second patrol, this time returning to St Nazaire. The third North Atlantic patrol had been in operation exactly a month, and at this time the boat was under the command of Oberleutnant Albrecht Gänge who had taken over as captain. The U-boat had been one of the twenty-four U-boats in the *Siegfried* Group which, as reported earlier, was split into three sections. *U-226*, with *U-842*, *U-575*, *U-373*, *U-709* and *U-648*, made up Section Three. They were ordered by Admiral Dönitz to find HX264.

While *Starling* and *Woodcock* were closing, *Kite* had obtained asdic contact and had carried out two attacks. The second, at 0300, was considered to have been on an SBT. Four minutes later *Starling* was in contact but the U-boat appeared to have gone deep. As the night was dark and asdic conditions were good, it was decided not to risk losing the U-boat in the depth charge disturbances from further attacks, but to remain in contact until daylight and then carry out a 'creeping' attack.

For the next four hours *Starling* stationed herself 1,500 yards astern of *U-226*, proceeding on a south-westerly course, with *Kite* and *Woodcock* in close attendance.

At dawn *Woodcock* commenced a 'creeping' attack with *Starling* acting as the directing ship. The crews of all three sloops were at action stations with depth charge crews standing by. As it was estimated that *U-226* was at 700 feet the charges had been set for between 600 and 800 feet. The 'creeping' attack consisted of stationing one sloop directly over the target and another behind. The second one, in this case Walker in *Starling*, directed the first one. By computing the distance and speed and estimating the course the first sloop, *Woodcock*, was instructed to fire. Directors swung on the bearing and twenty-six depth charges were ordered to be fired. A few minutes later breaking up noises were reported by the asdic operators. A patch of oil hit the surface followed by debris, including an unprepared torpedo. This and other bits were retrieved. The good news was signalled to the Admiralty and repeated to *Wild Goose*. Another, much more popular, signal followed when 'Splice the mainbrace' was hoisted and all those with G for Grog on their ship's card received a double rum ration that day.

Some two hours later an aircraft reported a U-boat diving twenty miles to the west of the group. This time *Woodcock* and *Kite* were detailed to protect *Tracker* while *Wild Goose* and *Magpie* set off at full speed with *Starling* to the reported position.

The U-boat was *U-842*. It had left Bergen on its first patrol a month earlier. A Type IXC boat launched from the AG Weser yard at Bremen a year earlier, it was under the command of Korvettenkapitän Wolfgang Heller. Its initial three-day patrol took it from Kiel up to Bergen on 14 September.

A Liberator from No 10 RCAF Squadron and a Swordfish from *Tracker* were over the reported position as Captain Walker and his team of three arrived. Neither aircraft found anything and it was assumed that the U-boat had dived immediately after making a signal. Eventually the asdic operator on *Wild Goose* reported a U-boat contact. This was confirmed by *Starling*. *Magpie* was ordered to carry out a square search. A loud underwater explosion was heard, this was probably a gnat at the end of its run.

Captain Walker made his first attack with a one ton pattern, but in so doing damaged his gyro compass and put his asdic out of action. The U-boat, which had been driven deep, was tracked by the other two sloops for ninety minutes until *Starling* was repaired and ready to take charge again. This time *Wild Goose* was ordered to carry out the attack. Through a malfunction only half the charges were released, but it was soon seen that these had been sufficient to account for *U-842*. Again part of a torpedo hit the surface and this, with much wreckage and human remains, was sufficient proof of the U-boat's destruction. Thus two U-boats had been sunk by the group in less than eight hours.

For the next two days the group provided distant cover, about sixty miles to the northward of convoy HX264, with *Tracker*'s aircraft on patrol. As the convoy did not appear to be threatened, the group left at noon on the 8th in very heavy weather.

In mid-evening *Tracker* was missed by a torpedo fired from *U-648* which exploded on the surface about a thousand yards on her port quarter; it had been a long shot from down moon and could not be avenged due to the sloop's fuel state and the foul weather. Later in the evening the wind changed and before midnight a full 80 mph gale was blowing, forcing the group to heave to for the rest of the night and the following day. It was one of the worst storms ever recorded and the ships suffered much weather damage.

By the early hours of the 10th the weather had moderated and course was set for Argentia at eleven knots. After twenty-four hours of fog on the Newfoundland Banks *Tracker* and the 2nd Support Group arrived at the Canadian base just before midday on 12 November.

The ships were repaired and refuelled and the crew given time to catch up on lost sleep and fit in a run ashore to purchase Christmas presents for their families at home.

With hindsight it can now be seen that the group could have been just as effective, if not more so, without the escort carrier. Each time a U-boat was reported *Tracker* had to be protected by two of the group, and when bad weather had been forecast the carrier was ordered to smoother water to avoid its aircraft being damaged. With the occupation of the Azores, from which a Fortress destroyed *U-707* on 9 November, the story of forty-four days of the autumn is concluded. Thirty-four U-boats had been sunk.

The British and United States escort carriers, sea and air escorts, continued with their good work. As has already been seen the larger groups of U-boats had been split into smaller sections. By the end of the month Admiral Dönitz had decided that these large groups were exactly the targets that the escort and support groups welcomed. The U-boats continued operating in smaller concentrations of independent acting groups, so it can be fairly said that with the breaking up of the wolf packs it was the *Autumn of the U-Boats*.

Boats and Personnel

While writing the book I was struck by the number of U-boats outward bound from Bergen that were sunk, so I collated the statistics. Of the 34 U-boat sinkings covered in the book, eight were of boats that had left Bergen.

Between 8 September and 5 October 1943 the following U-boats, *U-220*, *U-422*, *U-419*, *U-643*, *U-470*, *U-282*, *U-540*, and *U-842*, left on their first patrol and all were sunk. It seems extraordinary that all these boats, out from the Norwegian port on their very first war patrol should have been sunk. I cannot find any reason for it, or any common link, so have put it down to coincidence.

Tom Goddard, the East End seaman who served aboard *Oribi* from July 1941 until March 1945, has now retired. He is a member of the 17th Destroyer Flotilla Association (*Onslow, Onslaught, Obdurate, Oribi, Offa, Opportune, Obedient* and *Orwell*).

Douglas Gowland, the signalman in *Oribi*, escorting convoy SC143, which picked up U-boat survivors, had been in the destroyer earlier when it rather fortuitously rammed *U-531* in May. (see *The Month of the Lost U-boats*). As a result of the ramming *Oribi* had to put into Boston Navy Yard to have a new bow fitted. While on shore leave the eighteen-year-old signalman was so impressed by 'the land of plenty' that after his demobilisation he persuaded his family to emigrate there. They did exceptionally well. Returning to this country after thirteen years, Douglas settled down in a rural area. His telephone number was 531, the same as the U-boat that had been rammed! He says he owes a great deal to that chance encounter with the U-boat. After landing the U-boat prisoners at Greenock *Oribi* steamed north to Spitzbergen, with *Orwell*, to change the garrison, before returning to Scapa and Greenock for a boiler clean and five days leave. *Oribi* joined the Turkish Navy in 1946.

Ian Scrymgeour-Wedderburn, the Sub-Lieutenant in *Orwell*, is now a retired commander and resides in Scotland. He has recently met John Pelly, the officer on watch with him at the time *U-643* was sunk, who is now domiciled in Canada. He has also seen Pat Adam, the doctor who tended the U-boat wounded, who brought news that John Hodges, their captain, is very ill in hospital. *Orwell* survived until mid-1965 when she was scrapped.

After being landed at Greenock by *Orwell*, Hans Speidel, captain of *U-643*, and the other officers were taken to London for interrogation. He was then sent to a prisoner of war camp in the Midlands until March 1944 when he was transferred to Canada. After hostilities he was put on board the four funnelled *Aquitania*, for its very last voyage to Southampton. He was then confined in a variety of English camps until being released in September 1947. He now runs a business in a German port.

Two ex-*Byard* ratings, Able Seaman McPhail, living in London, and Signalman Phillip Norfield in Lancashire, remember their Captain Class frigate as a friendly ship in which no one asked for a transfer. There were different captains and officers who soon found she was a lively ship – in fact *Byard* was known as 'The Spirited Horse'. *Byard* completed 100,000 miles on active service by 5 March 1945, an average of 5,000 miles a month since commissioning. She was returned to the United States on cessation of her commission to the Royal Navy on 10 September 1945. Lieutenant-Commander L. H. Phillips RN and Lieutenant C. J. T. Edwards RN were awarded the DSC 'for outstanding bravery, enterprise and devotion to duty in acting with enemy submarines'. Four ratings received DSM's and four men were Mentioned in Despatches.

Phillip Norfield says, 'Since those days I have had five coronary thromboses and two strokes but I feel very well.'

Block Island became the only United States carrier to be lost in the Atlantic theatre of war when it was torpedoed by *U-549* with some loss of life in May 1944.

Hedley Kett, captain of HMs/m *Ultimatum* served as a navigator in *Oberon* and *Clyde* and for a short while in *H.32*. For nearly two years he served as first lieutenant, under Commander Ingram, in the Mediterranean and South Atlantic aboard *Clyde*, the large 'River' Class submarine. He was consulted about the possibility of carrying petrol to Malta, and indeed made six voyages to Malta with petrol in the ballast tanks of *Clyde*. Petrol being lighter than water, the submarine was able to carry ammunition, aerial torpedoes and food which was also urgently needed. Hedley Kett commanded *Ultimatum* from April 1942 until December 1944. He now lives on the East Coast, is a member of the local branch of the Submarine Old Comrades Association and has taken up art, recently holding two exhibitions.

J. A. Wade, a telegraphist aboard *Ultimatum* from December 1942 until June 1946, now lives in Leicestershire and is a Lieutenant (SCC) RNR Retired. *Ultimatum* was scrapped early in 1950.

Wilhelm Dommes, hunter and farmowner, former captain of *U-431* sunk by *Ultimatum*, went on to command *U-178* until November 1943. He then took over the U-boat base in Penang, then went to Tokyo as liaison officer for the U-boat arm in Japan.

A. R. Davies, as ERA in *Active*, spent three years in the Mediterranean in various ships. He is now a member of the Royal Naval Association in Llanelli.

Leonard Silvester had been aboard *Fleetwood* when it sank *U-528* in May, described in my book *The Month of the Lost U-boats*. Before May the ship was engaged in long distance work operating from Londonderry to Freetown escorting 8-knot convoys. The prisoners taken aboard from *U-340* were landed in Gibraltar. Leonard Silvester now lives in South Yorkshire.

I have described how Oberleutnant Klaus, captain of *U-340*, changed his mind about firing a gnat when *Fleetwood* was within range. In view of later events the captain was probably very prudent, for if he had fired his gnat, then picked up speed, he could have been hit by his own torpedo, as is shown by the next paragraph.

Some other U-boats mentioned in the book did not survive the winter. *U-377*, on its eleventh war patrol, was lost in January 'cause unknown' in most reference books. British Intelligence picked up a signal from the boat saying it had been torpedoed, which was most unusual. A U-boat was depth-charged from the air or at sea, attacked by gunfire or hedgehog, but torpedoed? There were no British submarines in the area and the only conclusion is that the gnat was no respecter of nationality and that another U-boat in the group fired the gnat that torpedoed *U-377*. No signal was received by U-boat headquarters. Gerhart Kluth was lost with his boat, he had made a good recovery from a severed artery when shot through the arm at the end of September. Jumbo Gerke, who took command of the boat when he was injured, left when the boat returned to Brest. He later went on to the commanding officers' training course and subsequently commanded *U-673* and *U-3035*. He now lives on the north German coast.

In February *U-264*, the U-boat that tried to cover the last milch-cow *U-460*, was sunk by Captain Walker's Group, but the telegraphist who had served in both U-boats and the whole of of Kapitänleutnant Hartwig Looks' successful crew were saved. The busy *U-91*, featured throughout this book, on its sixth war patrol out of Brest, was also a February victim in the North Atlantic.

The two U-boats that escaped the 'Battle of the Strait' and entered the Mediterranean did not last long. *U-450* was sunk in March 1944 off Anzio and four months later *U-642* was bombed in Toulon by American aircraft.

The successful Captain F. J. Walker CB, DSO and Bar, of *Starling* and North Atlantic fame died in July 1944 of 'overstrain, overwork and war weariness'. He had driven himself beyond all limits.

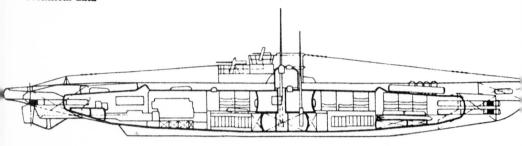

Type VIIC
Displacement: 769/871 tons.
Dimensions: 220 1/4 x 20 1/4 x 15 3/4 feet
Machinery: 2-shaft diesel/electric motors BHP/SHP. 2800/750 17,0/7,6 knots.

Bunkers and radius: Oil fuel 113, 5 tons, 9400/130 miles at 10/2 knots.

Armament: One 3.5 inch, two 20mm AA guns, five 21-inch TT
            (4 fwd, 1 aft), twelve torpedoes
Complement: 44-48.

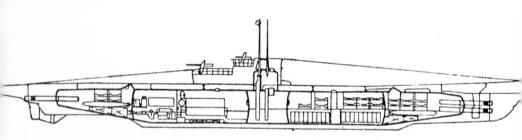

Type IXC
Displacement: 1120/1232 tons.
Dimensions: 252 x 22 1/4 x 15 1/2 feet
Machinery: 2 shaft diesel/electric motors BHP/SHP, 4400/1000, 18.3/7.3 knots.

Bunkers and radius: Oil fuel 208, 2 tons, 16300/128 miles at 10/2 knots.

Armament: One 4.1 inch, two 20mm AA guns, six 21-inch TT
            (4 fwd, 2 aft), 19 torpedoes
Complement: 48

Type IX/C-40
Displacement: 1144/1257 tons.
Dimensions: 252 x 21 3/4 x 15 1/4 feet
Machinery: 2 shaft diesel/electric motors BHP/SHP. 4400/1000, 18.3/7.3 knots.

Bunkers and radius: Oil fuel 214, 0 tons, 16800/128 miles at 10/2 knots.

Armament: One 4.1 inch, two 20mm AA guns, six 21-inch TT
            (4 fwd, 2 aft), 22 torpedoes.
Complement: 48.

Glossary

A/S	Anti-submarine
Asdic	Device for detecting submerged submarines from initials of Allied Submarine Detection Investigation Committee
DA	Director Angle
D/F	Direction finding
ERA	Engine Room Artificer
Gnat or T5	Acoustic or homing torpedo fired from U-boat
HE	Hydrophone effect
H/F	High frequency
1WO	First Watch Officer
2WO	Second Watch Officer
MAC	Merchant Aircraft Carrier
M/F	Medium frequency
OOW	Officer of the Watch
ORP	*Okret Rzeczypospolites Polskiej* (warship of the Republic of Poland)
PO	Petty Officer
RCAF	Royal Canadian Air Force
RCN	Royal Canadian Navy
RFA	Royal Fleet Auxiliary
RNR	Royal Naval Reserve
RNVR	Royal Naval Volunteer Reserve
RP	Rocket Projectile
rpm	revs per minute
R/T	Radio Telephony
SBT	Submarine Bubble Target, *Pillenwerfer* – a device that ejected chemical pills which activated on contact with sea water and created a disturbance which effected a false asdic target
SNO	Senior Naval Officer
USAAF	United States Army Air Force
USN	United States Navy
USS	United States Ship
VLR	Very Long Range
W/T	Wireless Telegraphy

NAVAL EXPRESSIONS

Bunting tosser	Signalman
Chin strap	put down to keep sailor's cap on in windy conditions
Chinese Wedding Cake	Rice Pudding
Dhobying	Washing clothes (from Hindi)
Uckers	Ludo

COMPARATIVE RANKS

Leutnant	Sub-Lieutenant
Oberleutnant	Lieutenant (junior)
Kapitänleutnant	Lieutenant
Korvettenkapitän	Lieutenant-Commander

Index

Accrington HMS 109
Achilles A. K/L, 19 20 35
Active HMS 189 214
Adam P. A. Lt. 88 213
Admiral Scheer 58
Afrika 60
Aircraft:
  Anson 43
  Avenger 54 56 57 61 62 146 148 150
    153 155-157
  Bisley 136-138
  Blenheim 136
  Boston 136
  BV222 92 181
  Catalina 44 142 143
  Condor 46
  Do24 186
  Fortress 41 100 104 106 107 211
  Halifax 22-27 29 30 37
  Hudson 43 63 64 67 68 101 117 128
    157
  Ju87 (Stuka) 181
  Liberator 16 28 29 37 39-51 61 63 66
    67 70 75 76 85 110 111 113
    115-118 128 129 131 139 140-143
    159 161 172 210
  Mariner 19-22
  Mitchell 142
  Mosquito 136 174
  Sunderland 37 43 92-95 130 131
  Swordfish 106 161 210
  Ventura 22 63-66
  Wellington 37 70 170 172-174 178
    191 193 195 200 201 204 206
  Wildcat 54 56 148 150 153 155
Aldwinckle R. M. F/L 159-161
Alexandria 175
Alexandria 184
Algiers 181 186
Alisma HMS 189
Alison T. Lt 178 179 185
Allsop G. C. F/S 67
Andrea F. Luckenbach 28
Anemone HMS 44

Angelus 19
Antares HMS 69
Anthony HMS 189
Antigona 60
APY Plymouth 173
Aratu 19 20
Argentia 211
Ark Royal HMS 79
Arndale RFA 176
Avery H. M. L/Cdr 61
Badger USS 146
Badoglio Marshal 38
Balliett L. S. Lt 157 158
Barber O/L 151
Barker USS 146
Baron Semple 139
Barrow 37 175
Barry USS 54
Bazeley HMS 109
Beagle HMS 189
Bealer R/O 21
Beamish R. P/O 160
Beckville 106
Beech F. Major 38
Beirut 186
Belfast 133 151
Belknap USS 147
Benalder 19
Bender W. K/L 135
Bentinck HMS 109 119 128 132 133
Bergen 37 56 83 105 119 128 151 161 210
  212
Berry USS 109 161
Bevin Ernie 37
Billings J. W/O 16
Birnie F/L 191
Blackwood HMS 109
Bland F/L 110 111
Block Island USS 151 153 156 213
Bluebell HMS 202
Boadicea HMS 189
Böhme O/L 191 195
Bombay 136
Bonneville 161

Bonymgre Sgt 137
Bordeaux 23 37 52 53
Borie USS 54 62 158 161 163-165 167
Boscombe 43
Bremen 110 135 139 210
Bremerhaven 19
Brest 15 16 23 37 44 52 64 65 105 156 159
172 173 195 196 215
Brett Ensign 21 22
Brewer C. W. Lt-Cmdr 148
Brünning K/L 174
Bulldog HMS 189
Bulloch T. M. S/Ldr 23 43 45-48
Bulmer USS 146
Burcher C. F/O 85
Burges HMS 109
Byard HMS 109 132 133 135 213
Canadian Star 29
Card USS 53 54 57 61 62 64 67 146 156 161
Carlsen K. P. O/L 196 199
Casablanca 62
Castle Archdale 93 130
Ceuta 202
Chapman L. Sgt 137 138
Chew Sgt 191
Churchill Winston 53 132 176
Cisne Branco 20
City of Perth 184
Clampitt G. Lt 197
Clyde HMs/m 176 213
Cologne 86
Colombo 136
Commandant Detroyat 189
Core USS 146-148 151
Cornish D. M. Sgt 172-174
Cunningham A. Sir 37
Curie 175
Currie R. A. Cmdr 109
Cyclops HMS 187
Cythera USS 58
Daghild 60
Dahlia HMS 64
Dalcroy 58
Dalmatia L 175
Danzig 35 79 82 159 183 191 196
Darling Adm 132
Darling Lady 132
Davies A. R. ERA 189 214
Daytona 43
Deecke J. K/L 157
Delise 153
Deutschland 82
Deveron HMS 109
Devonport 132 176

Dommes W. K/L 184 214
Dönitz K. Adm 34 37 54 57 136 148 169
211
Dorval 43 49
Douglas HMS 199 206
Drumheller HMS 69
Drummond R. P. F/L 104 106 107
Drury HMS 109 131
Duckworth HMS 69
Dudley J. R. Capt 147
Duncan HMS 109-111 113-119 159
Dundee 188
Du Pont USS 54
Egersund 83
Ellis F/O 201
Elser S. E. F/O 28 46
Emden 64
Empire Antelope 58
Empire Knight 28
Empire Leopard 58
Empire Oil 156
Empire Sunrise 58
Eocene 184
Ericsson USS 147
Essex Lance 116 130
Fame HMS 109
Fayal 100 104
Feiler K/L 45
Fencer HMS 100 161
Ferro O. O/L 95
Fina 173
Finke K/L 67
Fishguard 188
Fjordaas 208
Fleetwood HMS 189 190 202 203 206 214
Forester HMS 118
Forstner von S. KK 58-62
Fort Cumberland HMS 143
Fowler W. S. Lt 156-158
Franke H. K/L 106
Freyberg W. von K/L 93 95
Frizzle J. R. W/Cdr 93-95
Gamble G. F/O 128 129
Gander 16 48 159
Gänge A. O/L 209
Gateshead HMS 69
Gdynia 82
Gentian HMS 60
George VI King 69
Geranium HMS 104 105
Gerke E. O/L 15 214
Gibraltar 70 101 104 146 169 170 172
174-178 186 189 190 193 200 201 204
214

Giersberg D. O/L 75 76
Gilardone H. K/L 27
Gillespie USS 146
Goddard T. C. A/B 77 86 212
Goff USS 54 57 161
Goldsborough USS 147
Govan 69
Gowland D. Sig 77 212
Grado 60
Grave G. O/L 113
Greene USS 147
Greenock 98 212 213
Greer M. R. Capt 146
Grenville R. Sir 100
Gresswell J. H. W/Cdr 204
Gretschel G. O/L 106
Gretton P. Cmdr 109
H.32 176 213
Haifa 175
Halifax 69 93
Hallfried 106
Hamburg 40 46 61 79 94 106 115 128
    138 156 172
Hamburg 82
Handshuh H. L. 153 154
Harrison P. R. H. Lt 175
Hartley E. F/O 26 27 29 30 32
Harvey P. S/Lt 176 179
Hatherly G. L. F/L 131
Haugesund 83
Havelock HMS 106
Havre 184
Hayman R. W. Lt 148
Hela 79 82
Heilmann S. K/L 68
Heller H. KK 210
Hennig H. K/L 137
Henry Mallory 60
Heyse U. K/L 20
Highlander HMS 195
Hodges J. Capt 86 213
Hodgkinson D. B. S/L 191
Holmsley South 26 32
Hopmann R. H. KK 161 168
Hornkohl H. K/L 173
Hummerjohann E. O/L 128
Hunger H. K/L 64 65
Hutchins L/Cdr 163
Icarus HMS 69 72
Imperialist HMS 186 189 197 198 206
Isaac Sweers 184
Isbell Capt 54
Itapage 20
Jackson I. Sgt 160

Jamaica 28
James O'Hara USS 146
Jask 137
Jeffrey W. 197
Jones F/O 64
Jordan G. K/L 117
Joubert P. Sir 23 26
Kaipara 105
Kalliopi 60
Kamloops HMCS 69 95
Kasch K/L 40
Kerrigan R. F. F/L 113
Kett W. H. Lt 175 176 181 184 188 191
    213
Kiel 19 27 44 52 64 68 82 105 113 147
    151 156 159 161 172 200 209 210
Kingston Amber HMS 175 176
Kirkenes 147
Kite HMS 208-210
Klaus H. J. O/L 200 214
Kluth G. O/L 15 16 214
Knowles E. F/L 115
Kretschmer O. KK 35 44 58
Kristiansand 83 159 200
Kristiansund 147
Krüger J. O/L 115 116
La Baule 29 191
La Pallice 23 37 44 52 58-61 148
La Rochelle 52
Ladds K. F/Sgt 32 33
Lady Hogarth HMS 189
Lagens 100 101
Lawton G. Evans 28
LCT 2341 161
Leigh H. de V. S/L 179
Letitia 44
Lexington USS 151
Libau 82
Lisbon 196
Llangibby Castle 58
Loch Oskaig HMS 189 197 198
Lohmann D. K/L 44
Londonderry 109 208 214
Loney F/L 113
Looks H. K/L 56 215
Loosestrife HMS 109 115-120
Lorient 19 23 37 52 137 159 172 209
Love Mr 133
Lübeck 45
MacIntyre D. Capt 60
Maddalena 186 187
Madeira 200
Mäder E. K/L 147 148
Magpie HMS 207

Mahratta HMS 32
Maidstone HMS 181 186
Malta 37 115 176 186 213
Man o'War HMS 189
Marblehead USS 143
Marseilles 178
Martin 184
McAuslan Lt 157 158
McEwen W. J. P. F/L 66
McPhail T. W. A/B 133 213
Mead R. G/Capt 27 30-32
Millo 175
Minerve 175
Mitchell D. Capt 51
Mitchell Sgt 191
ML 170 189
ML 172 189
ML 175 189
Möller G. O/L 110
Mombasa 136
Montreal 42 51
Morden HMS 69
Moscow 79
Müller R. O/L 119
Murray F. M. Lt 153
Murrell Sgt 138
Musketeer HMS 69 73
Myrmidon HMS 69
Needham L. T. F/S 131
Nene HMS 64
Newark 70
Newton Ash 60
New York 54 151
Norfield P. Sgmn 133 213
Norfolk, Virginia 54 146 147 151 173
Northern Sky HMS 109
Northern Wave HMS 109
Nürnberg 58
Oberon HMs/m 176 213
Oliver J. 184
Oporto 172
Oribi HMS 69 70 72 76-78 86 88 90 212
Orkan ORP 69 70 72 74 88 89 93 95 147 148 151
Orwell HMS 69 77 78 87 88 90 212 213
Oulton W. W/Cdr 26
P.34 175 176
Patterson H. Lt 20
Peck B. E. F/L 113
Pelly J. S/Lt 212
Penolver 153
Phibbs K. H. L/Cdr 206
Phillips L. H. L/Cdr 132 213
Phoebe 19

Pickering F/O 200
Piggott W. B. Cmdr 206
Pink HMS 109 111 115 118 119
Plymouth 77
Poeschel O/L 56
Polyanthus HMS 61
Poppy HMS 202
Potentilla HMS 28
Pound D. Sir 37
Prestwick 42 43 51
Price F/O 191
Prien G. KK 35
RAAF Squadron
   10 26 159 210
RCAF Squadrons:
   10   16 56
  422   93 130
  423   93
RAF Squadrons:
  58   26 30 33
  59   40 110 111 113 115
  86   75 85 110
 120   28 40 47 51 66 85 113 115 131 172
 172   70 101
 179   101 170 172 178 191 195 200 201
 206   101
 220   100 101 104 106
 224   116 117 159
 231   51
 232   172
 233   102
 244   136 137
 269   64 67
 814   174
R. E. Hopkins 60
Ramsey L. C. Capt 151
Rapana HMS 72 75
Reese H. J. O/L 159
Reich C. K/L 116
Renoncule FFS 15
Revenge HMS 100
Reykjavik 45-47 49 67
Rinos 58
Ripley 19
Robertson G. P. F/L 107
Rochester 92
Rodgers B. H. C. L/Cmdr 197 199 206
Rollmann W. KK 139
Roosevelt F. D. Pres 53
Roselys FFS 15
Rothesay 187
Russell A. H. F/O 93 94

Rysegrave L/Cmdr 208
Sackville HMS 69
Sandanger 29
San Diego Calif. 42 53 146
Sargent P. T. F/L 130
Scapa Flow 78
Schäfer K/L 56
Schepke J. KK 35
Schnoor K/L 56
Schöneboom D. O/L 184
Scottish HMS 189
Sharjah 136 137
Sheela B. C. Ensign 62
Silvester L. 189 202 203 214
Simpson S. P. AVM 204
Sikorski W. Gen. 70
Slessor Sir J. AM 26
Smith P/O 64
Southern Empress 27
Speidel H. H. K/L 79 83 89 213
Spirea HMS 189
Spitzbergen 39
St Eval 104
St Johns 38 116 118 153
St Nazaire 23 29 37 52 53 93 106 161 183
  184 191 200 209
St Usk 19
Starling HMS 207 209 210 215
Stearns R. Lt 54 56
Steeves C. B. F/O 131
Steinart H. K/L 20
Stephen C. Foster 28
Stevenson R. R. P/O 159
Sunflower HMS 109 115-119
Swinemünde 80
Sydney Nova Scotia 38
Sydney NSW 85
Sykes J. B. Capt 53
Tacoma Wash. 53 146
Tangiers 201
Techand O/L 64
Tennyson A. Sir 100
Thalassa HMS 189
Thomas W. J. F/O 110
Tiesenhausen H. D. von KK 58
Tirpitz 38 147
Tjileboet 19
Tobruk 79
Toronto 130
Toulon 173 174 178 181 183-185
  187-189 195 196 215
Toward 60
Tracker HMS 207 208 211
Trojer H. K/L 27-29 33 35

Trondheim 37 67 135 147 161 183
Trotha C. von K/L 105
Truant HMs/m 175
Tucurinca 28
Turnbull B. W. W/O 115
U-boats:
  U-3 27
  U-34 27
  U-59 58
  U-67 27 146
  U-81 79
  U-84 147
  U-89 44
  U-91 70 92 95 156 163 215
  U-99 44 58
  U-117 54
  U-128 20
  U-132 47
  U-161 19 22
  U-178 214
  U-185 147
  U-194 50
  U-211 104 106
  U-220 151 153 155 156 212
  U-221 27-30 33
  U-226 209
  U-228 106
  U-231 129
  U-254 27 28
  U-256 15 153
  U-260 63 67 70 72
  U-262 104-106
  U-264 54 56 57 214
  U-274 117 159
  U-275 63 64 70 75 98
  U-279 63 66 67 70 95
  U-282 119 212
  U-305 63
  U-306 104 105
  U-309 58 70
  U-331 58
  U-333 104-106
  U-336 63-67 70 95
  U-340 189 196 199-204 214
  U-341 63
  U-373 209
  U-377 15 16 19 61 214
  U-378 63 70 72 74 147 148 150
  U-388 63 95
  U-389 63 67 68
  U-402 16 57-63
  U-405 161 165 167 168
  U-413 207
  U-419 63 70 75 76 85 95 98 212

U-420 159
U-422 54 56 67 212
U-426 116
U-431 183 184 188
U-437 75 93
U-439 70
U-441 104
U-448 63 70 72 95
U-450 189 191 193 195 196 199 215
U-455 54 56
U-459 52 70
U-460 52-54 56 67 214
U-463 26 44 52
U-464 52
U-466 104-106
U-470 113 114 212
U-487 146
U-516 38
U-525 54
U-528 214
U-531 77 212
U-533 137 138
U-537 39
U-539 63 64 70 72
U-540 40 41 51 115 212
U-544 44
U-549 213
U-566 172 173 189
U-575 209
U-579 44
U-584 63 156 158 163
U-597 46
U-603 63 70 92 153
U-608 161
U-610 63 70 74 75 92-95
U-631 63 70 74 115
U-632 85
U-641 63 70 75
U-642 174 189 215
U-643 63 70 79 82 83 85 88-90 92 93 95 98 212
U-645 63 70 95
U-646 157
U-648 209 210
U-653 45
U-659 156
U-661 46
U-663 26
U-664 54
U-666 64 67
U-673 24 63
U-707 104-107 211
U-709 209
U-731 63 64 70 72

U-732 186 189 195-199
U-758 63 67 72 95
U-762 70 72 92
U-841 134 135
U-842 209 210 212
U-844 110 113
U-847 54
U-848 139 143
U-952 63 67
U-953 104 106
U-964 128 129
U-967 208
U-3035 214
Ultimatum HMs/m 175-181 183 184 186-188 191 197 213 214
USN Squadron 128 65
Vanquisher HMS 109 116
Velox HMS 189 195 196
Vidette HMS 109 114-120 159
Vigo 173
Vogelsang K/L 47
Voorhess G. Capt 51
Wade Hampton 161
Wade J. Tel 178 214
Walker F. J. Capt 207 209 210 214 215
Walters D. S/Lt 178 184 185
Walter Q. Gresham 28
Wanklyn D. L/Cdr 176
Waters USS 146
Webber F/O 85
Wedderburn I. S/Lt 78 86 212
Wemyss D. E. G. Cmdr 209
Westhof Cmdr 64 65
West Humhaw 19
Whitehall HMS 104 105
Wild Goose HMS 207 210
Williams R. Lt 146 147
Wilson Sgt 191 195
Wishart HMS 189 201
Witherington HMS 189 195 199 201
Wolfe HMS 175
Wood Sir Kingsley 38
Woodcock HMS 207 209 210
Woodwark P. A. S. F/Lt 130
Wright J. P/O 75
Wulff H. Lt 156 157
Yorkmar 95
Youell Capt. 42